STOP THE PRESSES
(So I Can Get Off)

Fire Ant Books

STOP THE PRESSES
(So I Can Get Off)

Tales from Forty Years of Sportswriting

CLYDE BOLTON

THE UNIVERSITY OF ALABAMA PRESS TUSCALOOSA

For Lily and Hannah

Manufactured in the United States of America

Typeface: AGaramond
∞

The paper on which this book is printed meets the minimum requirements of American National Standard for Information Sciences—Permanence of Paper for Printed Library Materials, ANSI Z39.48–1984.

Library of Congress Cataloging-in-Publication Data

Bolton, Clyde.
Stop the presses (so I can get off) : tales from forty years of sportswriting / Clyde Bolton.
p. cm.
"Fire Ant books."
Includes index.
ISBN 0-8173-5252-X (pbk. : alk. paper)
1. Bolton, Clyde. 2. Sportswriters—United States—Biography. 3. Sports journalism—United States. I. Title.
GV742.42.B65A3 2005
070.4′49796′092—dc22

2005002968

Contents

Stop the Presses (So I Can Get Off) 1
Photographs *following page* 127
Index 265

Chapter 1

My grandmother Netta Bolton who lived in Lawrenceville, Georgia, had one of the first television sets I ever saw, and she loved to watch professional wrestling. Her sister Jewel Cooper would visit from Atlanta, and those two old ladies would get down on the carpet, on their hands and knees, in front of the TV and try to see up the legs of the wrestlers' tights.

I tell you this for two reasons. One is to let you know that I come from good, inquisitive stock. The other is because the first thing you learn in Journalism 101 is to try to capture the reader in the opening sentences or you might not capture him at all. I thought the image of my grandma and my aunt as elderly voyeurs would capture you.

Not that I ever studied Journalism 101. Or Journalism Anything. I never had a class in journalism or writing. Wait. I take that back. The *Birmingham News* once imported a so-called expert to lecture the staff on writing. I think he was from Florida. It must have been such seminars that birthed the cynical old saying, what is an expert? An expert is someone from out of town. I asked the managing editor, Tom Bailey, if he really expected me to attend the class, even offering this bit of logic: "If I haven't learned to write in thirty years of newspapering do you expect me to learn in two hours?" But he said I must attend.

The lecturer droned on and on until, finally, he said something that caused my friend and fellow wordsmith Jimmy Bryan to elbow me in the ribs. He said that before a reporter begins a story the writer should make an outline, just like you learned in elementary school. "Wouldn't you like to see him at a night football game in Tiger Stadium at LSU with fifteen minutes to write a story, and he's making an outline?" Bryan said.

I couldn't resist it. I raised my hand and asked: "What newspapers have you worked for?"

The teacher hesitated and then said: "Well, I haven't ever actually worked for a newspaper."

No kidding. I have. I worked for five of them, and there is nothing else like it on earth. Selling sofas is like selling shoes, and raising hogs is like raising cattle, but writing for newspapers isn't like anything else.

A reporter must be fast and accurate—and those two qualities are natural enemies, like the cobra and the mongoose. Many who begin newspaper careers find they aren't cut out to live life under the deadline gun, and they desert for slower-paced jobs, such as teaching or public relations. Haste does make waste, but a reporter who can't get the facts and still turn out a story in a hurry is headed for a seat on the copydesk where he'll read the stories of those who can.

I once heard my friend Lewis Grizzard, the humor columnist–author–speaker, address the question of newspapers getting it right: "People want truth and accuracy in newspapers," he said. "Hell, a newspaper doesn't cost but 50 cents. Truth and accuracy would be $3.95." That's funny. But that's all it is. Truth and accuracy are also supposed to be 50 cents.

The clock isn't the only obstacle. Frequently the reporter must write the story despite being knee-deep in an uncomfortable, adversarial situation. Not everyone wants to help your story along.

The University of Alabama football team opened its 1962 season by beating the University of Georgia football team 35–0 in Birmingham's

Legion Field. The Crimson Tide's sophomore quarterback, Joe Namath, made his eagerly anticipated debut by throwing three touchdown passes. I was writing the dressing room story, and naturally I went straight to Namath, the star of the game. I began interviewing him at his locker. The players were singing and shouting and popping butts with towels and doing all the things players do after a satisfying victory, and it was difficult to hear Joe Willie's answers to my questions. It wasn't difficult to hear the voice that boomed across the dressing room, though. "Get away from that goddamn boy!" Coach Bear Bryant screamed. "You'll ruin him!"

The room fell silent, as suddenly as if someone had hit the mute button on a TV's remote control. Every eye of every player and of every assistant coach landed on me. Namath sheepishly turned away and continued dressing. End of interview. Bryant then barked words that would have been hilarious if the situation hadn't been so supercharged: "If you want to talk to somebody, talk to somebody who did something. Talk to Jack Hurlbut." Hurlbut was a sub quarterback who had mopped up after Namath had won the game.

I never knew why Bryant pitched such a fit. I recently checked the microfilmed copies of the *News* and saw that after the last Alabama game—the January 1, 1962, Sugar Bowl win over Arkansas—I had interviewed Pat Trammell, Mike Fracchia, Billy Neighbors, Tommy Booker, Tim Davis, and Jack Rutledge, and there was no problem. Maybe Bryant was afraid of what the free-spirited Namath might say. Maybe he remembered an utterance of Murray Trimble, one of his Texas A&M players.

Bryant was always talking about the importance of "good mamas and papas." After A&M beat Texas someone asked Trimble what he thought of the Longhorns. He answered: "Well, not much. They probably don't have good mamas and papas." Perhaps propelled by those words, the Longhorns upset Texas A&M the next season.

Anyway, Bryant's tantrum and the embarrassment it caused me didn't exactly make the words flow from my typewriter when I returned to the press box to write my story for Sunday's *Birmingham News.* I told my boss, Benny Marshall, the sports editor of the *News,* about Bryant's tirade, assuming Marshall would confront him and demand to know why he would jump one of his reporters who, after all, was just doing his job, but it never happened. I was surprised at the time that Benny let it slide, but I hadn't been at the *News* long. I later realized that Marshall idolized Bryant.

Three things come to mind when I recall Bryant's explosion. One is something Abe Lemmons, the Texas basketball coach–wit said. John Wooden used to guard his UCLA star Lew Alcindor from the press, saying a nineteen-year-old was not equipped to handle the pressure. Lemmons thought that was a hoot. He wisecracked: "Back when I was nineteen and scrooched down in a foxhole on Guadalcanal, I was sure thankful I wasn't playing college basketball." Another is that when I was Namath's age I was married and supporting a wife and child on a pittance as the sports editor of a daily newspaper. I *was* the press. The third is the most un-Bryant-like statement I ever heard Bear speak. On his television review a decade or so later, when Richard Todd was a sophomore quarterback, Bryant told his TV audience that Todd would make Alabama fans forget Joe Namath. In his autobiography, *Bear,* the coach said he had had a tooth pulled and was on pain pills that day. Well, I did think his speech was slurred.

I remain mystified as to why my interviewing Namath would ruin him while Bryant's putting such pressure on a young quarterback would be beneficial to Todd. Anyway, Namath soldiered on, despite the debilitating effect of my attention. He was named to the all-time Alabama team, led the New York Jets to a memorable Super Bowl victory, and was inducted into the Pro Football Hall of Fame. Todd, too, became a fine player in college and in the National Football League, but he didn't make anyone forget Joe Namath.

But I learned to write under any conditions. I once had to get the sports information director at LSU to remove a student who was standing at the edge of the basketball court after a game, reading my story upside down as I typed it on a portable typewriter at the press table and telling me how dumb I was. I covered a World Series in Kansas City in an "auxiliary press box"—meaning a roped-off area in the grandstand—while drunk fans walked up and down the aisle, reaching over to peck at the keys of my word processor. I once wired a flashlight to my hat, like a miner's light, and typed an article in a car while photographer Tom Self drove through the night from Nashville to Birmingham.

And I have written stories that weren't really written. I mastered the knack of dictating accounts of basketball games over the telephone to a typist back in the office, just forming the stories in my mind and speaking them without actually writing a word. It was an emergency measure, but it saved ten or fifteen precious minutes. Nowadays, of course, sportswriters compose a story on a computer and transmit it instantly over a phone line to a computer system in the office. (Speaking of methods of transmission, some people I have told this to refuse to believe it. They wait for the punch line, as if it were a joke. But it is true, though it happened before my time. There used to be a pigeon coop on the roof of the *Birmingham News* building, and reporters would take pigeons with them to Legion Field. They would attach their stories to the pigeons' legs and the birds would fly them back to the paper.)

I not only learned to write under any conditions, I learned to interview under any conditions. Namath, by then a star for the Jets, was in Tuscaloosa during an off-season, working out in the university's weight room. I was interviewing him for my book *The Crimson Tide* as he lifted weights and threw footballs with his lawyer, Mike Bite. "I've got to go to the bathroom," Namath suddenly announced. He had already told me he was on a tight schedule, and I knew any minutes lost while he was perched on the throne would be irretrievable. So I followed him, and as I stood outside the stall quizzing him, Joe Willie Namath sat on the commode inside the stall, answering simultaneously the call of nature and my questions. I've interviewed football players at Sugar, Orange, Cotton, Fiesta, and Gator Bowls, but Namath is the only one I've interviewed at the toilet bowl.

A smart-aleck New York reporter once asked Namath if he studied basket weaving at Alabama. "Naw," he answered, "I studied journalism. It was easier." Good line, Joe, but I doubt if a basket weaver ever interviewed you while you took a, er, timeout from lifting weights.

Years later I read that Lyndon Johnson frequently required his female secretary to take notes from him as he sat on the commode. Well, I did it once, but I wouldn't want to make a habit of it. Still, a little humility never hurt anyone. In fact, I have found that humility can help a sportswriter get the story. If you're dumb about a subject, just admit it, and someone will feel sorry for you. Don't fake it.

I was assigned to write a story about a tennis tournament in Birmingham. I introduced myself to the public relations director and said, "I don't know one thing about tennis. I don't even understand how you keep score. But if you will steer me to a feature story I can write it and tack the scores onto the bottom of the story, because I do know how to write about people." Several girls from New Zealand or somewhere were playing in the tournament. The PR director seated them at a table with me, told them I knew nothing about tennis, and they had a jolly good time educating me. It made a nice story. If I had tried to fake it, the story and the day would have been miserable flops.

Alabama's basketball team lost to Bobby Knight's Indiana club in the Mideast Regional in Baton Rouge in 1976. Several reporters came to Coach C. M. Newton's motel room the next morning to hear Newton's postmortem on the game for their follow-up stories. One writer, Mike McKenzie, launched into a monologue on the technicalities of the game. All he needed was a blackboard and some chalk and he would have been drawing up plays. Newton sighed. I avoided eye contact with the writer, trying not to laugh. When McKenzie left the room Newton chuckled and summed up the scene with one of his priceless lines: "I know that no sportswriter knows anything about basketball, because half the coaches don't know anything about basketball."

One year Newton decided to educate those of us who wrote about Alabama basketball. He had a chalk-talk clinic in a conference room before the season began, demonstrating such tactics as clearing a side and zone-trap defense. After all the Xs and Os, I still didn't get it, and I didn't mind admitting it. "I know less about basketball now than when you started," I told him. "I still can't write about the stack play, but I can write about people."

"That's what your subscribers would rather read about anyway," Newton said.

Writers should, indeed, write about people. Who cares what kind of defense the losing team was in with 2:47 to play?

Well, a fellow who used to write sports for the *Birmingham News* cared. Al O'Brien had played college basketball, and when he covered a game he went into the technicalities. He was not pleased that I got more of the good basketball assignments than he did, and he cited his playing experience in a complaint. "I used to write obituaries," I told him, "but I've never died. You don't have to play basketball to cover basketball any more than you have to die to write obituaries."

I can understand coaches being irked when writers pretend they're experts in the technicalities. I don't like it when a civilian intrudes on my area of expertise. I've had readers tell me, "I could write a column." No doubt they could. Maybe they could write two columns, maybe even five. The question is can they write two hundred a year for more than thirty years as I did? I've written seventeen books, and I sigh when someone tells me, "I've always wanted to write a book"—as if that makes us brothers in some authors' fraternity. I simply reply, "I've always wanted to be an alchemist."

God help the sportswriter who tried to impress Bear Bryant with his knowledge of football. God help the sportswriter who even ventured the opinion that a football was made of leather. Bryant knew everything, and a writer wasn't supposed to know anything. I watched an Alabama practice one afternoon, and you've never seen such a bloodletting. The pads and helmets were popping, and the scene was as electric as a Super Bowl. It was the kind of practices coaches dream about.

Bryant always spoke to the press for a few minutes after each day's practice. Writers just sat there and waited for him to speak while he torched an unfiltered Chesterfield and spat miniature ribbons of tobacco onto the floor. I don't know why I did it, because the years had taught me better, but before Bryant could tell us how great the practice had been I piped up and said, "Boy, they were really hitting out there today, weren't they?"

Bryant jerked his cigarette from his lips and growled, "Shhhiiittt. You call that hitting? There wasn't a decent lick passed all day. They won't even need to take a shower, because they're as fresh as they were when practice started. Hitting? Haw!" Bryant was the only person I ever knew who could stretch "shit" into an eight-syllable word.

But a writer could kid some coaches about the incredible technicalities of football. I once walked into a room in which Mike DuBose and Curley Hallman, then defensive coaches at Alabama, were sitting at a table drawing up diagrams. I don't know where they could possibly have hung another one. Because all four walls of the room were plastered with them.

"Boys, you're overengineering," I told them. "When I played in high school we had just two defenses. If we thought they were going to run we went to a six-man line; if we thought they were going to pass we went to a five-man line. We were undefeated, and y'all aren't." DuBose grinned and said, "There may be more good sense in that than you think."

One time a "coach" actually gave me credit for having some technical knowledge—but it was undeserved credit. Gary Nelson was the crew chief for stock car driver Geoff Bodine, and the team was conducting a private test at Talladega Superspeedway. I was observing the mechanics at work—without having a clue what they were doing—when Nelson said, "Clyde, I'd appreciate it if you wouldn't watch this. We're doing some experimental work on this hub."

I thought he was kidding but then realized he wasn't. I laughed and said, "Gary, on a good day I might be able to tell a tire from a motor. I didn't even know that thing was called a hub." My wife and kids love that story, because they are well aware that as little as I know about tennis, it's more than I know about using a tool. Any tool. You don't have to be a mechanic to cover racing any more than you have to be a basketball player to cover basketball or a corpse to write obits.

I actually have coached college football—well, sort of. Several years ago, when Jim Hilyer was head coach at UAB, he asked me to be an honorary coach of one side of the Blazers in the spring game at Legion Field. I said sure. Alas, I was not allowed to actually make any decisions. "Let's fake a punt," I boldly suggested to Snoozy Jones, the assistant coach who was really in charge of our team. "Punt," Jones told the boys. Our side lost (no doubt because we didn't run any fake punts), but as the game reached its final seconds and I watched the opposing honorary coach's players creep up behind him with a barrel of water I realized I had scored a moral victory. He got soaked; I drove home warm and dry.

Jack Crowe, the head coach at Jacksonville State, asked if I'd be an honorary coach in the 2001 JSU spring game. I was pleased, because what little college education I acquired came under the auspices of Jax State, and I would be retiring from the newspaper business in a few months. It was a thoughtful gesture by a fellow I've known for many years.

It was a fun day. I gave our side a contrived pregame pep talk that lampooned Knute Rockne and provided the players with a belly laugh, and then I ran onto the field with them on my heels, hoping I wouldn't trip and be trampled by half a football team. Crowe made a special day even more special by telling my thirteen-year-old grandson Cory Bolton he could stand on the sidelines with granddaddy. A thoughtful assistant coach named Matt Wannebo even rounded up a JSU game jersey for Cory to wear.

During the game a huge player lumbered to the sideline after a bad play and bellowed, "Aw, excrement!" He hoped I had noted he hadn't used a bad word, and he asked if his refined exclamation met with my approval. I assured him it did.

Later on an official threw a yellow flag at my feet for no apparent reason. "What was that for?" I demanded. "I remember one time you wrote a bad story about officials," he explained. "That's a five-yard penalty." I called another official to the sideline. "Don't tell your colleague," I said, "but a bad story about officials is supposed to be a fifteen-yard penalty."

Again, my side lost. Again, the opposing players dumped a barrel of water over the head of the victorious honorary coach. Again, I drove home warm and dry, secure in the conviction that winning isn't everything.

Later, I would contrast that afternoon of fun with the football-is-life-or-death mode that grips our state when the season begins, and the name Mike Donahue popped into my mind. Donahue was Auburn's first great coach. He was a charter inductee into the Alabama Sports Hall of Fame. Donahue arrived on campus in 1904, stayed through the 1922 season, and made Auburn a power in southern football. Clearly, the sport wasn't just fun for him (from the first game in 1913 to the seventh game in 1915 his Tigers won twenty-two, lost none, and tied one), but he saw it as less than life or death, as a suggestion he made to his colleagues proved.

I once wrote a column declaring that if I could have lunch with any member of the Alabama Sports Hall of Fame, I would choose Mike Donahue. Here's why. At a meeting of the Southern Intercollegiate Athletic Association, Donahue startled his contemporaries by proposing that conducting the games be in the hands of the players. He wanted coaches barred from the field during the games, forced to sit in the stands. The other coaches said no thanks, they'd stay on the field.

Donahue explained his position: "My firm belief is that intercollegiate football will be a forward impulse toward a desirable goal when the coach is not permitted to sit on the sidelines. What is the theoretical aim of competitive college sports? Why, the encouragement of resource and initiative among those who participate. How is this aim accomplished when the coach from a vantage point on the sidelines practically directs the play at important junctures, if not throughout? Personally, I had rather develop one man—I mean a rounded man, a man who can use his brain as well as his muscles—than a dozen all-American stars who have learned to depend upon the intellect of a nonparticipant." One can only imagine what football would be like today if Donahue's noble idea had been implemented and if it had spread across the land.

Jack Crowe, incidentally, came up with a radical idea of his own before the 2001 season. He had watched a JSU soccer player named Ashley Martin pulverize the round, checkered ball. The girl from Sharpsburg, Georgia, had been a placekicker for the football team at East Coweta High School, and Crowe asked her to lend a hand—I mean a foot—to his team. She did. She became the backup placekicker for the Gamecocks. On August 30, 2001, she kicked three extra points as JSU mashed Cumberland. I watched from the grandstand, and I was glad I was there, for she became the first woman to play in an NCAA football game.

Crowe's promotional savvy and Ashley's foot created incredible publicity for Jacksonville State University. *Good Morning America* featured her live from Jacksonville. She went to New York and appeared on *Live with Regis and Kelly.* She even kicked a couple of extra points through a goal that was erected on the street at the studio. She was on a show called *Pure Oxygen* while she was in New York, and ESPN and Fox Sports came visiting in Jacksonville. She was featured in *USA Today,* the *Boston Globe,* the *Washington Post, People, Newsweek,* the *Sporting News,* and *ESPN The Magazine.*

I suspect old Mike Donahue would have been delighted.

Chapter 2

Sometimes when you've got it good, you don't realize how good you've got it.

I joined the sports staff of the *Birmingham News* on September 4, 1961, and retired on September 7, 2001. Ralph Jordan became Auburn's head football coach before the 1951 season and retired after the 1975 season. Paul Bryant became Alabama's head football coach before the 1958 season and retired after the 1982 season. So I covered Jordan for fifteen seasons and Bryant for twenty-two. They were the coaches, just as Samford Hall and Denny Chimes were the schools' landmarks, and you didn't give much thought to the inevitable day when they no longer would be the coaches.

A blanket indictment, in the view of the public, is that sportswriters thrive on controversy, that they love it like a hog loves slop. It is true of a small percentage of sportswriters, but a huge majority don't like controversy. They dread it. They prefer a routine of simply covering ball games, of writing feature stories about good guys, of knowing they don't have to extract information from the police blotter, of knowing their phone won't ring at 3 A.M., their sleepy brains having to compute the orders of some editor who is assigning them to a breaking story of human folly. Wouldn't you prefer that if you were a sportswriter?

An off-field story that has become too commonplace is the firing of a coach and the hiring of another. Coaches are paid so much money and the demand for winning has become so unrealistic that at the end of any season the college football scene resembles a canning factory. (You know, coaches getting canned.) Reporters wince when they hear the words "coaching change." They must try to pin down the circumstances of the dismissal of the old coach and scoop everyone else on the identity of the new coach. Who are the leading "candidates" for the job? What will happen to the old assistants? Who will the new assistants be? What is the reaction of the public? What do the people back at the new coach's old location say about him? Beat men covering coaching changes had best prepare for plenty of fourteen-hour workdays. God help any who haven't nurtured a network of contacts.

I was fortunate to cover the same two football coaches at Auburn and Alabama for many years. I recall that interval as the good old days.

Jordan and Bryant were alike in that they were hard disciplinarians who believed mean, physically conditioned, team-oriented players were the instruments of victory. They must be grounded in fundamentals, willing to play with pain, and unquestioningly accept the dictates of their coaches. But beyond that Jordan and Bryant were quite different.

I liked Jordan much better than Bryant. Jordan liked me much better than Bryant did. But that isn't saying so much about my relationship with either as about each coach's relationship with the press in general. Jordan liked the press. After he retired from coaching he kept an office in Auburn's athletic department. One day he told me, "You know what I miss? I miss the newspapermen dropping by to talk to me." I said, "Coach, I'll remember that. I'll always drop by to see you when I'm in Auburn." And I did.

At best, Bryant considered the press a necessary evil. At worst, he considered it an unnecessary evil. One of his pronouncements about the press was: "If you're winning, they can't hurt you; if you're losing, they can't help you." Bryant might have been fairly close to two or three writers—Al Browning of the *Tuscaloosa News* comes to mind—but that's about it.

His journalist of choice, at least in Alabama, was Benny Marshall. Even Bryant thought it politic to be on good terms with the sports editor of the state's biggest newspaper, the *Birmingham News.* Benny, frankly, worshipped the coach. He wrote a flattering book about Bryant titled *Winning Isn't Everything,* even dedicated it to Bryant.

Benny was a florid, dramatic writer who did more than any other person to manufacture the legend of Bear Bryant. His columns—which were never even mildly critical of the coach—portrayed one of American folklore's most endearing archetypes, the country boy who outfoxes the slickers, the lad in worn but clean overalls who, through hard work, perseverance, and native intelligence, rises to the top of his profession. Bryant was Honest Abe with a whistle around his neck. His most pedestrian, self-serving pronouncements became holy writ in Benny's hands.

When the *Saturday Evening Post* charged that former Bulldogs coach Wally Butts betrayed Georgia by feeding Bryant inside information over the telephone before the 1962 Alabama-Georgia game, Benny rushed to Bryant's side, angry typewriter smoking, writing columns that adamantly declared it couldn't have happened. The possibility that it could have happened wasn't entertained for a second.

But even Benny wasn't exempt from Bryant's scorn. Marshall hired a young sportswriter named Paul Hemphill, who later became an author and magazine writer of some prominence. As Benny told the story, he took Hemphill to Tuscaloosa to meet Bryant. Benny decided to impress Hemphill by getting out his notebook and pen and firing some questions at the coach. Didn't work. Bryant's answer to each of Benny's first five questions was the same: "Shit!"

Actually, covering Bryant for twenty-two seasons was like covering two different men. The stern, distant younger coach became a friendlier older coach in his final seasons. I think Bryant wanted to cultivate a kindly old grandpa image in his later years, to be remembered (and chronicled) by the press as a good fellow, not just as an ornery, obsessed dictator of a coach.

On October 3, 1980, Alabama played Kentucky in Birmingham's Legion Field. There was no doubt Bryant would win the three hundredth game of his career. (He did, by a score of 45–0.) My assignment was to shadow Bryant and write about what he did on that historic day. It was tradition that Bryant strolled around the playing field before a game. He did it early, before most of the crowd arrived. He and I were chatting on the sidelines when he surprised me by saying, "Come on and take my walk with me." So off we went, Bear Bryant and Clyde Bolton, on a rectangular trip around the floor of the Old Gray Lady of Graymont Avenue. The Alabama students had been admitted early, and they had rushed to claim the seats in the student section. Except for them, the grandstands were virtually empty. When Bryant and I walked in front of the crimson-clad students, they rose as one and gave him a standing ovation, clapping and yelling.

Bryant turned to me and said with a grin, "Damn, you've got a lot of fans!" That will always be a fond memory. He was, I'm convinced, the greatest college football coach who ever lived, and even after twenty-five years in the newspaper business I wasn't so jaded that I couldn't appreciate that moment.

Bryant sent me a copy of his autobiography, *Bear.* It is inscribed "To Clyde Bolton, a great writer and a true friend of sports. Sincerely, Paul 'Bear' Bryant." I'm glad he did. But in all the years that I covered Bryant I never had a conversation with him that wasn't about football. I said he was obsessed with football, and that's true. Of course, his obsession made him an extraordinary coach. The world belongs to the single-minded.

He was a man perpetually on a football mission—and I felt sorry for one well-meaning fan who got in the way of that mission. I guess it was in the 1960s. The Tide was in Athens to play Georgia, and I was sitting in the lobby of the old Georgian Hotel. So was an excited fan who was cradling a present for the coach, a crimson blazer. He had either had the coat made or he was a tailor who had made it himself, and he was waiting for Bryant to make an appearance. Finally, Bryant strode through the lobby, toward the front door. The man, smiling, got to his feet and intercepted the tall figure, telling him he had a gift for him and asking him to try it on. Bryant said he was in a hurry. If he would just slip it on, the fan said, he could see whether it fit, whether it required altering. Wouldn't take a minute. He began draping it onto the coach's shoulders. Bryant snatched the coat, threw it onto the floor, and bellowed, "I don't want that goddamned thing!" He continued out the front door. The fan, stunned and hurt, picked up his coat and slunk to his room.

When some chamber of commerce types greeted Bryant and his players at the airport in Knoxville and handed out tourist maps and trinkets, Bryant threw his gifts to the ground and said, "We're here to play a football game, not go sightseeing in the Smoky Mountains!"

Football was Bryant's reason to exist. Jordan, on the other hand, was a man of broad interests, a captivating conversationalist. On the wall of his office was a map of Ireland, the country of his ancestors. He loved history, and he frequently flavored his talks to his players with historical references. He quoted Winston Churchill: "Never in the field of human conflict was so much owed by so many to so few." He admired Gen. George Patton and summoned up lessons from the Normandy invasion and the Battle of the Bulge. He quoted from the Bible—particularly Ecclesiastes—and from Shakespeare. A favorite poem was Tennyson's "Charge of the Light Brigade."

Jordan knew firsthand about war. As an army engineer he participated in four major invasions during World War II. He was wounded at Normandy and was awarded the Purple Heart. Jordan refused immediate surgery for shrapnel in his shoulder because it would have removed him from the fighting. Four days later, his arm useless and his fever raging, he went under the surgeon's knife.

Jordan could tell funny stories about serious situations. He was on a ship, waiting for orders to begin the landing at Salerno in Italy, when a volcano erupted. A Texan who was notorious for spinning tall tales about the Lone Star State stood beside him. "I bet you don't have anything like that in Texas," Jordan said. "Nope," the fellow replied, "but the Dallas fire department could put it out."

I enjoyed Jordan's company, whether in his office, on the practice field, or in his home drinking buttermilk, a beverage we both fancied. During one visit I was pleased to note that a book I had written and signed for him was prominently displayed on a shelf in his house. The title: *The Crimson Tide.* I wonder how many coaches would have had the grace, the class—the guts—to stock a bookshelf with a history of a bitter rival, as Jordan did. But it was a gift from a friend, and if some visiting Auburn fan wanted to frown, let him frown.

I realize these are subjective conclusions, but I never felt Jordan hated Alabama; I think Bryant hated Auburn. Jordan could take the more detached view of a historian. Once I mentioned some stupid thing that an Alabama fan had said or done and he replied, "Well, neither side has a lock on the bastards."

Jordan casually mentioned to me one day: "The year 1922 was pivotal in the history of football in this state." He was right. The great coach Mike Donahue left Auburn for LSU after the 1922 season, and the program went to pot. In 1922 Alabama upset Pennsylvania 9–7 in Philadelphia to earn the national spotlight for the first time. It also was the final season for the dying coach Xen Scott, who was replaced by Wallace Wade, the man who would take Alabama to new heights and coach its first three Rose Bowl squads. Jordan knew the history of football at both universities. (Jordan, incidentally, suspected that activities of the Ku Klux Klan influenced Donahue, a Catholic, to leave Auburn for the friendlier Louisiana.)

Gracing Jordan's homestead were pecan trees that were planted when he took the job of head football coach at Auburn. The story goes that he was so certain of success that he provided for a bounty of nuts for future years. "That's the story everyone tells, but that's not what happened," Jordan told me. "What actually happened was this: I came home and found my wife, Evelyn, planting the pecan trees, and I said, 'You've got a hell of a lot more confidence that we're going to succeed at Auburn than I have.'" Jordan had a great sense of the comic, the ironic.

Nowadays SEC coaches and selected players gather in Birmingham for preseason interrogation by the southern and national sporting press. Used to be, the journalists assembled in Birmingham and flew to the various schools to interview the coaches and players. When the Skywriters visited Auburn in 1968, Jordan appeared drawn after losing twenty-five pounds in a successful bout with cancer. One writer asked him about his physical condition and then told the coach he wouldn't believe him if he said he was okay. Whereupon Jordan got off the best line in Skywriters history: "If I had only thirty-three days to live I damn sure wouldn't be spending any of them with you guys."

Jordan's wry sense of humor could blossom during a game, too. The 1957 club, the one that earned a national championship, led Houston 22–0 and was threatening again late in the second period. Jordan sent his first-team quarterback Lloyd Nix back into the game with the instruction "Get it in the end zone!" Alas, Nix threw a pass that a Houston player intercepted and returned eighty-nine yards for a touchdown. When Nix returned to the sidelines, Jordan grabbed his shoulder pads and said, "Damn it, Lloyd, I meant the other end zone!"

Jordan was left-handed, a circumstance well known during his undergraduate days at Auburn since he played football, basketball, and baseball. He is remembered today as the left-handed center of the football team, but his best sport was basketball. He even led the Southern Conference in scoring as a sophomore. The school yearbook noted that basketball was his "first love."

Jordan acquired the nickname Shug as a boy in his hometown of Selma. A fellow could buy a stalk of sugar cane at a store for five cents. Jordan devotedly spent his nickels thusly, chewing on the sweet, juicy cane. (I could relate to that because I used to do the same thing as a kid in Statham, Georgia.) Bryant, of course, became Bear because, as a lad, he wrestled a bear on the stage of the Lyric Theatre in Fordyce, Arkansas. I used to kid Jordan that Bryant wrestled a bear but that Shug merely wrestled a stalk of sugar cane. Anyway, Jordan's nickname of Shug had to share billing with another nickname during his playing days at Auburn. He became known as Lefty.

Jordan had an unusual talent. He could write with both hands simultaneously. In fact, he could write "Jordan" backward with his right hand while writing "Ralph" forward with his left hand. Another of his talents was coaching basketball—though Gene Lorendo loved to make light of that skill. Jordan, in fact, was head basketball coach at both Georgia and

Auburn. Lorendo (who would become a member of Jordan's original Auburn football coaching staff) played basketball for him at Georgia. As Lorendo told it, he'd make a point of sitting next to Jordan on the bench to assure himself of playing time. As they watched the action on the court their exchange would go something like this:

"Gene, who committed that foul?"

"That was Smith, Coach."

"Who missed that layup?"

"Smith missed it, Coach."

"Whose man just made that shot?"

"It was Smith's man, Coach."

"Lorendo, go in for Smith."

Lorendo, who would become the most famous assistant football coach in Auburn history, wasn't into the delicacies of basketball. He told me that during practice he got into a fight with the star of Jordan's Georgia team, chasing him around the gym before the guy hightailed it into the street, never to return to the squad. "The best player on the team," Jordan is supposed to have told Lorendo, "and the worst player on the team runs him off. Damn!" (Lorendo, a Minnesotan, told me he played two years of junior college football and basketball and a year of professional basketball before enrolling at Georgia as a freshman. He said they purposely dropped his file behind the file cabinet so they could plead ignorance of the facts if there was ever an investigation into his eligibility.)

Jordan had winning records as a basketball coach at Auburn and at Georgia. He went 95–77 on the Plain and 44–39 in Athens. He was Auburn's eighth coach and, when he left for Georgia after the 1945–46 season, its winningest.

The basketball palaces of today were barely dreamed of then, at least in the Deep South. Georgia played its home games in Woodruff Hall, a legendary dump in which (so the joke went) the wind was a factor. An Atlanta newspaper once did a revealing story on Woodruff Hall. A reporter placed a basketball on the center circle, removed his hand from the ball—and, lo, it rolled off the court. Jordan's Auburn teams played in an upstairs closet called Alumni Gym. There was a dead spot the size of a desktop in the floor. To Jordan it amounted to a sixth defender, for he coached his players to lunge for the ball when an unsuspecting opponent dribbled onto the dead spot.

Jordan once told me a story that graphically illustrated the sad state of SEC hoops when he was Georgia's basketball coach under Athletics Director Wally Butts. "For some reason they had stored war surplus beds in Woodruff Hall," he recalled. "There were bedsprings and double-decker beds all over the place. The court was covered. We were in the middle of this great football season, but we needed to get basketball practice started. I kept after Coach Butts about those beds, but he wouldn't do anything about it. Finally, there were only two weeks before we opened the season in Madison Square Garden, and we hadn't been able to practice for those beds. I told him we just had to get some practice, that it was a big thing, playing in Madison Square Garden.

"He looked at me and said, 'My gosh, you've got two whole weeks to practice. What's the rush?' "

Jordan's Auburn basketball players didn't have financial aid—unless you count Shag Hawkins's "scholarship." "There was a soft drink machine near the coaches' office," Jordan told me. "It produced about fifteen bucks a month, and we gave the money to Shag. That was his 'scholarship.' "

Chapter 3

I WAS JOGGING ON THE TRACK that encircles the high school football field in Trussville, Alabama, where I live, and I struck up a conversation with another jogger. Sheryl Davidson told me she played with the Huntsville-based Alabama Renegades of the National Women's Football League. Naturally, I interviewed her for a column. Even in the twenty-first century it's not every day that you meet a female football player.

"There are a lot of divorced women in the league, and they like to hit," said Davidson, who had never been married. "I don't know what their husbands did to them, but they bring it to the field." I knew motivation comes in packages of all sizes and shapes, but I'd never heard that one before. Maybe Alabama and Auburn should sign some divorced women for their football teams.

Unmotivated talent is a sad sight in sports and in real life. I remember a heralded quarterback who signed with Alabama and never delivered on his promise. When practice began he couldn't even run the mile in the specified time, a failure that, in the view of his teammates, must have erased him as a leader. "He signed that scholarship, and that was all he wanted," an assistant coach told me. "He thought he'd done his job." Another aide interjected a note of wry humor into the conversation: "When he came to Alabama he could stand on the fifty-yard line and with a flick of the wrist throw the ball through the goal posts. Unfortunately, when he left Alabama the only thing he could do was stand on the fifty-yard line and with a flick of the wrist throw the ball through the goal posts."

I remember something Ralph Jordan told me as we passed a rainy winter afternoon in his office: "If I could just see into their hearts, I could let Alabama sign forty and let Auburn sign forty, and then I could take forty from what was left and beat them both." It was an exaggeration, of course, but it was a point well made.

Jack Crowe, the Jacksonville State head coach, was an assistant at Auburn when AU signed a celebrated running back, one of those guys every school had to have. "I remember the look in his eyes the first time he ran the ball in practice and got hit," Crowe said. "I thought, 'Uh oh.' Sometimes a back is bigger and faster than everybody else in high school, and he never really gets hit. Then when he gets hit in college he isn't prepared for it." The fellow transferred from Auburn to a small school and never became a solid college player.

Bob Davis, the former Auburn basketball coach, told me a story that illustrated the difficulty of keeping motivation alive. Davis was coaching at Georgetown—the little Georgetown in Kentucky—and he had a superb team. His squad was about to play in the NAIA national tournament. "As the coach at such a small school, I had to do everything," Davis said. "I was wrapping my captain's ankles before our first tournament game, and I told him, 'This is going to be a great week. I believe we're going all the way. I believe we're going to win the national championship.'

"To which the boy replied: 'Aw, I don't know, Coach. It just doesn't mean as much to me as it used to.'

"I turned to our manager and said, 'Cancel our motel rooms after tonight. We won't be needing them.' And we didn't."

Davis told me another story that was an object lesson in how to unmotivate a team. Georgetown was playing at a college that had one of those old-fashioned gymnasiums with a balcony that encircled the court. Miniskirts were in full flower, and a bunch of the home team's female students seated themselves indecorously in the balcony behind the Georgetown goal. "My guys came down the court, looked up in that balcony, and shot the ball over the backboard," Davis said. "The officials wouldn't call a foul on the defense because they were too busy looking up in the balcony. Passes were hitting my guys in the face because they weren't watching for the ball. They were watching something else. I was willing to dismiss it as a coincidence—but at halftime, when the teams swapped goals, those girls moved to the other end of the court."

I've said I believe Paul Bryant was the greatest college football coach who ever lived. Much of his success was rooted in his ability to motivate his players. He was so persuasive that he could have sold last year's calendar. I've always been intrigued and curious about his propensity to get the best out of his men. When Bryant arrived at Texas A&M he went to an outdoor theater to speak to some five thousand students. He took off his coat and stomped on it. He rolled up his sleeves. Then he introduced himself and said he was ready to go to work. The kids went nuts. As Dee Powell, one of his players, later said, "he cast a spell on everybody."

Alabama won the national championship in 1965, and seeing their angry, purposeful coach break down a door had a motivating effect on the players, Jim Goostree, Bryant's trainer, believed. Alabama lost its opener to Georgia 18–17 and then played Tennessee to a 7–7 deadlock on the third Saturday in October, blowing the game in the final moments when Kenny "Snake" Stabler, thinking it was third down, threw a pass out of bounds to set up a game field goal attempt. Only trouble, it was fourth down, not third. After the tie with the Vols, Bryant and his team returned to the dressing room in Legion Field to find the door secured by a heavy chain and huge padlock.

Bryant, fuming, told the manager to unlock it; the manager didn't have a key. Bryant told a state trooper to shoot the lock off; the officer was reluctant to fire because of obvious danger. So Bryant got a running start, and with his big foot kicked the door in. Splinters flew everywhere, and the door fell prone onto the cement floor. With his bare hands Bryant tore the chain and padlock out of the frame. The players gulped. From then on, Alabama played with more purpose, Goostree said, and in the end it overcame Nebraska in the Orange Bowl to win the national title.

Georgia Tech fans threw liquor bottles at Bryant in Grant Field. So he appeared on the sideline in a suit and tie—and Alabama football helmet. You think that didn't motivate his players? My gosh, the man even called on Ann Landers, the syndicated advice columnist, to motivate his Tidesmen. He read her column every morning—even before he turned to the sports pages—and when he found one that was appropriate he read it to his guys. She and Bryant corresponded, and she confessed she was flattered by his attention. He once called Ann Landers and asked for a copy of a special column, one he had been reading to his freshmen football players for twelve years. He had misplaced his copy. It was titled "Dead at 17," and it was a fantasy about a boy who drives recklessly and is killed in an automobile crash and sees himself buried. She told Bryant she'd rerun the column.

Jerry Duncan was one of my all-time favorite Alabama players, and he and I have remained friends over the years. He has been tortured by rheumatoid arthritis, but Bryant's motivation has been at work in him for a long time, like some time-release capsule. "With this arthritis thing, there have been so many times I just wanted to sit down and quit," Duncan once told me. "But I believe having been under Coach Bryant and having been disciplined by him has helped me.

"I remember one time somebody went to one of the assistant coaches and told him Coach Bryant had been running us too much and we were bruised and tired. 'Can't you get him to ease up on us a little bit?' The assistant told Coach Bryant this. That day at the meeting Coach Bryant came in and said, 'Somebody tells me y'all are tired. Well, I'm tired, too. I'm tired of listening to that crap. I'm fifty-five years old. I'm tired of y'all. I'm tired of working. But what am I going to do?

"'Let me tell you something: if you think you're tired now just wait fifteen years when you owe the bank fifty thousand dollars and you come home one day from work and your house is on fire and your wife has left town with the drummer and you've got three kids to take care of. Then you're gonna really be tired. That's gonna check you.'

"I've thought about that a lot."

There were, of course, some that Bryant never could motivate. Most outspoken among them was Steve Wright, a lineman from Louisville, Kentucky, who trashed Bryant and his methods in his 1974 book *I'd Rather Be Wright.* Wright was never a starter at Alabama. In fact, the only games he played in were the final six of his senior season. Yet he went on to play for Vince Lombardi's Green Bay Packers, helping win three NFL titles and two Super Bowls (he said he loved Lombardi), and the New York Giants, Washington Redskins, Chicago Bears, St. Louis Cardinals, and Philadelphia Eagles.

Wright began his book by saying he spits whenever he thinks of the University of Alabama. There is a mutual hatred, he declared, and he remembers when it all started downhill. It was on a hot afternoon in 1961, when he was a sophomore and he was working in a certain drill. Wright said he had done everything he was supposed to do, completed the routine perfectly, and he was on his hands and knees, trying to get some air, when Pat James, an assistant coach, told him he had done pretty well except for one thing. When Wright asked what it was, James told him he wasn't mean enough and smacked him in the face with a forearm.

Wright said both his lips were split and his nose was smashed. It was a traumatic experience for an eighteen-year-old boy, and it damaged his ego. He said the coaches frequently "beat up" on the players, but that he made up his mind that anyone who hit him was going to get hit, and the situation snowballed from that point.

The linemen had two-bar face masks on their helmets, and the coaches jerked the players around by those handles, Wright said, but when a coach grabbed his mask he would knock the coach's hand away, which didn't exactly endear him to the coaches. Wright said he infuriated the Alabama martinets by grinning at them when they yelled at him.

Wright felt he was dealing with shallow people who could get away with whatever they wanted, that they couldn't communicate except on an animalistic level, and that they certainly weren't educators.

Sometimes the best-laid motivational plans of mice and men aren't plans at all.

When Bryant was coaching Kentucky his team met one of Sid Gillman's fine Cincinnati clubs on the road. When the Wildcats went out to warm up, Bryant noticed no one was in the stands. When his men finished their warmup, the Cincinnati players hadn't even taken the field. When the Wildcats returned to the dressing room, Bryant realized he had messed up, that he got his team to the stadium an hour earlier than he intended.

The players sat there for an hour, smoldering like volcanoes. When they finally returned to the field, they erupted and stomped favored Cincinnati 27–7. Assistant coaches Carney Laslie and Frank Moseley spoke to many clubs over the years, and they always cited Bryant's creation of that dead time as a brilliant psychological move. It was years later when Bryant finally confessed to them that he had simply made a mistake in timing, that it was all just plain luck.

Bryant liked to tell another story about motivation. On a Thursday before his Kentucky team was to play LSU, he had his appendix removed. He certainly couldn't attend the game, his doctor said. But on Friday one of his players visited him and asked, "Coach, you'll be there tomorrow, won't you?" When the time came, Bryant got out of bed, and two attendants took him to the sideline. His Wildcats were excited to see their coach giving his all for them. So they dashed out onto the field, ready for battle—and got stomped 34–7.

I suspect some of Bryant's motivational skills filtered down from the most famous motivator of all, Notre Dame's Knute Rockne. After all, Bryant's coach at Alabama, Frank Thomas, played for Rockne and roomed with George Gipp at Notre Dame. Rockne's "win one for the Gipper" speech is the most renowned motivational spiel in football history. Surely Bryant must have learned something from Thomas, who must have learned something from Rockne.

Bryant's success as a motivator was rooted in fear. Players—and assistant coaches and other employees—were simply afraid not to produce. He was a fearsome man, the Intimidator long before the nickname was applied to Dale Earnhardt. In my wildest exercise of imagination I cannot picture players pouring a bucket of Gatorade over his head. (He was shooting craps in Las Vegas one night when a man tried to pick his pocket. Bryant grabbed the thief's arm with his right hand and with his left hand hoisted him onto the craps table, smashing his face into a pile of chips.) But scaring folks isn't a sufficient explanation of why Paul Bryant could motivate. Plenty of scary coaches end up selling insurance for a living. A coach can be scary and not really scare. I'm thinking of one scary coach whose drunken players vomited in the shoes he left outside his room to be shined, another who was decked flat on the practice field by a right cross delivered by a fed-up lineman. Georgia Tech's Bobby Dodd wasn't scary, but he was a great coach. I've never heard a satisfactory analysis of why Bryant was a master motivator—but I've remembered something Gene Stallings told me a few years ago, and I'm sure it's a clue. "You just wanted to please him" Stallings said, obviously savoring those six words decades after the fact.

I could relate to that, because I wanted to please Benny Marshall, the sports editor who hired me at the *Birmingham News.* Pleasing some of my subsequent bosses was not a priority (except as was necessary to keep my job) because I knew more about what was going on than they did. I wanted to please Benny because I respected his skills, his devotion, and his work ethic. He knew the business and applied his knowledge to the best advantage. He delivered, and I believed that if I did it his way I would be delivering, too. He didn't just talk the talk; he walked the walk. You knew that no matter how hard you worked, Benny worked just as hard (and probably harder) that week. And he had passion. He was never just picking up a paycheck. Bryant's players and assistants must have seen him in a similar light.

Oh, I didn't agree with everything Benny said and did, any more than Bryant's lieutenants agreed with everything he said and did. I thought Benny made some foolish moves, and I know Bryant's assistants thought their boss did, too. But the story about the old hall of fame umpire Bill

Klem would apply to Bryant and Marshall, too. When he retired someone asked Klem if he ever missed a call. "Not in my heart, I didn't," he answered.

I'll leave it at that, the search for the answer as to why Paul Bryant was a great motivator, I mean. Even he said, in his autobiography, *Bear,* that he didn't know what motivates a team to rise to the occasion, what makes it respond when the going gets tough.

Attempts to solve the bigger mystery of why he was the greatest college football coach usually bog down in clichés: he came from poverty and was driven not to return; he was obsessed with being the best; he was fearless; he was a brilliant tactician; he could motivate—but, hey, all that can be said about any number of coaches. It's impossible to explain why Bryant was a masterpiece, just as it's impossible to explain why a painting is a masterpiece. Bryant didn't help much there, either. He said he wasn't smarter than anybody else, but maybe he worked a little harder. But lots of coaches work hard.

Perhaps we should leave it where Bobby Marks, one of his players and assistant coaches, did. "I don't know what he had," said Marks, "but he had a lot of it."

Chapter 4

In 1985 I won the American Motorsports Award of Excellence for the best story in the nation on Nextel Cup (formerly Winston Cup) racing. One of the prizes was a thousand dollars in scholarship money to be given to the college of my choice. I asked the sponsor to send the grand to Jacksonville State. Why JSU? Well, I spent a few months as a student there, which is a few months more than I spent at any other college.

College wasn't for me, and I dropped out my freshman year. I lived eight miles from Alexandria High School and rode a school bus. I lived eight miles from JSU, and since my family couldn't afford for me to stay in a campus dormitory, I drove an old Kaiser automobile to Jacksonville. Four more years of traveling sixteen miles a day for book learning had all the appeal of Chinese water torture. I wanted to be out in the real world, married to my high school sweetheart, and holding down a job, so I bid JSU farewell.

That old Kaiser was part of the problem. It burned two quarts of motor oil in the eight miles between my home and JSU and another two quarts on the return trip. Of course, I couldn't afford four quarts of oil a day. If I could have afforded the oil I could have afforded a better car. What I did was this: I got an acquaintance who had a service station to save the stuff for me when he changed oil in a customer's car. I fed my old Kaiser used motor oil—or, as I preferred to refer to it, experienced motor oil.

In the morning before I left for JSU I'd pour two quarts of oil into the crankcase. I'd take two quarts of oil in fruit jars with me and pour those two quarts into the thing before I drove home. One day the motor exploded with all the clatter and smoke of a motor blowing at Talladega Superspeedway, and my car went to Kaiser heaven. More likely, Kaiser hell. After that I got to JSU as best I could, riding with a pipe fitter who was working on a campus building, hitchhiking, bumming rides with other commuting students, whatever.

ROTC was mandatory, and I hated it. I had the cleanest hands at JSU because I was constantly working off demerits by washing the windows of the ROTC building. I never learned to take an M-1 rifle apart, and inspection on the quadrangle was a nightmare because I knew I could be—and usually was—cited for any number of violations. I couldn't do college algebra, and it was suggested I take a high school course, which I wasn't about to do. Even now, when I speak to groups, I say there are three kinds of people—those who understand math and those who don't. It always takes a few seconds before the audience understands the joke. Some never do.

I did learn some physics during my college days. I learned that if you strike the cue ball off center it will affect the angle at which it bounces off the rail. In fact, I was spending as much time in the poolroom on the town square as I was in classes. My lack of interest, lack of qualifications, and lack of transportation led to my flunking out of JSU and looking for work. To be precise, I quit before I was shown the door. I've never regretted it. I was simply able to get a head start of three years–plus on my profession.

They say life is what happens instead of what you had planned. That's certainly true in my case.

When I was at Alexandria High School I was president of the Future

Teachers of America. I particularly admired Reuben Boozer, one of my teachers, so I wanted to be a teacher. Then I read a novel, *Arrowsmith,* by Sinclair Lewis, about a doctor, and decided I wanted to be in the medical field. So I enrolled in prepharmacy at Jacksonville State. In other words, I didn't know what I wanted to be, and when I quit college I simply started pounding the pavement in Gadsden and Anniston, asking for a job. I haunted the main drags, Broad Street and Noble Street, and their tributaries.

With a break here or there I could have become an employee of Alabama Power, the phone company, the post office, a supermarket, Sears, Goodyear, or any number of businesses as easily as I became a newspaperman. I heard the Goodyear plant in Gadsden was hiring, so I presented myself at the main building as a candidate to build tires. There was a guard post but no guard, so I strolled into an office.

"What are you doing back here?" a white-collar man yelled. "How did you get past the guard?" I told him I was looking for a job, and there wasn't any guard. Fussing and fuming, he grabbed me by the arm and escorted me from the building, as if all his problems—including the negligence of the guard—were my fault. "And don't come back," he said, punctuating the bum's rush with a cliché from a Three Stooges flick. I wonder what would have happened to me if that guard hadn't chosen that moment to go pee. Maybe I would have built racing tires for a living instead of covering racing.

A series of heads-or-tails events such as that one affected the course of my life. An atheist might say that's just the way things turned out; I prefer to think the hand of God was involved, because I strongly believe I was supposed to be a writer of newspaper articles and books.

One incident was literally heads or tails. In a moment of high school mischievousness, a pal and I decided to ask a fellow student's girlfriend for a date, just to see if she would go out with one of us. We flipped a coin to see who would have to ask her. I lost. I asked Sandra for a date, and she accepted. Now we've been married fifty years. When I'm speaking to groups, I usually add: "I sometimes have to remind her she not only was the result of a coin flip, but a coin flip that I lost."

Actually, I can't imagine anyone having a better marriage. We've always been in love, and we still are. "We've been a great team," she said not long ago. That summed it up. She is the best woman I know, a giver who is happiest when she's helping others. I've often wondered how my life would have turned out if that coin had fallen heads instead of tails. We wouldn't have married. Our three sons wouldn't exist. Neither would our four grandchildren. The women our sons married would have married other men. A coin flip in a country school more than half a century ago even affected you, for you wouldn't be reading these words if it had turned out differently.

But back to my hunt for my first permanent job. I walked into the *Anniston Star,* an eighteen-year-old seeking employment. I was shown to the office of an executive named Ralph Callahan. Callahan wore a seersucker suit and smoked a pipe, every bit the picture of a southern newspaper boss. He said there was an opening for a flunky's job (my term, not his) in the circulation department. From across his desk, Callahan gazed into my eyes, unblinking, as if he were trying to decide whether to hire me to be publisher of the paper instead of a grunt worker. I made up my mind I wouldn't blink, either. I gazed into his eyes, as if I might be trying to decide whether to accept the job of publisher. My eyes burned, but I held steady. Maybe Callahan liked that, I don't know. In any event, he told me I had the job. I wiped my eyes with the back of my hand. It paid $39.50 a week, he said—and to this day I don't know why the *Star* didn't kick in another fifty cents to make it a buck an hour.

On May 5, 1955, I reported for work at the *Anniston Star.* I was a newspaperman. I did whatever no one else in the circulation department wanted to do—kept records, swept the sidewalk, counted out papers to the carriers. The latter was particularly onerous. The papers came off the press in an old unair-conditioned room out back. The carriers lined up, each signifying the number of copies he needed, and I counted them out, trying to match the speed at which they were coming off the press. I fanned them in the crook of my left arm and quickly counted them with my right thumb. The heat was oppressive, and I wore jeans and no shirt. Talk about an ink-stained wretch—I could have held up a mirror and read the front page off my chest.

I hung around the sports department and the city room of the *Star* in my spare time. I was captivated by the news operation, by reporters coming in off their beats, loosening their ties, flipping open their notebooks, and crafting the hieroglyphics into stories on manual Underwood and Royal typewriters, by editors penciling headlines of exact length to the letter, by men who could watch a football game and condense the action and color into thirteen column inches—and I damn sure didn't intend to count out papers to carrier boys for a living. I told Taylor Smith, the managing editor, that I'd like to become a reporter, and I asked for advice. "My advice is don't become a reporter," he said.

But John Cathey, the sports editor, said he needed someone to cover church league softball at Ezell Park, to write four- and five-paragraph stories. He wouldn't pay me anything, but I could keep the score book, and the league paid the scorer three bucks a night. When you're making $39.50 a week, three dollars two or three nights a week is a substantial perk. So I began writing brief softball stories for the *Star,* and I was, at least technically, a sportswriter. I still have some of the clippings.

Labor Day 1955 rolled around, and Arthur Phillips, the circulation manager, told me I would have to labor. Everyone else in the department had the day off. I was miffed, and I said to myself that Phillips could make me be in the office, but he couldn't make me do much of anything. I bought an *Atlanta Constitution* off a rack on Noble Street, propped my feet on a desk, and began reading it. I was thumbing through the classifieds, not actually looking for a job, when an ad jumped out at me. The *LaGrange Daily News* in Georgia wanted a sports editor.

I applied for the job, went for an interview, and was hired in October 1955. I had just turned nineteen and I was, I think, the youngest sports editor of a daily paper in the United States. Now I was a real newspaperman—if only for forty-five dollars a week. Actually, I *was* the sports department. I covered everything from LaGrange High's state championship football team to the Southern Peach swim meet to kiddie leagues. I went to work at 5 A.M. and stripped the AP wire machine and edited copy and wrote headlines and laid out pages, and in the afternoon and at night I covered whatever had to be covered. It was great training, but I was perpetually sleepy.

On the morning of October 8, 1956, I asked Phil Harrison, the editor of the *Daily News,* if I could have the afternoon off to watch the World Series game between the New York Yankees and the Brooklyn Dodgers on television. Actually, I had no such intention. I was bushed, and I planned to take a long nap. That evening my telephone rang. I answered and Harrison didn't even bother to say hello. He simply blurted, "How about that!"

"Uh, how about what?" I answered lamely.

"Why, Don Larsen's perfect game, of course," the man who had given me the afternoon off to watch the World Series said suspiciously.

I recovered nicely, though. "Oh, yeah, that was something, wasn't it? I thought you meant something big had happened in LaGrange."

While I snoozed, the Yankees' Larsen had pitched the only perfect game in World Series history, beating the Dodgers 2–0 in game five.

LaGrange High School met Richmond Academy of Augusta in the Georgia football playoffs while I worked at the *Daily News,* and one of the Richmond stars was Pat Dye. Years later, when Dye was Auburn's coach and he would become miffed at me, I'd remind him: "Hey, boy, I covered you when you played in high school." And I'd add: "But you were probably older than I was."

When my young wife and I moved to LaGrange (and out of my daddy and mother's house) we had a car my parents had given us, a TV set my grandparents had given us, and little of anything else except love. We moved into a three-room furnished apartment. We allowed ourselves a dollar's worth of gasoline a week, and when that was nearly gone we walked. We had mere pennies for entertainment. We bought a coloring book for ten cents and a pack of crayons for ten cents. We'd open the book on the kitchen table, and Sandra would color one page and I'd color the opposite page. Mike, the first of our three children (Mark and Mitch are the other two) was born while we lived in LaGrange, which made us pinch our pennies that much harder.

The editorial staff of the *LaGrange Daily News* consisted of the editor, the sports editor, the main news reporter, the society editor, and the photographer. The main news reporter resigned, and after a little more than a year as sports editor I asked for the job of main news reporter. I wanted to acquire as broad a background in the business as possible. So I began covering city and county governments, the police, the sheriff's department and the highway patrol, civic club speeches (I welcomed the free lunches), and the courts and writing feature stories. The fellow who had been hired to replace me as sports editor was a washout, and Phil Harrison, the editor of the paper, told me he had an idea. "We both need more money," he said. "Suppose I tell the boss not to replace the sports editor. Suppose I tell him to split the sports editor's salary between you and me, and we will split the sports editor's workload."

Compared to the salary I was making, the widow's mite in the Bible story seemed lavish. I didn't know how I could possibly do more work than I was doing, but I welcomed the opportunity to earn more money, so I bought into Harrison's scheme. Harrison approached Bill Coker, the general manger of the *LaGrange Daily News,* with his plan. He came out of the meeting shaking his head in amazement. "Bill agreed to half of it," Harrison told me. "He said you and I will split the sports editor's workload, but we won't be paid any more money."

Newspapers have a reputation for being chintzy. They know there are enough idealistic, intelligent, adventurous folks who will forgo the opportunity to make more money in other fields just to be part of what they perceive as a glamorous profession, and newspapers capitalize on that situation. But I've always been grateful to the *LaGrange Daily News* for giving me the opportunity to become grounded in the business. I learned to cover everything from a basketball game to a murder to a county commission meeting, to write headlines and lay out pages, and to interview coaches and cops and criminals. A small paper is a fine starting point for young newsfolks.

I was homesick and ready to move on to a larger newspaper, so in 1957 I applied for, and got, a job as a reporter with the *Gadsden Times.* I soon became city editor. I was filled with the aforementioned spirit of adventure, and something was always hot in our circulation area.

A Seaboard railroad freight car containing sixty tons of 105-millimeter howitzer artillery shells caught fire, and hundreds of the shells exploded, causing some 150 homes in Piedmont to be evacuated. I crept within a hundred yards of the fire to shoot pictures. A fellow staffer who had seen combat in the navy, who knew what explosives could do, told me I was crazy. He was probably right.

I covered the Torso Murders, a grisly affair that "incited more emotion and imagination than any other crime in Alabama history," and I don't believe my description was exaggerated. A woman named Viola Hyatt shotgunned a couple of brothers, Lee and Emmett Harper, cut off their arms and legs and scattered them over a wide area. Terror gripped our readers when the first torso was found, but soon afterward when the headline screamed "Second Torso Found" folks checked the windows to be certain they were locked, wedged chairs under doorknobs, and made sure all guns were loaded. Severed limbs turned up periodically, and fear had a vise grip on Etowah and surrounding countries.

I like a joke as well as the next fellow, but I thought an acquaintance of mine went too far when, in the midst of the hysteria, he somehow acquired a department store mannequin's leg, and his wife came home to find it sticking out of the oven.

Viola was arrested, and she finally pleaded guilty in return for a life sentence. She never really explained her motivation behind the crimes. I interviewed her father, and the story won first place for features in the Alabama Associated Press Newswriting Contest.

A high school boy threw an incendiary bomb at a synagogue and shot two men, wounding them after they ran through the front door, over which was framed the inscription, Love Thy Neighbor as Thyself. In his statement he referred to "Jewish swine." My story on the attack won first place for spot news in the state AP contest.

A rumor that black civil rights demonstrators would stage a lunch counter sit-in at a local store sent me and my camera to the scene. Klan members showed up, too, and one warned me not to shoot any photos of Klansmen if there was a fight. I made up my mind I'd do my job, and if that meant getting my butt whipped, so be it. I was relieved the demonstrators didn't materialize.

I had another close call in Gadsden. Some creep from our circulation area was scheduled to die in the electric chair, and Charles Ryan, the managing editor, told me to cover the execution. I wasn't going to watch the guy die, I told Ryan respectfully. When I was a little boy I saw what was left of a man who had been hit by a train, and the sight haunted me for years. Ryan said keeping my job might depend on my covering the execution. I told my wife Sandra we might be looking for a new job because I wasn't going to watch a man being electrocuted. I don't remember the details, but the execution was canceled or postponed, saving me and the criminal.

I didn't stay saved, though. Frank Helderman Jr.—"Buster"—the son of the publisher of the *Gadsden Times,* Frank Helderman, fired me. The employees had known Buster as the boss's kid, hanging around the paper, and they tended to treat him as a kid. Then he graduated from college, worked briefly in several departments of the *Times,* and his daddy gave him a position of authority (I think he was called general manger). I still considered him a kid, but now he had power, and evidently he was itching to use it.

One day a reporter got something wrong, and Buster was dressing the older man down in the newsroom, in front of everybody. The reporter was embarrassed at first, and then he began to seethe, and I was afraid the situation might turn physical. "Let me handle this," I told my young boss. "I'm the city editor, and I'll get it straightened out." Buster stormed off to his office.

The next day he said to me, "Don't you think you'd be happier working somewhere else?"

"Yes, I do," I said.

"Then take as long as you need and find another job."

I was surprised but not shocked. Firings were commonplace at the

Gadsden Times. Having been canned by the *Times* became sort of a badge of honor in state newspaper circles. Several outstanding journalists got the ax at the *Times,* where an independent spirit wasn't welcome. A couple of *Birmingham News* stars—sportswriter Jimmy Bryan and political writer Al Fox—and I used to sit around the *News* and laugh about our firings at the *Times.* I spoke at a meeting of the Gadsden Quarterback Club in 2001. I began my talk by saying, "The best thing that ever happened to me happened right here. I got fired from the *Gadsden Times.*" The quarterbackers loved it.

Gadsden wasn't a wash, though. The two first-place awards in the Alabama Associated Press Newswriting Contest helped establish my name in the state. Our second child, Mark, was born in Gadsden. And for the first time, I made a hundred dollars a week, which I counted as a milestone.

The *Montgomery Advertiser* hired me as a copy editor. I reported for work in February 1961, excited about the new job, but I was immediately deflated. L. P. Patterson, the managing editor, said the post of state editor had come open since we talked, and he wanted me to take it instead of the copy editor's job. I would have to work six nights a week instead of five—but they would pay me $5 a week more than we had originally agreed upon. Gee, I would make $115 instead of $110, and I would only have to work one more night for the extra five bucks. I've told that story many times, hoping to add to newspapering's aforementioned reputation for chintzy dealings.

I had already moved my family—Sandra and sons, Mike and Mark—to Montgomery, so I was stuck. At least for awhile. I had a terrible job. As state editor I was charged with keeping up with what was going on in Alabama—with minimal help. I talked Arthur Shaw, who had worked with me at the *Gadsden Times,* into coming to Montgomery as my assistant, but he recognized a bad thing when he saw it, and he soon returned to the *Times.*

This may sound funny now, but it wasn't funny then. Some thirty-seven funeral homes in south Alabama phoned in obituaries, collect, to the state desk of the *Advertiser.* Shaw or I would take the information. This wasn't as bad as it sounds because the funeral homes in the smaller towns sometimes went for days without a burial, so there would be no calls.

But the *Advertiser* installed something new called a WATS line while I was there. Now, to save money, we had to call the funeral homes instead of accepting collect calls from them. Sometimes no one answered, and we'd have to call back. Sometimes the person who answered would say the boss had gone to supper, and only he could give out the information. So the thirty-seven calls might, on a given night, mushroom into fifty. I was swamped by this obit business. It sabotaged the work a state editor should have been doing. I thought of myself as the newspaper equivalent of a football coach who didn't have time to coach the players because he was always busy lacing up their shoulder pads. In speeches in later years I would be moved to declare that I had written more stories about dead people than about live ones.

Ah, newspapers!

The publisher of the *Gadsden Times,* Frank Helderman, loved what I derisively called "business is good" stories. He personally assigned them, and it sometimes fell to my lot to have to write them. I'd phone several merchants and ask them about business and write a story quoting them. They knew the drill, and they'd invariably say business was good, even if it was bad. Helderman believed positive ink would nudge the economy and the paper would sell more advertising. Never mind about a little technicality known as the truth.

When I joined the *Montgomery Advertiser,* the managing editor, L. P. Patterson, told me to interview some official in some state office and write a story about Alabama's economy. The official painted a rather negative picture, and I quoted him. It was refreshing to know I was working for a paper that expected me to write the facts about the economy. Or so I thought. Patterson disapproved of my story and told me such negative information could only have a counterproductive effect on the economy. He, too, had simply wanted me to write a "business is good" story, but I was too naive to realize it.

Arch McKay was a jovial staffer for Montgomery's afternoon paper, the *Alabama Journal.* One day he told me authorities had pulled a body from the Alabama River near Montgomery and asked if I wanted to ride with him to the site. Sure. We parked as close as we could to the grisly scene, but we still had to make our way through considerable undergrowth. We came upon a stalwart barbed wire farm fence, and I crawled under the bottom strand.

Arch pronounced me a poltroon, a coward, and a sissy and announced he would hurdle the fence in the manner of the immortal Jesse Owens. He got a running start, became airborne—and hooked the toe of his canvas shoe in the top strand. He fell with a thud on his arm. The next day he came to work wearing a shiny white cast. Did I tell everyone on both newspapers how he broke his arm? You bet.

I covered a terrifying race riot in Montgomery on the night of May 21, 1961. The Freedom Riders had come to town, and they were inside the black First Baptist Church on North Ripley Street, along with hundreds of other people. Outside, a car had been turned upside down and set afire. Hundreds of federal marshals tried to guard the church against a white mob estimated to number one thousand. Gov. John Patterson had invoked martial law, and National Guardsmen with fixed bayonets were a chilling sight.

A reporter didn't dare dress the part, because the last thing the racist thugs wanted was exposure, so I dressed in blue jeans and a white T-shirt—and a federal marshal hit me in the back with a tear gas canister. I was admitted to the church. I suppose my press card must have done the trick. I remembered the surreal feeling of being in a house of God while outside an ungodly mob wanted to murder the people who sat in the pews and listened to the words of the brave man in the pulpit—Martin Luther King Jr.

I told another reporter to station himself in a nearby phone booth, and I would try to feed him information that he could relay back to the office. When I returned to the site there was no reporter and no phone booth, just a pile of broken glass and twisted aluminum framing. I wished I were back in the office, phoning funeral homes in Opp and Elba on the WATS line, rather than running the risk of ending up in a funeral home. Several newsmen had been attacked the day before, May 20, when the Freedom Riders arrived at Montgomery's Greyhound bus station and a riot broke out. I knew these hate-filled whites were deadly serious. The sense of adventure that had lured me near the burning bomb train in Piedmont had given way to common sense.

On Sunday, March 23, 2003, my days as an *Advertiser* staffer long behind me, I was in Montgomery for an afternoon book signing. Barnes and Noble was hosting the event for my new novel, *Turn Left on Green.* I was killing time before the signing, and I drove along North Ripley and remembered that fearsome night in 1961. There had been a park in front of the church, and it was in the park that I took the tear gas canister in the back. I remembered dropping flat and pressing my nose against the ground, in the grass, trying to breathe. Now, in 2003, a Montgomery police department building occupied the site. If there was a moral in that, a moralist would have to find it.

It was a glorious springlike morning, and the members were going to church. I parked my car and read about the 1961 race riot in the upraised letters of a cast-iron historical marker, and then I entered First Baptist, too. An usher directed me to a seat.

It's an old church. Its flaking red bricks have weathered untold storms and summers of punishing Alabama sunshine. The pews are curved, in the old style, and their patina is reassuring, for you know many prayers have been offered up from them. A speaker in the pulpit asked if there were any visitors. Obviously there was one. Would the visitor stand and give his name and tell the congregation why he had come to First Baptist?

"My name is Clyde Bolton, and I recently retired from the *Birmingham News,*" I said. "In May 1961 I worked for the *Montgomery Advertiser,* and I covered a race riot at this church. It was a terrifying night." There was a buzz in the audience, a few bitter, knowing chuckles. No one had to guess what I was talking about.

"This morning, forty-two years later, I wanted to return to this church and worship with you folks," I said. Some of the members applauded lightly. "Welcome, welcome," a woman in the pew behind me whispered, patting me on the shoulder.

The people sang the old tried-and-true hymns, and E. Baxter Morris, the pastor, proclaimed the old tried-and-true Good News. They held my hands and included me in their prayer circle near the end of the service, and we were dismissed with the reassuring words of one of my favorite songs, "God Be with You." It was quite an experience, returning to that former war zone in peace and brotherhood. I'll always remember it fondly.

But back to 1961 . . .

The *Advertiser* was a morning paper, and I never adjusted to working at night. All I did was work, read books from the time I got off until daybreak, and sleep until time to go back to work. I lost thirty pounds in seven months—without trying. (Please, no cracks about how I should go back to Montgomery for seven months.)

I had to get out of that miserable job. One day I boarded my 1954 Chevrolet, drove to Birmingham, and, unannounced, presented myself as a candidate for a job on the state's biggest newspaper, the *Birmingham News.* John Bloomer, the managing editor, cordially showed me around the office, but he said there were no openings on the staff. He walked me back to the elevator, and as I was stepping into it he said, "Well, we do have an opening in the sports department, but I'm sure you wouldn't be interested in that."

I had been out of sports for five years and had no intention of returning to the Toy Department, but I would have scrubbed commodes to have escaped from the *Montgomery Advertiser.* I forearmed the closing elevator doors and said, "Oh, yes, sir, I would be interested in that." Bloomer introduced me to Benny Marshall, the sports editor, and they hired me. I was so desperate that I offered to come to the *Birmingham News* for the same salary I was making in Montgomery, $115 a week. If you think the *News* said, "Oh, we'll pay you more than Montgomery is paying you," you're mistaken.

I joined the *News* at age twenty-five on September 4, 1961, and retired at age sixty-five on September 7, 2001. I've often wondered what my life would have been like if those elevator doors had closed, if John Bloomer hadn't said, as an afterthought, that were was an opening on the sports staff.

I'll never forget what L. P. Patterson, the *Advertiser*'s managing editor, said when I gave him my two weeks' notice. He didn't say we're sorry to lose you or good luck in Birmingham. He said, "Are you out of your goddamn mind? The way to the top is through editing, not writing." I bit my lip and let it slide. After all, I was at his mercy for two more weeks, and I thought I might need him for a reference some day. Why burn that bridge behind me? Years later, when I became the featured sports columnist of the *Birmingham News,* I smiled and said to myself: "This may not be the top, but it's closer to the top than being managing editor of the *Montgomery Advertiser* is."

Chapter 5

When I reported to work at the *Birmingham News* on September 4, 1961, four days after my twenty-fifth birthday, I stepped into a newsroom that was straight out of *The Front Page,* one of those old movies that used to glamorize the newspaper business.

There was a horseshoe-shaped copydesk, presided over by a slot man who, from his position in the shoe, farmed out copy to be edited and headlined by those on its rim. A couple of female telephone operators sat at an ole-timey switchboard and stabbed plugs into holes so reporters could talk on gooseneck phones. Manual typewriters on reporters' desks rat-a-tat-tatted like so many machine guns, and pneumatic tubes crisscrossed the ceiling, sucking stories from the hands of editors and dispatching them to the composing room to be set in type. Everybody smoked; everybody's collar was unbuttoned and necktie loosened; and some even wore green plastic eyeshades. Editors yelled, "Copy!" and copyboys got off their duffs and walked stories from one desk to another or fetched copy paper or coffee. The furniture was old and scarred, to match some of the reporters.

It was loud and it was romantic, a far cry from today's newsroom, which is punctuated with computer screens like so many streetlights coming on at dusk and which is indistinguishable in appearance (and, for the most part, in spirit) from an insurance company's office. It's been a long while since I heard anyone use the term "the newspaper game."

There was a time when I could take friends through the Birmingham News building and show them a Linotype machine spitting out lines of lead type and let them smell the metallic stink of plates being cast for the press and explain the entire process of how a newspaper was produced. In my later years at the paper, when everything became computerized, I didn't have a clue how it was produced.

Benny Marshall, the sports editor–columnist, welcomed me that first day and assigned me a desk. It was a blocky, wooden, grayish blue thing that looked as if it might have been bought secondhand from a navy surplus store. Inside the desk was a manual Royal typewriter that appeared or disappeared with the pull of a wooden lever. My typewriter was out of sight, and when I moved the lever a hideous machine rose from the bowels of the desk, like a rotted corpse escaping a grave in a horror movie. It was a typewriter, all right, but it was covered in what I soon learned was ancient, encrusted tobacco spit.

"It was Zipp Newman's," said Ace Kabase, the guy who laid out the sports pages. He explained that Newman, who retired in 1959 after some forty years as sports editor, always had a cigar in his mouth. He chewed the things. And spat the resulting goop onto his typewriter (even when he listened to opera on the radio, as he did on nonfootball Saturday afternoons). The desk hadn't been used since he retired. The next day, armed with a box of cleaning supplies and instructions from my wife on how to use them, I restored Zipp's old machine to a reasonable facsimile of a working typewriter.

As sports editor emeritus, Zipp still wrote a weekly column, at home, for the paper. One day he strolled into the office delivering his column—and everyone immediately got busy. I soon realized why. They didn't want to invite his attention. Zipp spotted me and walked over to my desk and introduced himself. Sure enough, a gooey cigar hung between his teeth, and threads of tan juice crept from the corners of his mouth. I had on a long-sleeved white dress shirt. Zipp took the cigar from his mouth, grasped my arm in welcome—and left a long brown stain the length of my sleeve. It never did come out.

So what? I was in the big time, or at least what passed for the big time in Alabama. The other members of Benny Marshall's staff were Kabase, Ronald Weathers, Jerry Bryan, Alf Van Hoose, Jim Martin, Frank McGowan, and Walton Lowry. The staff was too small then, and it would remain too small for the forty years I was on board.

I always said that if I were starting up a newspaper Ron Weathers would be the first person I would hire. He would cover without complaint the stuff no one else wanted to cover—tennis, high schools, Samford, and Birmingham-Southern.

Jerry Bryan was a colorful character from Reform, Alabama. He had been the heavyweight boxing champion of Pickens County, and he had become a hero of the newspaper game by knocking an editor of the *Birmingham Age-Herald* through a window. Jerry and I were going to cover a football game in Jackson, Mississippi, one day when we came upon a funeral procession. It was an abnormally long procession in a small town, and we were struck at the tail end of it. Jerry's impatience and newspaperman's curiosity got the best of him, and he floored the accelerator, passed all the mourners, and pulled up beside the lead car—which was driven by an angry policeman who had spotted us in his rearview mirror. "What happened?" Jerry demanded. "Some big shot die?" I was afraid we might die. The fuming cop not only didn't let us go ahead of the procession, he made us park and dared us to move before the procession was out of sight.

Van Hoose had been the speaker at my high school football banquet, and now I was on the *Birmingham News* sports staff with him. Small world. He was a walking fire hazard. He smoked a pipe, and fires would blaze up periodically when he'd tap the ashes out into a paper-filled wastebasket. Sometimes he would forget to extinguish his pipe at all and drop it, burning, into his sport coat pocket with the predictable result. His shirts were dotted with tiny holes burned by coals from his pipe. "Alf must buy his clothes at a fire sale," an office wit remarked.

Jim Martin was an excellent wordsmith, one of the more entertaining golf writers I've ever read. He left the paper shortly after I arrived, but for years he wrote a golf column, as a freelancer, for the *News*. He not only could write golf, he could play it. He won Montgomery's city championship, set three course records (each with a round of 64), made three aces, and became a club pro.

I tend to think of Jimmy Bryan (no kin to Jerry) and Wayne Martin as members of that 1961 crew because we were on the staff together for so many years, but they came on board a little later. I once said in print that Jimmy's writing flowed like a mountain stream and that it was just as clear. He was a pleasure to read because he knew writing is communicating—a basic fact that somehow is lost on many of today's sportswriters. Jimmy wrote the best lead on a football game story that I ever read. It was after Alabama destroyed Vanderbilt 66–3 in 1979 when U.S. monetary inflation was in double digits: "Inflation killed the Commodores Saturday. Once the football was inflated, Vanderbilt was dead."

Wayne cemented his place in the history of the *News* by entertainingly covering one of the dramatic college basketball stories of the 1980s—the rapid ascension of the new kid on the block, UAB hoops under Gene Bartow.

Benny took me to Tuscaloosa to meet Paul Bryant and to Auburn to meet Ralph Jordan. Bryant was perfunctory and Jordan was cordial, asking me about my background and my family. Thus was set the tone for the relationship I would have with the two men over the years.

The first bylined story I ever wrote for the *Birmingham News* was about a local bowler named Joe McCorvey winning a big tournament, but the first football story that carried my byline in the *News* was written the day I met Bryant. He told me about a plague of injuries that had attacked the team. The 1961 edition of the Crimson Tide would open against underdog Georgia and its new coach, Johnny Griffith, in Athens, and I wondered if the injuries might be too much for Alabama to overcome. They weren't. Alabama stomped Georgia 32–6 en route to an undefeated season and a national title.

I soon learned that Bryant loved to applaud the upcoming opponent and moan about the inadequacies of his own team. During the preseason, he even referred to those 1961 Tidesmen as a bunch of "sissies." Somehow, I never could picture Lee Roy Jordan, Billy Neighbors, Tommy Brooker, and Pat Trammell as sissies. I had been raised on the legend of arch pessimist Wally Butts of Georgia, so I was used to a coach accentuating the negative to the point of being ridiculous. But there was a difference. The newspapers in Georgia tended to make a joke of Butts's crying, while the Alabama papers, for the most part, kept a straight face when Bryant declared his monsters had no chance against the Baptist Church Kindergarten's B-team. I mean, everyone called Butts "Weeping Wally," but no one would have considered calling Bryant "Bawling Bear." Today a coach who cried to the extent Bryant did would be ridiculed in column after column, but if it ever happened in those days I didn't read it.

I knew Bryant to kid about his poor-mouthing just one time. And he didn't smile then. He was asked how good his upcoming team would be, and he replied, "We'll go 0-and-12."

"But you only play eleven games," the reporter protested.

"We'll lose the bowl game, too," Bryant said.

In his autobiography, *Bear,* Bryant (actually sportswriter John Underwood) wrote that he used the press to help him win football games. He said something I found curious, given the widespread assumption that his players had unwavering faith in him and believed in every utterance that passed his lips. He said words in cold print in a newspaper could have a more profound effect on a player than the same words spoken by a coach.

Bryant said he could always get his message across to Benny Marshall. He would drop Benny a clue as to what he wanted written, and Benny would run with it. Bryant told how Marshall visited his hotel room late one night before the 1962 Sugar Bowl and found him sick and feverish. Benny penned an article telling how Bryant would answer the bell anyway.

(Shades of win one for the Gipper!) Benny's piece, according to Bryant, won the football game, but Benny never knew it. Bryant flatly said Alabama wouldn't have won except for that article.

To those whose voices were flavored with disapproval when they noted he "used" the press, Bryant said he would use anything to get the players to look and listen. In the old days the *Birmingham News* and other Alabama papers certainly made it easy for him, because they were willing to be used.

Weeping Wally Butts was responsible for the foremost con job ever perpetrated on a sportswriter. The 1946 Georgia team, featuring Charley Trippi, went undefeated, beat North Carolina in the Sugar Bowl, and won a national title. But before the fifth game, against Furman, Butts somehow convinced Scoop Latimer, a Greenville, South Carolina, sports editor, that his Bulldogs were too beaten up to survive the Purple Hurricane. Latimer, perhaps envisioning himself becoming a legend in the annals of prognostication, wrote a column picking Furman to win the game. Georgia won 70–7—and Latimer did, indeed, become a legend in the annals of prognostication.

(Time out: I am amazed that readers become so overwrought about something as inconsequential as columnists' predictions. If I picked Auburn or Alabama to lose and it won, I could count on receiving several childish letters from fans, telling me how stupid I was. Finally, I began suggesting in prediction columns that they should tell me before the game, not afterward, how stupid I am, since anyone can read the scoreboard. That put a stop to the notes.)

When I arrived at the *News,* Benny told me I'd be covering major college football and basketball. I was delighted, because I feared that as the new boy I might be stuck on high schools. My first football game was that 32–6 Alabama-Georgia thing in Athens. Benny did the game story and a column, and I wrote the dressing room stuff. Benny and I unexpectedly spent part of Friday night in an Athens hospital. We weren't sick, but Georgia's new coach, Johnny Griffith, was, and we were running down the story.

Griffith suffered an attack of appendicitis on Friday, and a surgeon removed his appendix. So he wasn't at Sanford Stadium for his first game as coach of the Bulldogs.

Nowadays the *Birmingham News* assigns beat men to cover Auburn and Alabama, but for years after I arrived it was handled differently. "You do an Alabama story for Tuesday and an Auburn story for Wednesday and Thursday," Marshall might tell me. He and Van Hoose and I and sometimes other staffers bounced from one team to the other. I liked that. It enabled me to get to know the coaches and players at both schools. I particularly liked a young Auburn assistant coach named Vince Dooley, and I made a point of dropping by his office when I was on the Plain. The *News* had a Mississippi edition in those days, and I spent a great deal of time in Starkville. I'd usually visit with a young Mississippi State assistant named John Majors.

When I came to the *News* in 1961 the SEC head football coaches were Bryant and Jordan, Florida's Ray Graves, Georgia's Johnny Griffith, Kentucky's Blanton Collier, LSU's Paul Dietzel, Mississippi's John Vaught, Mississippi State's Wade Walker, Tennessee's Bowden Wyatt, Vanderbilt's Art Guepe, Georgia Tech's Bobby Dodd, and Tulane's Andy Pilney. In all, I would cover eighty-six SEC head football coaches in my forty years at the *News*. I can't even remember what some of them looked like. (Trivia question: what's the second oldest Division I-A football stadium? Answer: Mississippi State's Scott Field. It dates back to 1914. Georgia Tech's Grant Field, which dates back to 1913, is the oldest.)

LaGrange High's football team won the Georgia state championship in 1955, my first year as a sportswriter. Alabama's football team won the national championship in 1961, my first year at the *Birmingham News*. Being a sportswriter was a fun way to make a living—if you could make a living.

I was even excited about Auburn and Alabama basketball in 1961—in fact, more excited than either school was. Neither made the commitment to have a strong program. Auburn played in a former airplane hangar called the Sports Arena that might have seated twenty-five hundred on its portable bleachers. Alabama's Foster Auditorium was a handsome old building but it, too, lacked seating capacity. "We used to call it five thousand but I doubt it would seat that many," Hayden Riley, who was coach in 1961, once told me.

Adolph Rupp's Kentucky had ruled the Southeastern Conference. When Rupp retired in 1972 after forty-one seasons as boss Wildcat, he was the winningest college coach with a record of 876–190 for 82.2 percent. He had four NCAA championships, twenty-seven SEC titles, and one Olympic gold medal. How dominating was that? Tennessee was second with five SEC titles. Alabama had two and Auburn one.

Auburn's coach was Joel Eaves, a tall, white-haired, distinguished-looking man whose 1960 club brought that Southeastern Conference championship to the Plain. Eaves made the best of smaller players, employing them in a patterned attack called the Shuffle Offense (which was featured in *Sports Illustrated,* I think on the cover). I thought Eaves was superior to the usual run of SEC basketball coaches of that era, and I was sorry I got to cover just two of his teams. He left after the 1963 season to be director of athletics of Georgia. His record over fourteen years at Auburn was a respectable 213–100.

Riley was a likable fellow who never got it going at Alabama. His final season was 1968, and in eight years he compiled a record of 102–104. Alabama was not a basketball state then and it still isn't. Interest will flare up when a team is exceptionally good, but it isn't sustained.

Mississippi State had a colorful coach named Babe McCarthy who was doing what few others had ever done—namely, developing a legitimate rivalry with Rupp. State won SEC titles outright in 1959, 1961, 1963, and tied the Wildcats in 1962. McCarthy and Rupp had a "feud" going, and it spiced up SEC hoops. I made numerous trips to Starkville to cover Babe's teams for the Mississippi edition of the *News.* I like small towns, and Starkville and Oxford are my two favorite Southeastern Conference venues. I always thought I would enjoy living in either one—and since I've read everything William Faulkner ever wrote, Oxford probably would be my first choice.

I especially liked traveling to football and basketball games with Benny Marshall. I felt I was in the presence of a master. At least a master of the gee-whiz coverage of that era. He was too kind a person, too concerned about others, to have been nearly as effective in this modern era of hard-nosed sports reporting and accentuating the negative.

Benny loved the *Birmingham News.* After many years of service in its behalf, he said it was still a thrill to walk through the front doors every day. He cared about writing, and he worked hard at it. He demanded of himself the precise word, and if he had to spend thirty minutes in pursuit of it, so be it. His was the kind of dedication that led to his being named Alabama's Sportswriter of the Year seven times.

Benny wrote a book titled *20 Grand.* It recounted twenty outstanding sports happenings in Alabama history. I've never read a finer sports story than the first chapter of that book, "September Memory," which captured the spirit of minor league baseball as it was in 1931 when the Birmingham Barons' aging Ray Caldwell met Houston's brash young Dizzy Dean in the Dixie Series at Rickwood Field. That book has been on my desk at home since it was published in 1968, and I still enjoy reading it.

Benny was a slight fellow who usually wore a suit and tie, though he didn't require his staffers to do so. It's funny what sticks in your mind, but I can still picture his tiny wrists. They looked as if they might break in two as he rapidly punched the typewriter keys with just his two forefingers.

Paul Hemphill, who had been one of Benny's protégés at the *News,* eloquently described his old boss in a magazine article:

> A witty gnome who could cry at the sight of a wino passed out in an alley, and then make you cry if he chose to write about it, Benny was a one-man show when I joined him as a high-school sportswriter in 1958; absolutely committed to reading, writing and planning the entire sports section. He would be in the office making up the paper at 6 o'clock in the morning, up in the composing room to oversee the makeup, back down to remake the home edition, out to Alabama football practice in the afternoon, and at his typewriter turning out his daily column as the sun went down. He became like a father to me, boosting my ego and covering up my mistakes and gently showing me the way.

At any rate, Benny was too good for the *Birmingham News* or most other newspapers. He was built more along the lines of a novelist or at least a shimmering magazine writer.

As his friend Tom McEwen of the *Tampa Tribune* wrote after Benny's death at age forty-nine: "Benny put his arm around you with his words and took you along whenever he went."

I don't know if prodigy is the correct word for Benny. Maybe so. In any case, he graduated from Mortimer Jordan High School when he was fourteen years old and entered Samford University the same year. He was genuinely concerned about people, bothered by the human tragedy. Everyone talked about the war in Vietnam, but Benny agonized over the suffering of fellow humans, even those in a land far away. Perhaps a couple of heart attacks he suffered had even sharpened his empathy. I don't know.

The last football game he ever covered for the *Birmingham News* was on September 20, 1969, at Auburn. The Tigers beat Wake Forest 57–0. A couple of fellows named Sullivan and Beasley made their debuts that day. You might have heard of them.

The next Thursday, Benny returned from New York, where he had covered the presentation of the all-time all-American football team. He stopped by the office, and it was obvious he'd been deep into the hooch. Then he went home, walked into the bathroom, and shortly after 5 P.M. pressed a .38 revolver to his temple and pulled the trigger.

I've been asked many times why Benny Marshall killed himself. I don't know. There were several other suicides in his family if that's a clue. His health wasn't great, but as far as I know it wasn't terrible. I mean, he was covering football games and going to New York. I just don't know why. I do know that something went out of my life that day, and I've never felt quite as optimistic since.

Benny was buried the next Saturday, his favorite day of the week because it meant college football. I was in Knoxville, covering Auburn-Tennessee. I would rather have been at his funeral. I don't remember who first called me at home with the news that Benny was dead. Maybe it was Jimmy Bryan. Maybe it was Wayne Martin. The news spread rapidly among the staff members. We didn't know what to do, so we drove from our respective homes to the office and cried on each other's shoulders.

Vincent Townsend was the autocratic vice president–assistant to the publisher of the *Birmingham News*. For some reason he didn't like Benny. Townsend used to chew him out in front of the sports staff. Those of us who loved Benny hurt for him. We were sorry he had to take that crap from a man who wasn't as valuable to the paper as Benny was.

Townsend's son Mickey was in charge of the newspaper's pick-the-winners football contest. Some fellow from Siluria had won the thing that week. While Benny's sports staff and his other friends on the paper wept in the office that night, Vincent Townsend demanded, "Did we get a picture of the football contest winner?" Then and there I made myself a promise. When I heard of Townsend's death I would immediately ask the question, "Did we get a picture of the football contest winner?"

One morning in 1978 I came to work at five o'clock and a writer asked, "Did you hear? Mr. Townsend died."

"Really?" I said, "Did we get a picture of the football contest winner?"

During my forty years at the *Birmingham News* I survived a succession of other sports editors, executive sports editors, and assistant sports editors, and they ranged from decent to bumbling to unable to find the front door of the News building with a map and compass. None was in Benny's league. When I was elected to the Alabama Sports Writers Hall of Fame in 2001 it was especially meaningful to me because I joined my best friend, Jimmy Bryan, and my best boss, Benny Marshall, in the ranks of the inductees.

Chapter 6

Neil Bonnett had been injured in a crash at Charlotte or Darlington or on some other thrill ride in the Nextel Cup carnival, and I dropped by his home in Hueytown. Maybe it was Tuesday or Wednesday after his car tried to knock down a concrete wall on Sunday. Bonnett was in his pj's and obviously aching. He explained in clipped words that his breastbone was broken in two. But then he asked me, "Do you reckon a doctor could put a metal plate across the break and screw some screws in there to hold my breastbone together so that I could drive this weekend?"

I looked at him for maybe ten seconds, then I said, "Neil, you're crazy as hell."

I'm convinced that race car drivers are crazy as hell—but they are fascinating and I admire them. Someone said the tragedy of modern man is that he lives and dies and never knows whether he was a coward. Race drivers know.

"Miss a bunt and you lose a ball game," Richard Petty said. "Miss a corner and you lose your life." That, in a nutshell, is what sets automobile racing apart from striking a ball with a stick, throwing a ball into an iron ring, punting a ball into the autumn sky. Hemingway said there are only three sports—auto racing, bullfighting, and mountain climbing. The rest are mere games. I wouldn't go that far, but I get his point.

A lot of sports editors didn't agree with Hemingway in the 1960s and before. They gave auto racing little or no coverage, ignoring the large crowds at local tracks and larger ones at superspeedways. So what if the hometown bullring attracted more fans in one night than the minor league baseball team pulled in two weeks? Everybody knew baseball was a sport and racing was just a daredevil show. Besides, the sports editors already understood baseball, and they'd have to go to the trouble of learning about racing.

Benny Marshall wasn't one of those stick-and-ball dinosaurs. He was farsighted, broad-minded. He saw subscribers and potential subscribers in the grandstands at the local tracks at the state fairgrounds and in suburban Midfield. Alabamians were flocking to the new superspeedway near Atlanta, and if they were attending races, they no doubt wanted to read about races. So he assigned me to cover racing. He dubbed me the first automobile racing writer of the *Birmingham News*—not with a sword to the shoulder but with a casual remark that befitted his style: "We need to cover car racing. You're our man."

"But I don't know anything about racing," I protested.

"You'll learn," Benny said.

And, of course, I did learn. I was the racing writer of the *News* from 1962 until 1990, and my name became so closely associated with the sport that for eight or ten years after I was off the beat some fans and even drivers blamed me for the paper's deteriorated coverage of local racing. I considered it a compliment.

A promoter named Tom Gloor took over Fairgrounds Speedway in 1962, gave the gravel-slinging half-mile racing surface a good asphalting, and renamed the joint Birmingham International Raceway (BIR). Gloor was a Chevrolet dealer, a sharp businessman and savvy marketer. He energized the place, and fans lined up at the ticket window. Later, he would expand the racing surface to five-eights of a mile and light the track and move the races from Sunday afternoons to Friday nights.

How smart was Tom Gloor? This smart: In the 1960s there was a wildly popular TV program titled *The Fugitive.* Actor David Janssen played Dr. Richard Kimble, who had escaped from custody after being unjustly convicted of the murder of his wife—who actually had been killed by a mysterious one-armed man. Dr. Kimble's nemesis was an Inspector Gerard, who pursued him each week. The final episode of *The Fugitive* was scheduled for a racing night and Gloor could imagine folks staying home to watch the denouement. So he announced that he would give a running account of the showdown at the races. And he did. Between each race he would bring the fans up to date, and they cheered wildly when Gloor announced that Dr. Kimble had prevailed over the one-armed villain.

The first race Gloor promoted was the first race I covered. They say timing is everything, and on that score Gloor was fortunate. For the first time, the *Birmingham News* was actually staffing local races, writing bylined advances and features, running a racing column, treating racing as a full-fledged sport. And his promotion of the old track coincided with the arrival of three invaders from the Miami area who would lift local racing to a new level.

At first, Bobby Allison and his brother Donnie and their pal Red Farmer commuted from south Florida to race in Alabama, but eventually they moved to Hueytown, a change of residence that led to its becoming known nationally as the biggest little town in racing. They raced furiously and expertly, frequently finishing 1-2-3. Most of the locals could be called semipros, men who worked regular jobs during the week and raced on weekends, but the Allisons and Farmer were professionals. (Farmer was an electrician before he devoted full time to racing.) Maybe they had to eat baloney sandwiches on a bad week, but they did nothing but race. Their Alabama opponents grudgingly referred to the Floridians as "those gypsies."

Cosby Hodges, a former race driver, had a used car lot, and he wanted to give Donnie Allison a helping hand by offering him a job. "I don't want a job," Donnie told him. "I'm going to win the Indianapolis 500 some day." He didn't win it, but he finished fourth in 1970 and was the Rookie of the Race.

B. J. Parker is better known as the founder of the Southern All Star Racing tour, but he was a local driver in the 1960s. I remember the day I met him. He was leading a long-distance race at BIR that was red-flagged. The Allisons and Farmer lurked behind him. I thought it would be neat to interview the leader while the race was stopped, so I walked onto the track, introduced myself, and asked him what he was thinking about at that juncture. I was surprised and amused by his answer. "I can't beat those professionals, can I?" Parker said with a grim chuckle. A defeatist attitude? Naw, he was just being realistic. Others in the race felt the same way about their chances.

The Florida trio set the benchmark by which local racing was measured. Once, for no reason, Donnie Allison bored three holes in his right front fender. The next week, several other cars showed up at BIR with three holes in their right front fenders.

The Allisons and Farmer traveled together, venturing into hotbed North Carolina and other locales. One night they pulled their racers through the infield gate of a speedway and a homeboy driver said, "Oh, hell, there's that Alabama gang." The name stuck, and the Allisons and Farmer became the original Alabama Gang. Bonnett and Davey Allison would be latter-day gangsters, and the term would even be expanded to loosely include all Nextel Cup drivers from the Heart of Dixie.

Nobody fears today's Alabama Gang. There was a time when, if you wanted to know how Alabama drivers fared in a Nextel Cup race, you'd start at the top of the finishing order in the paper and read down; now you start at the bottom and read up. (And that's on the rare occasions when an Alabamian drives in a Cup event.)

A Birmingham-Midfield-Montgomery-Huntsville NASCAR circuit provided ongoing short track drama in the state. Some drivers would even race at BIR on Sunday afternoon and then hightail it to Atlanta's Peach Bowl and race on Sunday night. Without benefit of an interstate highway, mind you.

Dixie Speedway in Midfield was a sporty quarter-mile track that no longer exists. Dixie hosted an annual 500-lap marathon. The scream of the motors played off metal advertising signs that lined the backstretch and the turns, and my ears rang for three days afterward. I had finally got the ringing off my mind when my wife, Sandra, asked, "Are your ears still ringing?"

"They weren't," I said, "but they are now."

Fans saw horsepower of a different sort one night at the Midfield track when B. J. Parker was the promoter. Parker was going to have a drawing for a pony between races. He led the male animal onto the frontstretch for the fans to observe. As he rubbed its back, the pony became, er, infatuated. The evidence of its increasing infatuation was clearly visible to the fans in the grandstand but not to B. J., who was standing over the pony.

"B. J., you'd better quit petting that pony," said public address announcer R. V. Parker, who was no relation.

The fans howled, but B. J., blissfully unaware, just grinned.

"B. J., that pony is falling in love," R. V. Parker said.

And B. J. just grinned.

At a quarter-mile in length, Dixie Speedway was an action track that sometimes couldn't hold the buzz bombs that barely exited one turn before entering another. The most spectacular wreck at Dixie occurred when a race car soared over the guardrail and through the advertising fence and finally came to rest atop a Lincoln Continental in the parking lot. Police and track employees worked hard to keep spectators away from the crash site, but one young man was especially anxious to get into the parking lot. Johnnie Morris, a racing official, asked him why he was so fretful.

"I turned sixteen today and got my driver's license," he said. "My daddy let me drive his car, and it's somewhere in that parking lot."

"What kind of car is it?" Morris asked.

"A Lincoln Continental," the boy replied.

"Son," Morris said, "you'd better go call your daddy."

The Allisons and Farmer were as competitive against each other as against outsiders. There was a weekend when the Allisons' brotherly love wasn't so brotherly or so lovey. "At the time we were racing Modifieds,

Bobby and I were our own best competition," Donnie recalled. "When you have competition, you have trouble. I think the trouble was that I wanted to beat Bobby more than I wanted to beat anyone else, and he wanted to keep me from beating him more than anybody else. We let things get out of hand before we finally sat down and had a talk. We agreed it was both of our faults."

It was during a Saturday night–Sunday afternoon of Montgomery-Birmingham racing that their rivalry turned ugly. "I had wrecked my car, and I was pretty broke," Donnie said. "I told a good friend I would drive his car until I got enough money to put mine back together. "At Montgomery they made Bobby start in the rear, and he was aggravated. Bobby and I got together, and I ended up spinning and hitting the fence. I told Bobby, 'I'll get even with you for that.' We worked all night to get the car ready for Birmingham's hundred-lapper the next day. Well, we had a caution flag about the ninetieth lap, and on the restart the injector sucked some air and Bobby passed me.

"I kept telling myself if I was going to spin him out, now was the time to do it. We got the white flag, and I said to myself, 'I've only got four corners left to do it.' I spun him, and he finished second, and I won. He shook his fist at me, but I figured that just evened the score. Then my father came over to me, and he said, 'We didn't bring you kids up to act like that. It's time you got together.'" Ed Allison's intervention led to peace talks. "And from that day to this," Donnie said, "We've never had a cross word."

Widespread recognition of Alabama short track racing came when Bobby Allison won NASCAR's national Modified championship in 1964 and repeated in 1965. Farmer had won the same title in 1956 before he ever raced in Alabama. Sportsman cars replaced the Modifieds as the top short track division in Alabama and most of the South, and Farmer won NASCAR's national Sportsman championship in 1969, 1970, and 1971.

It was a dazzling accomplishment, winning national titles in three decades, the '50s, '60s, and '70s. It required incredible skill, stamina, and willingness to travel and go without sleep. There was no limit to the number of races in which a man could drive, and the champion was simply the one who compiled the most points. In 1969 Farmer competed in eighty-three races and won thirty-one of them. He swamped runner-up Harry Gant (a future Nextel Cup star) 8,276 points to 5,495.

The man who won a national championship when Dwight Eisenhower was president of the United States still races, backed by his longtime sponsor Long-Lewis Ford. Farmer competes in several dirt track events each year, racing mainly at Talladega Short Track. He can still win. I was amused on a summer's day in 2003 to read in a newspaper that he had started on the pole and led all fifty laps of the race in Dothan, Alabama. He started racing in 1949, so he has raced in seven decades.

Farmer makes a joke of not revealing his age, and I've always gone along with it. What's the harm? The *Birmingham Post-Herald* once revealed Farmer's age, though. Gee, what a brilliant piece of investigative journalism. I was reminded of the tag Brock Yates, the *Car and Driver* magazine columnist, applied to modern sportswriters: "the no-fun police."

Farmer won the 1971 national championship despite being injured in a crash at Maryville, Tennessee. His kneecap was removed at a Birmingham hospital. Lying there in bed, he dug deep for a silver lining. "Maybe I won't have to drive with a cast. Since there's no bone anymore, I don't have to wait for the bone to heal."

While Farmer was hospitalized I asked him for an accounting of the injuries he had suffered during his racing career. He came up with: Broken right ankle. Broken right foot. Left leg broken on three occasions. Left kneecap removed. Two vertebrae in back broken. Six ribs broken. Cheekbone broken with subsequent loss of feeling in the left side of his face. Burns on 40 percent of his body. That list was current more than thirty years ago. It has grown since. Oh, and Farmer wears a hearing aid because he is partly deaf from exhaust noise. "I got the hearing aid and didn't tell my family," he joked. "I changed my will three times in two weeks."

Football players play hurt. Race drivers play broken. Farmer performed an extraordinary act of willpower and courage one night in 1962 at Dixie Speedway. Modified-Specials raced in a few tracks in Alabama, Tennessee, and Georgia in those days. It wasn't a true national division, but its championship trophy was something both Bobby Allison and Farmer wanted for their mantels. On July 20 Bobby held a slim lead over the redhead.

Farmer's accelerator hung, and he crashed in practice. His foot was broken. Surely that cinched the championship for Allison. Surely his chief competitor would be out of action. Farmer left the speedway to the tune of a wailing ambulance siren, but just before the feature race a pickup truck pulled into the pits and Farmer got out. A bright new cast weighted down his foot and leg. The crowd gave him a standing ovation. They appreciated the guts required to leave the hospital and watch a race.

Somebody left the pits, came upstairs, and whispered something into the public address announcer's ear. The stunned PA man then told the crowd Farmer wasn't there as a spectator. He planned to drive.

Red borrowed a hobby car, an entry-level racer that was much slower than the Modified-Specials. It was all that was available. He bit his lip and tears crept from his wincing eyes as friends helped him through the window and into the bucket seat. Farmer finished last that night, but he earned a few championship points. I don't remember who won the race. That seemed as unimportant then as it does now.

Farmer drove the rest of the season with his right leg resting in a special metal trough that was built into the car. His mechanics coated the trough with oil additive so his leg would slip up and down and operate the accelerator. He couldn't keep Allison from winning the championship, but he never stopped trying.

As Farmer reclined in that hospital bed in 1971, I wondered how a man who had been broken so many times could climb into a race car and drive it fast. "It's hard to explain," he said. "I just love it. I'd get into one this weekend if I could. Nothing takes the place of it for me. The other day when Alton Jones and I had that real close race at BIR, I really enjoyed that. It was just as thrilling for me to run a race like that as it was for the spectators to watch it. I just wish there had been a couple more cars up there with our fenders banging and sparks flying.

"I've seen people have wrecks and never be good drivers again, but none of my wrecks has ever bothered me as far as letting up on the gas."

I asked him if he worried about being killed.

"It doesn't enter my mind," Farmer said. "You can get killed walking down the street. Somebody can blow a tire and jump a curb and run over you. I'm an electrician, and I could get electrocuted. One thing, if I'm going to go in racing, that's the way I want to go. There's no good way to go, is there?"

He had been an adventurer outside the race track, too. "We used to skip school and go to this abandoned strip mine," Farmer recalled of his teen years in Florida. "We'd climb these Australian pines that were thirty or forty feet high and do flips off them into the water. Alligators would be sunning themselves on the banks, and we'd grab their tails and try to pull them into the water."

Wasn't that perilous? "Well, if they were over five or six feet long we'd let them alone."

I have never met a more positive man than Charles "Red" Farmer. Norman Vincent Peale must have had him in mind when he wrote *The Power of Positive Thinking.* You can't be around Farmer and be "down." He is still as excited as a kid when he goes to the race track or his shop.

I know Farmer could have been a star on the Nextel Cup circuit, but when he was young a great short-tracker could do as well financially as all but a handful of Cup drivers, and he chose to be his own boss. Though he never made a name for himself on the Cup circuit, he was named one of the fifty greatest NASCAR drivers of all time in 1998, and in 2004 he was inducted into the International Motorsports Hall of Fame, joining such luminaries as Juan Manuel Fangio, Jim Clark, Enzo Ferrari, Dan Gurney, David Pearson, Mario Andretti, Curtis Turner, and Dale Earnhardt.

Farmer could drive the monster tracks as well as the bullrings. He won a Saturday Sportsman race at Daytona International Speedway and two Saturday ARCA events at Talladega Superspeedway—though he didn't delight the powers that be when he compared the hovering dangers of driving ARCA on the big courses to "sitting in an electric chair while a drunk plays with the switch."

There was a time when I would have put BIR racing up against short-tracking anywhere in the United States. I looked forward to Sunday afternoons and later Friday nights at the old track. (It's the oldest speedway in the South, and just a mile from BIR sits Rickwood Field, the oldest baseball park in the nation. One reason they survived is that they were made of concrete and steel rather than wood, as so many of their contemporary facilities were.) When I was covering racing there, BIR hosted Friday Hassler, Jody Ridley, Alton Jones, Jerry Lawley, Richard Orton, Neil Bonnett, Jimmy Means, Dave Mader and his son "Little Dave," Freddy Fryar, Bill Sternenberg, Ray Putnam, Bill Gregg, Bo Anthony, Don Anthony, Henry Brook, Jerry McCormack, Denny Rewis, Darrell Waltrip, and others who could drive with the best at any bullring. "It's like a hornet's nest in Birmingham," Daytona 500–winner Buddy Baker said after he drove in a Sportsman race at BIR. "If you can win in Birmingham you can win anywhere."

I almost played a key role in Neil Bonnett's career when he was showing his stuff at BIR. I asked him if he'd like to drive at Talladega Superspeedway if I could arrange a ride for him. Of course, he would. I confess that my motive was partly selfish. I knew Neil was going to be a great one, and I wanted to be able to say I had arranged his first Nextel Cup ride. I told Don Naman, who was president of the world's largest track, "You won't always have Bobby and Donnie Allison to help you draw fans. You need to help in bringing along other Alabama drivers. I know just the guy. His name is Neil Bonnett, and he's going to be a star some day."

Naman agreed, and he arranged for some independent car owner–driver to bring a second car to the next Talladega event for Neil. Alas, the driver wrecked his primary car in a race before Talladega's and had to use his second car himself. Neil would have to wait to make his Nextel Cup debut.

A few years ago Darrell Waltrip and I were recalling the times he'd pull his Sportsman car from his home in Owensboro, Kentucky, and drive at BIR. "That's where the best competition was," Waltrip said, "and I wanted to test myself against the best competition." And yes, he remembered the drive-in theater adjacent to the track, the one that showed dirty movies. "I'd be going down the backstretch and look up at the screen and there'd be a naked woman. I knew the drivers in front of me and beside me and behind me were looking at that screen, too, and I always hoped nobody would forget to turn left at the next corner."

BIR was old when I started covering racing in 1962. Horses were raced at the state fairgrounds as early as 1889, on a one-mile dirt track that ran parallel to Third Avenue West. In 1925 the present speedway opened, and visitors to the state fair were awed by the sight of a ten-thousand-seat covered grandstand that was fronted by a half-mile dirt track. Construction cost two hundred thousand dollars.

Horse racing moved to the new facility, but more importantly the speedway ushered in the era of organized automobile racing. During the 1925 fair, thousands of spectators filled the grandstand and clustered around the track to watch an automobile extravaganza at which the Chevrolet brothers of Indianapolis showed their new Frontenac, a car designed for racing on short dirt tracks.

Word of the majestic new speedway spread, and soon the nation's leading drivers were coming to Birmingham to dare the track. Cigar-chomping Barney Oldfield raced there, and a list of the stars who competed at the fairgrounds eventually would include Fireball Roberts, A. J. Foyt, Richard Petty, Tom Sneva, Tony Bettenhausen, Troy Ruttman, Alec Sloan, Eddie Sachs, Buck Baker, Junior Johnson, Cale Yarborough, Ned Jarrett, and Marshall Teague.

For years car racing was primarily a state fair thing, but in the late 1940s J. P. Rotton began promoting weekly events at the speedway. A new era began. Men such as Bill Latham, Nero Steptoe, Jack Smith, Bob Reuther, Calvin Cobb, Carl Jones, Charlie Griffith, Malcolm Brady, Bob Kieran, Gene Tapia, Fletcher Ford, Joe Holley, Joe Lee Johnson, Charlie Parrish, Gober Sosebee, Tommy Wells, Fred Thompson, Earl Abts, Jake Hatcher, Bones Brasher, Ed Samples, and Sonny Black chased the checkers on a weekly basis.

One story has it that Hooker Hood got tired of making the long trip from his home in Memphis only to be roughed up by the locals. At a prerace drivers' meeting he supposedly said, "I'm tired of being spun out and wrecked, and I'm going to read a list of drivers whose asses I'm going to whip." When he spoke one leadfoot's name, the guy protested, "Hooker, you can't whip my ass." Whereupon Hood replied, "Then I'll take you off the list."

Big Bill France, the founder of NASCAR, promoted a race at the fairgrounds in 1948 and pronounced the facility "the biggest I had ever seen in the South." Fans came from all over the state to watch the races at Alabama's premier race track. Folks from Anniston, Gadsden, Montgomery, Decatur, Florence, and Tuscaloosa made regular pilgrimages—and there must have been a million of them in the stands the day that Nero Steptoe won a race after losing his right front wheel with two or three laps to go, because that many have told me they were there.

Readers Digest used to have a regular feature titled "The Most Unforgettable Character I Ever Met." If I had written an installment it would have been about Grayson "Pappy" Rose. Rose was a mechanical genius, a race car owner who would go to any lengths for a practical joke. I've attended two funerals at which there was more laughing than crying. One was Grayson's, the other was Lewis Grizzard's. (I hope mine will be the third.) Rose was the model for colorful crew chief Pappy Draper in my novel *Turn Left on Green.*

When most of Alabama was legally dry, Rose souped up cars for both revenuers and bootleggers. I asked him if he made one faster than the other. "Well, if I did a five-hundred-dollar job for a bootlegger he'd pay me in cash and give me a hundred-dollar tip. If I did a five-hundred-dollar job for a revenuer I'd have to fill out all these papers in triplicate and send them in to the government, and maybe I'd get paid in ninety days and maybe I wouldn't. Which one would you have made faster?"

He had an alternate answer: "As long as the bootlegger outran the revenuer, we all three had a job. Which one would you have made faster?"

Rose headed to Daytona for Speed Weeks one February, and in his possession was a possum. Along the way he stopped at a mom-and-pop motel. He tied the possum under the bed in his room and phoned the proprietor and told him there was a mouse under the bed. The owner came to the room, got down on his hands and knees and pointed his flashlight under the bed—and bolted from the room screaming at the sight of the monster "mouse."

Rose always carried a pair of pliers in his pocket. You could call it a peculiarity or you could call it being prepared. Tommy Charles, a local radio and TV personality who also was a pilot, and Rose were flying to Daytona when they smelled smoke in the cabin of their small plane. There was a wiring problem, and Grayson used his pliers to make temporary repairs. They landed at a tiny dirt airport in South Georgia. An attendant told them he couldn't get the plane fixed until the next day. He'd drive them to a little motel where they could spend the night. Rose asked him to stop at a liquor store. Couldn't, the man said; it was a dry county. Once in the motel, Rose phoned the local sheriff and asked for the phone number of the nearest bootlegger. "I knew that you, being the sheriff, would know how to get in touch with all the bootleggers," he said. The sheriff told him to go to hell.

There was no taxi service in the town, so Rose called the local undertaker and said he'd pay handsomely if the fellow would have a hearse pick them up and take them to the airport the next day. It did.

Rose was driving to the Atlanta 500 one Sunday when he was stopped in Ranburne, Alabama, a dry town. He had a case of beer in his car, and he was ordered to appear before a magistrate. The magistrate fined him—and then Grayson offered to match him double or nothing for the amount of the fine. The infuriated judge told him he'd better not ever see him in Ranburne again.

Grayson planted turnip greens in a strip of soil between his transmission shop and the street and told the neighborhood busybody it was marijuana. "Whatever you do, please don't call the police," he begged. Sure enough, the cops arrived within half an hour. He used to weld quarters to nails and drive them into the sidewalk. We'd sit in his Woodlawn shop and watch bicycling kids slam on their brakes and leave black skid marks.

Rose's pride and joy was his "mongoose." The contraption consisted of a box designed to barely reveal the tip of a foxtail. The tail was rigged to a spring. Grayson told a fearsome story about the mongoose inside the box and, at the height of the yarn, he pushed a lever that flipped the foxtail onto the victim. He boasted about the time Alabama football hero Johnny Musso, attacked by the mongoose, ran screaming from his shop. And he was delighted that his mongoose caused a local television personality to pee on herself.

Rose's pals loved nothing better than turning the tables on him. Once he spotted some male employees taking a break behind a supermarket. He stopped to show them the mongoose. He was recounting the horrible history of the bloodthirsty animal when a pregnant woman walked up. "I was so far into the story," Rose told me later, "that I couldn't just stop. I didn't know what to do, but I went on with the story and flipped the mongoose on those guys." Whereupon the pregnant woman fainted dead away. That night Grayson's home phone rang, and a voice said, "Are you the man who scared my wife with that foxtail?"

"Yes, sir, I am," Rose said, "and I'd give a thousand dollars if that hadn't happened."

"A thousand dollars, hell," the caller said. "It's going to cost you a lot more than a thousand dollars."

Grayson's little girl, Grace, saw the expression on her pop's face and yelled to Pearl Rose, "Mama, Daddy's in trouble!" Actually, he wasn't in trouble. The caller was one of his racing buddies—who was, of course, accompanied by several others, who snickered in the background.

Once a friend brought a grizzled old logger dressed in overalls and snake boots to Rose's shop to see the mongoose. ("I should have known something was up when several other guys showed up at the same time," Grayson would say later.) Rose began telling his chilling tale of the dread mongoose, and the woodcutter even added to the tension by asking, "Is that thing pizen?"

"Oh, yes," Rose said, "it's one of the most poisonous animals on earth."

Came the climatic moment, and Rose flipped the mongoose on to the logger. The man screamed—and pulled a revolver from the bib of his overalls, pointed it at Rose, and fired five times.

"I thought I was dead," Grayson told me later. "I thought I could feel the blood running down my chest into my pants." The bullets, of course, were blanks, and the audience loved the show.

Rose had a saying: "A cheater doesn't always win, but a winner always cheats." He lived to slip something past the racing inspectors. "The biggest thing Grayson cheated on was fuel," Carl Jones, who drove briefly for Rose, told me. "We were supposed to run methanol, and there was no way they could check for nitro. I think a druggist friend of his figured out a formula to make nitro blend with methanol."

There was a bit of the con in Pappy Rose anyway. He learned that adding a little water to the racing fuel would actually increase a car's performance. So he sold bottles of a special "additive" called Rosetone to other racers, who were unaware they were buying water tinted with food coloring.

But it's been a long time since Bobby Allison and Grayson Rose and Tom Gloor graced BIR. It's been a long time since a big crowd gathered there to watch a race. Occasionally I'm asked if the halcyon days of BIR could be reprised. The answer is no. Times have changed. Air-conditioning wasn't in wide use back then, so we might as well be sweating at the race track on a Sunday afternoon as sweating at home. We had two or three television channels that never carried races, but now we have seventy-five channels, with racing a staple, including all the Nextel Cup events. There's a food channel, an animal channel, a golf channel, a game show channel, a cartoon channel—and the list goes on. The Birmingham papers do such a poor job of covering local racing that no interest is created in their pages. And when they opened that monster speedway at Talladega in 1969, the fairgrounds facility that Bill France once called "the biggest I had ever seen in the South" became just a flyspeck on the Alabama racing map.

Chapter 7

The first race on what is now called the Nextel Cup tour that I ever covered (or saw) was Darlington's Southern 500 of September 3, 1962. At that time the series was elegantly named Grand National, same as the English horse race. Two incidents that day caused me to fear for my life, and when the sun set I would have been delighted if Benny Marshall had taken me off the racing beat and assigned me to something more pleasant, like running a marathon in cowboy boots or pulling up poison ivy with my bare hands. I couldn't have dreamed that racing would become my favorite sport, that when I retired in 2001 I would have covered NASCAR's premier division for forty of the fifty-three years it had been in existence.

Tom Gloor, the new BIR promoter, his partner Willie Kelley and promoter Bob Harmon and I met at the Birmingham airport. We shoehorned ourselves into a rented single-engine plane that squatted on the runway. Gloor, the pilot, turned on the air so we wouldn't suffocate in the September heat. We immediately started gagging and scrambling out of the aircraft. A few days before, a bat had inserted its furry little self into a vent and gone to bat heaven. There is no experience quite like that of sitting in a compartment the size of a car trunk and breathing air that is traveling over a rotting bat on a summer day. Finally the plane was ventilated and made habitable again, and our delayed mission was airborne. We landed on an unpaved field next to Darlington Raceway.

I had never been inside a superspeedway. I was awed. But not by the press box. The press box was a scaffold and boards that teetered scant feet from the first turn guardrail. I climbed the ladder that led from the ground to the press box and saw that the earlier arrivals, those who hadn't been delayed by bat corpses, were sitting on the back rows. Great. I'd have a front-row seat. As I entered the press box, a man handed me plastic goggles. I looked at him blankly. He smiled. So did the veterans on the back rows.

The race started, and I soon realized the purpose of the goggles and why I had the front row all to myself. As the tires of the speeding cars bored through the first turn, they emitted a cloud of rubber dust. By fifty miles I looked like a performer in a minstrel show. My face was black except for the area under my goggles, which was pasty white. Only 450 more miles to go. As the sun dropped, it beamed its killer rays onto the lone occupant of the front row. Those behind me were content in the shade, their goggles in their briefcases, toys to be taken home to the kids with a "look what Daddy brought you." Now my face was lobster and black.

Just as I was about to pass out from sunburn and a rubber-coated respiratory system, I was jerked back into consciousness by a car that veered out of control at 150 miles an hour. It hit the first turn guardrail, directly in front of the press box. It began to climb the guardrail like a massive robot in a Japanese monster movie. I could have spit on the hood—if I hadn't been too dehydrated to spit. The driver's eyes met mine, and I could see he was wondering what a performer in a minstrel show was doing in the press box. All I could think was, Dear Lord, let those smart alecks on the back row get killed, too. At the last moment the car fell back onto the track with the fury of a safe that had been dropped from a third-floor window in a Charlie Chaplin film. My hand shook too furiously to make notes.

Finally, mercifully, the race ended. Junior Johnson was flagged the winner. While the paunchy bootlegger kissed the beauty queens and grinned in victory lane, flushed with the thrill of victory and money, I lay supine under a spigot behind a utility building, the water washing away the tire dust but not the sunburn.

We headed home, Gloor and Harmon in the front seats and Kelley and I in the backseats. The drone of the single engine drugged me to sleep. Then, all of a sudden, there was no drone. The engine stopped dead, and the plane began falling. I leaped into wakefulness. There is nothing as loud as a silent airplane engine at four thousand feet. You couldn't have driven a straight pin . . . well, let's just say I was terrified.

"Is it ice on the carburetor?" Gloor blurted.

"I think you're out of gas," said Kelley, who happened to be a pilot, too. I wished I was back in the press box, dodging race cars. The gauge showed there was plenty of fuel—but the gauge was as wrong as everything else on that day. As the plane plummeted, Gloor switched on a second fuel tank. The engine coughed, then came to life with a roar. The propeller spun. The plane leveled. I would see my wife and young'uns again.

As we neared Anniston, Gloor and Kelley got into an argument. One believed we could make it to Birmingham without stopping for fuel, the other didn't. Enough. I'd had e-damn-nuff. "If you'll land this piece of crap at the Anniston airport I'll get out and walk to Birmingham," I yelled. We did land, we got fuel, and we flew home.

I arrived at my house and embraced my family, my fingers leaving bruises on my wife's shoulders. Once I got my nerves under control, I wrote a story about Junior Johnson winning the Southern 500. I took the story to the office. I happened to glance at the Associated Press wire. It said that a recheck of scoring, hours after the race, showed that Larry Frank, not Johnson, was the winner. There was nothing to do but chunk my original story and begin the two-hour task of writing another one.

It was the end of a perfect day. A perfectly awful day, that is. As I covered my typewriter after writing that second story, I couldn't have guessed racing would lead two presidents of the United States to invite me to the White House or that it would introduce me to the most remarkable sports figure I would ever meet, Big Bill France.

(Postscript: I didn't know whether I could make myself get on another airplane, but I knew that if I was going to be a sportswriter for the *Birmingham News* I would have to fly and fly frequently. Before my next trip by air, I stopped at a state liquor store and bought a half-pint of courage. The only thing they had in half-pints was corn whiskey, so that would have to do. I went to the Birmingham airport terminal—the one that was in use before the current one—and when they called my flight I ducked into the restroom, chug-a-lugged that half pint, and tossed the bottle into a wastebasket. Then I got on board and read the Bible I'd brought with me.)

There's something else I want to say about that racing year of 1962. You can win a drink—of corn whiskey or whatever—by betting that a season's opener for NASCAR's premier division once was run right here in Birmingham. On November 4, 1962, Jim Paschal beat Richard Petty in a 100-mile race at BIR. In those days, races were sometimes added after the schedule had been posted and they were considered part of the following season's points competition. So that BIR event was officially the first of 1963. Subsequent 1962 races at Tampa and Randleman, North Carolina, also were counted in the 1963 season.

That seems remarkably quaint today, given the slick production that is Nextel Cup. The game has changed drastically, and there had to be changes if it was to become a mainstream television sport, but now it seems as much a gigantic exercise in capitalism as a game. Big money tends to squeeze the soul out of sports—not to mention human beings.

Jabe Thomas, who was called the Clown Prince of Racing, once pitted at Talladega and asked his crew for a candy bar. He pitted again on the next lap. "What's wrong? What's wrong?" his crew chief demanded. "Nothing's wrong," Thomas said, handing the fellow the candy wrapper. "You didn't want me to be a litterbug, did you?"

Donnie Allison was running away with a race at Bristol when Thomas pulled into Allison's pit and asked the car owner, Banjo Matthews, "What will you give me not to spin Donnie out?" Matthews shooed him back onto the track, but on the next lap Banjo held up a pit board with "50¢" scrawled on it. Thomas returned to Allison's pit and stuck out his hand, palm up. Matthews handed him two quarters, and he drove away laughing.

It's impossible to imagine that happening on today's Nextel Cup tour. Heck, it's impossible to imagine a driver being known as the Clown Prince of Racing. I'm glad I covered the roundy-round when both could happen.

Michael Waltrip might have been a clown prince if he had come along in an earlier era. He has a marvelous, ironic sense of humor. We were playing golf at the Anniston Country Club when he was new on the circuit, and I hit a tee shot into a swampy area. "Go get my ball and I'll write a column about you," I told the young driver. I was just kidding and had counted that ball among the missing in action, but Waltrip screamed in mock delight, flung his driver into the air, and bolted into the swamp. Everyone on surrounding greens and tees and fairways stopped to see what the alarm was all about. Waltrip mired up in mud to the top of his golf shoes and the cuff of his pants, but he reached my ball. Then he ran back to the tee and handed it to me, his eyes wide and imploring, his tongue out, panting like a puppy who was proud to have fetched the morning paper. "Now write a column about me," he said. When I recovered from the shock I did the only thing I could do—I interviewed him for a column.

I'm glad Michael finally started winning, in his seventeenth year on the circuit. He had raced 462 times before he won the 2001 Daytona 500. I know the constant contrasting of his career and his brother Darrell's was hard on him. A man who'll go into a swamp after a golf ball deserves some victories.

You know what I miss? I miss the old days when a team took a real passenger car and souped it up for racing. I enjoy strolling through the International Motorsports Hall of Fame's museum at Talladega and seeing the old cars with the dashboards and vinyl door panels and chrome trim intact. Today's cars are much safer—and that concern should override everything else—but they are purely and simply racing machines with vital organs and limbs of racing issue, and they never existed as passenger cars. Dead is the car make vs. car make aspect that used to be so important to NASCAR followers. Even the least informed fan has to realize these aren't really Fords, Chevrolets, and Dodges.

In 1963 I broke the story that Fireball Roberts was switching from Pontiac to Ford, and Pontiac fans were crestfallen. They felt betrayed. Several called—one in a kill-the-messenger tone—and said I must have my information wrong: "Farball wouldn't do that." Nobody would give a flip today, but in 1963 Roberts's switch created the kind of stir among stock car racing's fandom that Bear Bryant's becoming coach at Auburn would have created locally. (Okay, that's an exaggeration; a shooting war didn't break out.)

NASCAR has further eroded the importance of brand vs. brand by constantly tampering with the car specifications to ensure close competition among the makes. NASCAR sees it as simply being certain the hoops are the same height on both ends of the basketball court—and it's difficult to argue with the logic or the result—but there is a faint stench of contrivance about the practice. There's no point in a fan's bragging about his favorite marque's performance if it's on NASCAR-supplied steroids. Equalizing the various makes produces parity and lots of winners on the Nextel Cup tour, but I've never been one to worship at the altar of parity.

The history of fun and games has been that a sport is more captivating and more productive of buzz when there is a hotshot to love or hate—Lombardi's Packers, Babe Ruth, Muhammad Ali, Arnold Palmer, Jeff Gordon, Bill Russell's Celtics, Michael Jordan, Tiger Woods, Secretariat, Roger Maris, John Wooden's UCLA, Jack Nicklaus, Dale Earnhardt, Citation, Wayne Gretzky, Willie Shoemaker, Joe Louis, the Richard Petty who won twenty-seven races in 1967. I find an NFL season in which the Dolphins go 17–0 infinitely more interesting that one in which every team breaks even.

But, of course, Nextel Cup has grown from a sport that played primarily before on-site audiences into a television program watched by millions, and its TV "partners," who pay a king's ransom for the rights, want nose-to-tail, door-to-door racing every Sunday. Don't touch that remote control.

The rise of Bobby Allison whetted my appetite for stock car racing. He was immensely talented; he couldn't be intimidated; and he was obsessed with being the best. He and Paul Bryant were the most obsessed sports figures I've ever known. In fact, I once wrote, "If Bear Bryant had been a racing coach, Bobby Allison would have been his driver."

I heard the stories about Allison driving his passenger car in the dead of summer with the windows up and the heater raging to acclimate himself to superheated racing conditions. I heard how he raced in New Jersey and then drove straight through to Alabama to race again, employees of Huntsville Speedway coming to work and waking him as he slept in his pickup truck outside the pit gate. Who wouldn't be interested in such a fellow?

I think Bobby is the best stock car driver who ever lived. Now, it's easy to protest that I'm prejudiced in favor of a homeboy, but that isn't it. He is tied for third (with Darrell Waltrip) on the all-time Nextel Cup victory list with eighty-four, but some of his most impressive drives didn't end in victory lane. He could, say, take a tenth-place car and finish fourth.

He and I were discussing Jeff Gordon one day, and Bobby ventured that Gordon was the second-best driver of all time. "Who's first?" I asked. "You're looking at him," Bobby said with a mischievous grin. I agree.

Allison was a perfectionist, and the lives of perfectionists can be rocky. He gave 100 percent, and he couldn't abide anyone on a team—from owner to crew chief to janitor—who didn't. He knew more about making a race car perform then the mechanics did. He wouldn't suffer fools. For instance, he didn't pacify a millionaire owner who, despite having no racing background to speak of, thought he had superior ideas about making the car handle. As a result, Bobby wasn't always in a situation commensurate with his ability. He was, indeed, driving a tenth-place car to fourth place instead of driving a first-place car to first place. He and I once added up the number of Cup teams for which he raced, and I believe it was twenty-something. But maybe that figure included some he drove for twice.

I might become exasperated when Bobby left strong rides, but I admired his stubborn integrity, his readiness to swim against the flow if need be. It's a shame he and Junior Johnson couldn't get along when he drove for Junior. "If Allison had stayed with me," Johnson said, "he would have won 200 races and Richard Petty wouldn't have." I don't doubt it. Bobby drove for Junior one season, 1972, and in thirty-one races he finished first ten times and second twelve times.

Bobby set one of the most impressive records in all of sports in 1972, though it doesn't get much recognition. It seems to have somehow fallen through the cracks of public perception. He led the final nine races in 1971 and the first thirty of 1972. No one else has ever led thirty-nine consecutive Nextel Cup events. It compares favorably to Joe DiMaggio's fifty-six-game hitting streak.

Consider all that can happen in a race that is beyond the driver's control. Any number of mechanical failures can occur. A tire can blow. Another driver can crash in front of him. A foul-up in the pits can cost a lap. The car can simply not be up to leading the race. To lead thirty-nine in a row is downright incredible, and when you consider Alabama drivers rarely lead a lap anymore, Allison's feat is even more remarkable.

Bobby spoke his mind, which irritated NASCAR and other drivers and teams. We were chatting in the garage at Talladega one day when he pointed to the car in the next stall and said he believed there was water in the door. Its purpose was to cause the car to make the minimum weight in prerace inspection, but a push of a button after the race started would dump the water on the track and lighten the car. "I'm considering calling a NASCAR inspector over here and then getting a hammer and a punch and punching a hole in their car door and letting the inspector see the water run out," he told me. At first I thought he was kidding, but then I realized he was serious. "Bobby, It's going to be pretty embarrassing if you do that and no water runs out of that door," I said. "Besides, you might get your ass whipped." Anyway, he thought better of it and didn't attack the door.

Allison demonstrated his mechanical savvy on July 12, 1966, when he scored his first Nextel Cup victory, at Oxford, Maine. It was an era in which factory-backed cars dominated, but Bobby scored an upset in a racer he had built in the backyard garage at his home in Hueytown. He was the definitive "independent." It was the first victory for a Chevrolet since 1963. It was holy writ that Nextel Cup cars were powered by big-bore motors in the 427-cubic-inch neighborhood, but Allison showed up at the third-mile Oxford Plains Speedway in a Chevelle that was moved by the peppy 327-incher that had sent him to victory lane so many times in Modified and Sportsman racing. He couldn't surrender a hundred cubic inches on the vast superspeedways, but he figured his little motor might outjump the monsters on the short tracks. Besides, under NASCAR's cubic inches-to-weight formula, he got a break of more than nine hundred pounds. "It blew right by all the hot dogs," Allison noted. Indeed. He started on the pole, led all but a handful of the three hundred laps and lapped everyone else.

On July 16 he lapped the field twice at a fifth-mile track at Islip, New York, and on August 24 he won by a lap at a half-mile speedway in Beltsville, Maryland. Allison and his homemade Hueytown special scored three Nextel Cup victories in one season against the factory-backed boys. You had to know he was something special.

Equally memorable—and perhaps more important to his career—was a race he didn't win. On August 27, 1966, the Nextel Cup cars were dueling in the tight confines of a quarter-mile track at Winston-Salem, North Carolina. Allison, the newcomer, and Curtis Turner, the old veteran, got into a slamming match. It would have been easy for Allison to back off, but he didn't. Turner was in a Ford owned by Junior Johnson and financed by the big bucks of the factory, but Bobby was in his homemade Chevy, and he'd have to personally repair and pay for any damage to his car. Also, Turner was a famous driver whom *Sports Illustrated* had once called "the Babe Ruth of stock car racing," and Bobby was a relative unknown hoping to make a name for himself. Turner hit Bobby's car from the rear. Bobby let him by and began bumping Turner. Turner spun Bobby out. Bobby spun Turner out. Turner broadsided Bobby. As Turner came around under caution, Bobby broadsided him. Both drivers got out of their mangled racers and without a word returned to the pits.

The demolition derby helped influence *Sports Illustrated* to carry a full-length, admiring feature on Allison. The magazine recognized him as "the sport's newest hero." Said *SI*: "On the surface it was a minor incident, one that might happen a dozen times a year in the rough-and-tumble world of stock car racing. But this one was a bit different, for it strengthened an opinion held by just about every knowledgeable observer in stock car racing—namely that Bobby Allison of Hueytown, Ala., is on his way to becoming the next superstar of the Grand National circuit, right up there with Lorenzen and Petty and Johnson and Turner and even those heroes of the past—Fireball Roberts and Little Joe Weatherly. Not because he cracked up a car, of course. Anybody can do that. But because he didn't give way, which is often what automobile racing is about."

Stock Car Racing magazine wrote: "Both cars were wrecked, but Bobby established once and for all that he takes nothing off anybody on the race track. The youngster hadn't backed off from one of the great names in racing history, and that was important." NASCAR fined each driver one hundred dollars for "rough driving." Car owner Johnson warned Turner, "If that happens again, I'll pay the hundred dollars and you can pay for fixing the race car." Apparently Turner was favorably impressed by Allison's defiance: "Somebody told me that at the next short track race Curtis was sitting on top of a truck in the infield hollering for me," Bobby said.

If you think "obsessed" is too strong a word to describe Bobby Allison, consider this. In 1976, long after he had become a Cup star, he was driving in a Sportsman race on a third-mile track at Elko, Minnesota. His car hit a concrete wall, and he was seriously injured. He suffered three broken bones in his left foot, two broken bones in his right foot, three broken ribs, a broken nose, two facial fractures, and a blow-out fracture to the right eye socket that caused double vision. Forty stitches were required to close the laceration in his face. As he was being treated in a hospital in Minnesota, he had no feeling in his feet. He wondered if they had been cut off. "I asked myself if my racing career would be worth the loss of my feet," Bobby told me. "I decided it would."

After Bobby's son Davey started racing on the Nextel Cup circuit, some fans speculated that Bobby wouldn't really mind if Davey beat him in a race. I asked him about it, and I'll admit I was surprised by his answer: "If beating me in a race meant that Davey would go on to a great career, and if me beating him in a race meant that Davey wouldn't have much of a career, I'd still rather I won."

I believed in Bobby. I heard that Nextel Cup car owner Bud Moore would have a Mercury factory deal for 1967, and I phoned him at his shop in Spartanburg, South Carolina, and told him there was a superb young short-tracker named Bobby Allison who dazzled Alabama fans and who, indeed, had won three Nextel Cup bullring events in his homemade car. I asked Moore to give Bobby serious consideration as his driver. Eureka! Bobby got the ride. Now, don't misunderstand. I'm not saying I got Bobby Allison his first factory assignment, because I don't believe that's true. But it might have helped in some small way. Who knows? I remembered my phone call to Bud when Bobby, reunited with Moore in 1978, scored the first of his three victories in the Daytona 500.

Donnie Allison became the Nextel Cup Rookie of the Year in 1967. Driving a Holman-Moody Ford, Bobby Allison notched his first superspeedway victory in 1967. It was a very good year. The day after Bobby won that Rockingham race he thanked me for my support of his career. I've never forgotten that. An athlete's thanking a sportswriter is rare. So many seem to think the accolades are their God-given due.

Bobby won 84 races and Donnie won 10, and that's the all-time Nextel Cup record for brothers (unless you want to count Richard Petty's 200 and Maurice Petty's zero). The Flocks are second: Tim won 40; Fonty, 19; and Bob, 4. It's interesting to note that the Allison brothers ran 1–2 five times and Donnie won four of them. I suspect Donnie had as much raw talent as Bobby, but he wasn't so single-minded. Before the 1973 Daytona 500, Donnie told me, "I wouldn't say he is any more serious about it than I am, but he has no interests other than racing, with the possible exception of his airplane. Our father used to take us hunting, but all the brothers got away from it in later years except me. When Bobby goes hunting he enjoys it, but you can't get him to go. I think sometimes that's good, and sometimes I think not. He has no place to relieve the pressure of his occupation. He says the only place is flying his plane. But he's content. Like at night, when others might sit down and drink a beer, he's content to go to the shop and fool with his racer. It's something he has trained himself to do. That's something he enjoys doing, so he does it."

Accidents change the direction of many racers' lives. But an accident sent Donnie in a different direction before he became a racer. He won the Florida state AAU diving championship when he was a boy. At the swimming pool he met a horse trainer who was impressed by his small size—and probably by his fierce competitiveness. The fellow persuaded Donnie that he should become a jockey, and he began serving an apprenticeship as an exercise boy at Tropical Park near Miami. Sixteen-year-old Donnie Allison was riding his motorcycle on the way to feed a horse when a truck stopped in front of him and he crashed into it. His left leg was mangled. The bone stuck through the skin and into the pavement. "They wanted to amputate my leg," Donnie told me, "but my dad wouldn't go along with that. He told them if there was any chance to save it, he wanted them to. I think they just experimented on my leg, and it just happened to work." He was left with one leg that was shorter than the other, a crooked spine, and a limp.

He spent thirteen and a half weeks in the hospital. When he went in he weighed 100 pounds. When he was dismissed he weighed 125, "and from then on I grew like crazy." So it was good-bye jockey career. It was hello stock car career when a neighbor let him drive his amateur division car. His debut was unremarkable: "I started about fortieth and finished about forty-second."

After his stock car driving days were essentially over, Donnie and I stood in the garage area at Talladega and watched practice. It was a time in which the Nextel Cup talent level was extremely low. As I recall, Donnie was coaching some young driver. "It's a crying shame to see so many of these mediocre drivers with rides and a great one like you on the sideline," I told Donnie. He smiled grimly and said, "But you have to remember, I don't look good on television with a silk shirt open to the waist and gold chains hanging round my neck."

Bobby Allison's winning those three races and refusing to let Curtis Turner bully him weren't the only highlights of 1966 for Alabama racing fans. On September 4, 1966, I broke a story in the *Birmingham News* that a monster speedway would be built at Talladega. It was easy to close your eyes and picture homeboy Bobby zooming around steep banks right here at home.

Does anyone remember the working name of the track? It was "Alabama International Motor Sports and Testing Facility at Talladega." When the 2.66-mile speedway—the largest and fastest in the world—opened in 1969 it was christened with a name commensurate with its status, Alabama International Motor Speedway. Later, the name was changed to the disappointingly mundane Talladega Superspeedway.

William Henry Getty "Big Bill" France was the father of the new Alabama track. He was the founder of NASCAR and the builder of Daytona International Speedway—and a unique human being. He was the American dream on long legs—a high school dropout and former service station mechanic who by force of will and personality became the most powerful man in stock car racing.

France was like Bear Bryant in that when he entered a room everyone fell silent except to whisper, "There he is!" At six-foot-five he was even taller than Bryant, and women obviously were attracted to him, as they were to Bryant. He had as magnetic a personality as anyone I've ever known. France had a keen sense of humor; he was a marvelous storyteller with marvelous stories to tell and the only true genius I've ever known.

I always enjoyed his company. He'd call and I'd pick him up at the Birmingham airport and take him wherever he wanted to go. He'd bring me up to date on his plans for NASCAR and his race tracks, and because of our friendship I was able to break several stories, including the big one about construction of a speedway at Talladega.

I received a phone call regarding a family emergency before the 1972 Daytona 500, and I was exiting the press box at Daytona International Speedway as France was entering. "Where are you going?" he asked. "My mother called to tell me my dad may be dying," I said. "I'm going back to Birmingham."

"We'll fly you back," he said, and immediately he was calling the NASCAR hangar and telling the pilot to prepare for a flight to Birmingham. My wife, Sandra, and I checked out of our motel and flew home on the NASCAR plane. My friend Rex Sanders, a Chattanooga racing writer, drove our car to Birmingham. Now, you might scoff and say France did this only because I was a racing writer who could help him. But there was no other person or organization that I covered that would have volunteered to fly me five hundred miles, and France would have done the same favor for any number of his friends.

I don't think any other individual in the history of American sports was as important to his game as France was to stock car racing. Considering his background, that is truly amazing. He was born in Washington, D.C., and he quit high school after two years and went to work in a garage. He built a wooden car that was covered with canvas and raced it in Maryland. In later years he marveled that it didn't catch fire. France worked at a service station, and it was his lot to respond to cries for help from customers who couldn't get their cars started on cold mornings. "I decided that if I was going to have to fix automobiles for a living, I might as well fix them where it wasn't snowing," he said. "I decided I might as well do it in Florida."

He and his wife, Annie, and his son, Bill Jr. (who eventually would succeed him as the titan of stock car racing), set out in a Hupmobile with twenty-five dollars and a box of tools. They reached Daytona Beach; France marveled that it was the prettiest place he'd ever seen; and there they stayed. The legend grew that his car broke down in Daytona, and that changed the course of racing history. "I don't know who got that story started," France once told me, "but it's not true. I was a mechanic. I would have fixed the car."

"I know who got that story started," I told him. "Your publicity department at the speedway in Daytona sent it out."

France was a race driver, and after he opened a service station in Daytona it became a hangout for other race drivers. A couple of stock car races on a beach-road course had lost money, and the chamber of commerce asked him if he knew of anyone who might promote the event the next year. France tried to contact a promoter in Orange City, but the man refused to accept his fifteen-cent collect call—and history was made. France decided to promote it himself, and a career was born. If the man had accepted the call, there might be no NASCAR, no Daytona International Speedway, no Talladega Superspeedway.

France and I were sitting in the deserted stands at Talladega one day and I mentioned the phone call. "Do you think you might still have a filling station if he had accepted the call?" I asked. "I do have a filling station," he said, pointing to the one in the speedway's garage area. "It's right there."

I remembered that conversation when, years later, a member of his staff told me of sitting in the same empty grandstand of Talladega Superspeedway with France. The man who built the track didn't joke, though. Instead, he asked, "Where are we?" Alzheimer's disease is tragic in any instance, but to see it erode a great mind like Bill France's . . . well, it broke my heart.

France wanted me to write his biography, and I was excited about it. "We'll go out on my boat and stay two or three days," he said, "and I'll tell you some real stories." I knew it could be a dazzling book—not because of the author but because of the subject. Then one day during race week I dropped by his office at Talladega Superspeedway as I had done many times before, said howdy, made myself comfortable, and began chatting with France. He had little to say. He kept staring at me as if he was trying to place the face. After I left I told an employee, "Bill acted strange. He acted like he didn't know who I was."

"He probably didn't," the employee said. "Bill has Alzheimer's. It's supposed to be a secret, so don't say I told you." I was devastated. One of my aunts had suffered from the disease, and I knew how destructive it could be. Months later I was in Daytona, and I phoned Jim Foster, France's right-hand man and a former sports editor. "Jim, I'd like to have lunch with Bill one more time," I said. "Will you arrange it?" We met on Bill's boat and had sandwiches. He didn't know me. He asked if I wanted a glass for my beer. I said the can was fine. Five more times he asked if I wanted a glass for my beer, and five times I spoke the same answer. Foster mentioned that Joe Littlejohn, France's fast friend who helped him organize NASCAR, was coming from his home in Spartanburg, South Carolina, to Daytona for the races. France spoke four of the saddest words I've ever heard: "Who is Joe Littlejohn?"

Not being able to write Bill France's biography was the biggest disappointment of my professional career.

France died in 1992 at age eighty-two, but his legacy for Alabama is a speedway that draws the state's biggest sports crowds, that hosts the only major league sport we have. Its first Nextel Cup race was the Talladega 500 of September 11, 1969. I've never covered a crazier event.

A month before, the Professional Drivers Association had been formed, with Richard Petty as president. All the leading drivers except Bobby Isaac became members of the union. The cars attained unprecedented speeds of almost two hundred miles an hour, and the world's fastest speedway chewed up tires. The union members boycotted the race. France said there would be a Talladega 500 anyway. A makeshift field contested it, and a North Carolina farmer named Richard Brickhouse won it. That broke the back of the union, and it soon dissolved.

Frankly, I'm glad I wasn't writing an opinion column in 1969 because I didn't have a firm opinion on the issue, and I still don't. I understood France's contention that drivers had always raced according to the condition of a track. I understood the drivers' reluctance to race on a track that devoured tires. In his column, Benny Marshall sided with the speedway—but, then, it wasn't Benny's butt that would have been riding on disintegrating tires, was it?

But the bad times were soon over, and the speedway became a jewel in NASCAR's necklace of tracks. Neil Bonnett joined his Hueytown neighbors Bobby Allison and Donnie Allison on the circuit, and the Alabama Gang had a powerful triumvirate on the big league tour. It was a great time to be a racing fan in the Heart of Dixie.

I was a regular reader of the informed, voluminous coverage of the newspapers in Charlotte and Indianapolis, other cities with gleaming tracks, and I assumed the *News* would embrace the sport in the same manner. I was wrong. Before the Talladega track opened, Roger Bear, its promotion manager, came to Birmingham to meet Vincent Townsend, an executive who essentially ran the *Birmingham News*. I can still see the shocked look on Bear's face when he walked out of Townsend's office. "That man talked to me like I might be bringing some traveling daredevil show to town," Bear muttered. "He said the only interest he had in that speedway was in how much advertising we bought."

Maybe I should have expected as much. When I was covering Birmingham International Raceway's weekly events, Townsend told me to keep up with how much advertising the track bought and adjust my coverage to it. So much for newspapering's cardinal principle of advertising not affecting news coverage. I didn't keep up with it, though. Damned if I was going to be reduced to that. I told Townsend BIR bought lots of advertising.

Birmingham had the world's greatest speedway in its front yard and some of the world's greatest drivers in its backyard. A newspaper should have welcomed such an opportunity and covered racing in a big way—but the *News* didn't. It would send me to just seven Nextel Cup races a year—two Talladegas, two Atlantas, two Daytonas, and one Charlotte—occasionally adding another if there were special circumstances. Bobby Allison, Donnie Allison, Neil Bonnett, and later, Davey Allison won 131 Nextel Cup races. They are the only Alabama drivers ever to win on the circuit. In later years, with no Alabamian even competitive, the *News* would staff more than three times as many races. Go figure.

When Alf Van Hoose was sports editor–lead columnist of the *News* (1969–90) he never joined in the coverage of races at Talladega Superspeedway, not once. I was speaking to a library group recently when someone asked me what was the strangest thing I ever encountered in the newspaper business. I said: "The featured sports columnist of the biggest newspaper in Alabama never attended the sports event that draws the biggest crowd in Alabama, never saw the state's only major league sport."

My racing coverage earned me a couple of invitations to the White House. My jaw dropped when I read the telegram that came one morning in 1971. I was one of five or six racing writers Richard Nixon was inviting to the White House. William Faulkner once turned down an invitation from the Kennedys, saying it was too far to go for supper. I didn't think it was too far at all.

Nixon was going to "acknowledge" racing and host a reception for drivers, car owners, promoters, and sponsors. One hundred sixty-eight racing figures were invited, including such drivers as Bobby Allison, Donnie Allison, Parnelli Jones, Mario Andretti, Lothar Motschenbacher, Jackie Stewart, Richard Petty, and Al Unser. Nixon examined various race cars on the White House lawn, and then we went inside for chicken livers, shrimp, miniature shish kebabs, and other snacks. I don't remember the details, but I was surprised at how easily we had gained access to the president. The assassination of John Kennedy still lingered in the public's mind, and I remarked to someone, "You know, it seems like it would be fairly easy for someone to assassinate Nixon." Then I glanced at a huge potted plant on a pedestal beside me. Hidden in the leaves was a tape recorder, and it had taped my words. Gulp. I suppose it was taken for the innocent remark that it was, because nothing ever came of it.

Nixon was up on his football. "You have two great football coaches," he told me. "I don't know who will win that game, but Auburn is awfully strong." (Oops, Alabama won 31–7.)

Jimmy Carter invited the racing crowd to the White House in 1978, but it was his wife, Rosalyn, who greeted us. He had had a change of plans. "I'm glad you can be here tonight," she said. "I'm glad I can be here tonight. I'm sorry Jimmy can't be. It would take something of the magnitude of the Camp David summit to keep him away." I read later that Lee Petty said if a fellow invites you to his house, he should be there. I thought Carter's negotiating a peace treaty between Egyptian president Anwar Sadat and Israeli prime minister Menachem Begin might be a tad more important than entertaining the Boltons. It was a huge factor in his winning the Nobel Peace Prize in 2002.

Billy Carter was there. "I've already et," I heard him tell a man in the food line on the White House lawn. (What we et, on plain old picnic tables, was beef, ham, potato salad, cole slaw, bean salad, carrot cake, strawberry shortcake, and cornbread.) I introduced Billy to my wife. "Hi, Sandra. Glad to meet you, babe," the president's brother said.

Mrs. Carter was a gracious hostess who seemed to be enjoying herself in the presence of the unpretentious folks of racing. She told me she and her husband used to go to dirt tracks back in Georgia when they were first married. I swiped a toy race car from a picnic table centerpiece and took it home for a souvenir. I figured the U.S. government could afford it.

Chapter 8

There he was, Vince McMahon, the former owner of the XFL, in the center of a wrestling ring, lowering first his trousers and then the southern part of his undershorts and forcing a wrestler named William Regal to kiss his butt while a national TV audience looked on.

Birmingham had a team in the XFL, the Thunderbolts, and I thought that moment in the ring was somehow symbolic of our town's history of deceased professional sports franchises. The Magic City always ended up on its knees, puckering up its lips. McMahon's World Wrestling Federation and NBC were proprietors of the league, which lasted just one season, 2001. About all I remember about the XFL is that Gary DiNardo was Birmingham's coach; Jay Barker was one of its players; one team had a runner who went by the cryptic nickname of He Hate Me; and there was a helmeted cameraman on the field, prying into huddles and then chasing after the ball when the play began. I always hoped he'd get smeared by a big, fast linebacker.

I do remember when McMahon and his daughter Stephanie came to

Birmingham to announce that the city would be afflicted (my word, of course, not theirs) with yet another pro football franchise. As rasslin' villainesses go, Stephanie was right pretty. (This was before she got a monster boob job that made her look like someone shoplifting two basketballs.) I kidded her about some televised wrestling plot I'd seen a few days before, and, ever the promoter, ever her daddy's girl, she said, "Wait until you see what happens Thursday night."

I remember something else. I remember that at the announcement luncheon I sat at a table with a covey of young reporters, and they assured me this league would succeed. I said it would fold in two years (overestimating by a year), but I secretly envied their optimistic, naive attitude, because I had once felt the same way—when the World Football League and the Americans came to town in 1974.

Actually, I had twice felt the same way. The other time was when the World League of American Football (WLAF) brought the Fire to Birmingham before its 1991 season. The WLAF was the child of the National Football League, which spoke of it in loving, paternalistic words, and I thought that would guarantee stability. I was wrong. The WLAF played in 1991 and 1992, play was suspended for 1993 and 1994, and the league was reincarnated in 1995 as an all-European circuit. It's now called NFL Europe. The Birmingham Fire, of course, was extinguished in the process, and I learned not to trust the NFL.

Let's see, we've had the Americans and the Vulcans of the WFL, the Stallions of the United States Football League, the Fire of the WLAF, the Barracudas of the Canadian Football League, and the Bolts of the XFL. We've had a few other football representatives that could most accurately be described as semipro, including one that's still breathing, the Steeldogs. We've had the Bandits of the Continental Basketball Association. There was another gang of Bandits—these in some soccer league that never played a game. I remember that a "star" they had imported from Ireland or Scotland or somewhere across the pond came to the sports department of the *News* crying that he was stranded in a foreign country with no money to get home.

We had the original Bulls of the World Hockey Association who at least served some purpose by introducing Birmingham to that sport, which I enjoyed watching on occasion. Canadian John Bassett, whose wealth couldn't save him from a premature death by cancer, was the likable owner of those first Bulls. He enjoyed stationing himself anonymously in the stands and listening to the fans who were being exposed to hockey for the first time. He was sitting behind a couple of middle-aged women, one of whom kept referring to the "ball." Bassett learned over and said, "Pardon me, ma'am, but in hockey it's called a puck."

"Oh, I know it," the gentlewoman said, "but I just can't bring myself to say that word."

John was a member of a beer-brewing family, and he named a daughter Carling. I told him she was lucky he didn't brew Budweiser. He laughed. I was gratified because most people don't get my jokes.

Also interred in Birmingham's sports cemetery are other hockey franchises, an LPGA tournament, the original Birmingham Classic that featured Auburn and Alabama basketball teams in Boutwell Auditorium, the SEC championship football game, the SEC basketball tournament, the SEC track and field meet, horse racing, the All American Bowl, and from the mists of creation that you may not even know about—the Dixie Bowl. It played here twice, Arkansas beating William and Mary 21–19 in 1947 and Wake Forest beating Baylor 20–7 in 1948. We've lost Auburn football and Alabama football.

There was incredible excitement when the Americans of the World Football League arrived in 1974. As they say in horse racing, they broke our maiden. Later they would break our hearts, but for awhile all we knew was that we had a team in professional football, probably always would have, and we were in love with the concept.

The coach of the Americans was Jack Gotta, who remains one of my favorite sports figures of all time. Gotta was not only a solid coach but also a personality guy the city embraced. He knew the Americans needed publicity, and he made it easy for reporters. The Americans trained at Marion Institute, and the press stayed in some little white frame houses near the field. If you wanted to interview a player, the PR staff would escort him to your little white house after practice.

The Stallions needed publicity, too, but they seemed ignorant of that fact of life. It's funny now, but at the time it was dumbfounding. The Stallions and the USFL played three spring–summer seasons (1983–84–85). The 1983 club held preseason training in Daytona Beach. I wasn't the Stallions' beat man, but I was in Daytona in February covering the races, and I was assigned to drop by the team's camp one day and interview some players for feature stories. I knocked at the Stallions' office, and some fellow came to the door. I asked for the PR man. "The PR man's gone to the show," the guy said. I asked for a roster and biographical sketches of the players. "We don't have a roster or biographical sketches of the players," he said, never so much as inviting me inside and out of the cold.

I drove to a building where Jim Hilyer, the special teams–conditioning coach, was conducting workouts. Hilyer was an old friend from his days on Shug Jordan's Auburn staff, and I told him I wanted to interview some players. The team had just been assembled and his knowledge of the players was sketchy. He named a few, said he thought some others were so-and-so. "That fellow's a quarterback," he said, pointing to a nice-looking young man who was lifting weights, "but I don't know his name or anything about him."

Well, you can't go wrong writing about QBs, so I introduced myself to the player and said, "All I know about you is that you are a quarterback. I don't know your name, I don't have any idea where you played college football, or even if you played college football. I plead total ignorance where you are concerned—but I want to write a feature story about you." Bob Lane of Northeast Louisiana laughed and told me all about himself. He became one of my favorite Stallions, and I was pleased when he was named the team's MVP at the end of the season. Without even so much as a roster, I waded into several other interviews that day. Some of the players were helpful, some weren't.

When I got back to Birmingham after Speed Weeks in Daytona, Neal Sims, the executive sports editor, complained, "Your feature stories on the Stallions sure were short."

"No kidding," I said. "Gee, I can't imagine why."

On a scale of one to ten, in the matter of cooperation with the press, I'd rate Jack Gotta, coach of the Americans, a nine. I'd rate Rollie Dotsch, coach of the Stallions, a three. Instead of going out of his way to make players available, as Gotta had done, Dotsch mailed out written rules severely limiting their availability. That might have flown in the established NFL, but it was absurd in the USFL, a struggling league that desperately needed favorable publicity. No problem. I simply ignored the Stallions as much as possible and wrote columns about other subjects.

Dotsch was a tough old coach who had taught the offensive lines of two Pittsburgh Steelers Super Bowl champions, and it seemed strange that he was so thin-skinned where the press was concerned, especially considering that the coverage of the Stallions was generally positive. He got mad about something somebody wrote, and after some game he decided he wouldn't talk to the writers. The league wouldn't have it, though, and the USFL ordered him to be available for postgame quotes.

When the Americans arrived in 1974 the public was ecstatic. The fans loved the team's name and loved the red, white, and blue color scheme and believed Birmingham was in pro football to stay. The bitter lesson that such ventures probably won't last had yet to be learned.

Gotta (who is retired and living with his wife, Joanie, in Canada, near Calgary) was a story in himself, and if sheer force of personality could have saved a team and a league, the Americans and the WFL would be coexisting with the NFL today. He graduated from high school in Ironwood, Michigan, without having played football. His father and uncles were legendary players in that area, but Jack weighed just 112 pounds. "I was the first Gotta who never made a letter in high school sports," he told me recently. Remember what I said earlier about life? It's what happens instead of what you had planned.

Gotta enrolled in a General Motors training program, apparently destined to work at an uncle's dealership, but he was growing, and he started playing amateur football in the area and caught the attention of some colleges. Lo and behold, Oregon State signed him, and he played end on offense and defense. His final collegiate season was 1952. He played in the air force, and then played nine years in the Canadian Football League, as an offensive and defensive back.

Gotta coached Ottawa to the CFL championship, and then the notion of trying to duplicate the feat in a new league in a football hotbed appealed to him, so he came to Birmingham. And the Americans did, indeed, win the WFL title in 1974. "I was intrigued about going back to the States," Gotta said, "but I didn't want to go just anywhere. I felt that in going to Birmingham I was going to a place where football was number one." Everything seemed hunky-dory at first. Park board records show the Americans drew 43,031 for their home opener on July 10, 1974, against Southern California. Their largest home crowd was 56,453 against Memphis two weeks later. As late as September 7 they were pulling 49,245 to Legion Field for a game against Chicago. But the league's reputation was rotting, and toward the end of the season the Americans were attracting just 12,000 fans. They drew but 22,000 to Legion Field when they beat Florida 22–21 in the first and only World Bowl. Despite the shakiness of the league and the presence of sheriff's deputies who were repossessing the uniforms because the franchise wasn't paying its bills, it was a joyous dressing room that night.

I was writing a locker room article, and the players sprayed me with champagne and doused me with beer. On my expense account I turned in the price of a necktie and the cost of dry cleaning a suit. At the newspaper's Christmas party a few nights later, I was leaning over a punch bowl, filling a cup. My tie was dangling perilously close to the liquid. John Bloomer, the editor, walked over and said, "Look I approved one necktie on your expense account against my better judgment, but damned if I'm going to approve another one. You'd better keep that one out of the punch bowl."

The World Football League began play in 1974 with franchises in Birmingham, Chicago, Detroit, Orlando, Honolulu, Houston, Jacksonville, Memphis, New York, Philadelphia, Portland, and Anaheim. The league said it would "eventually encompass the entire world." Bill Putnam, a former navy underwater demolition expert, owned the Americans. His background included owning the Philadelphia Flyers of the National Hockey League and being president of a group that controlled the NFL's Atlanta Flames and the NBA's Atlanta Hawks.

Large crowds were reported at the WFL's opening games, but a damning revelation occurred in Philadelphia. The team announced a crowd of 55,534 for its opener and an audience of 64,719 for a game two weeks later, but the league's credibility took a major blow when it turned out the house had been papered. Actual paid attendance was more like 13,000 for the first game and 6,200 for the second. The other tickets had been given away. Two months into the season, four teams were on the rocks. The league assumed operation of the Jacksonville and Detroit franchises, and then both folded. Houston's franchise moved to Shreveport; New York's, to Charlotte. The WFL became a joke league.

Detroit's trainer had to borrow tape from the opponents, and the players had to bring their own towels. On opening night in New York, nobody could find the keys to the ticket booths in Downing Stadium, and they had to break open the booths to get to the tickets. Jack Pardee, coach of the Florida Blazers, and his assistants provided the toilet paper for the team's dressing room.

When Birmingham and Florida met in the 1974 World Bowl, the Blazers were the sentimental favorites because they had missed more paydays than the Americans had. The league had taken over operation of the Florida franchise. The World Bowl was played on a Thursday night. The Birmingham players skipped Monday's practice and threatened to boycott the championship game unless their back pay was made up, but they reconsidered and took the field.

Quarterbacks Matthew Reed and George Mira led the Americans to a 22–21 victory, and Mira was named the game's MVP. The Reverend Denny Duron, the team's third-string quarterback and first-string hotline to heaven, thanked the Lord for holding the Americans together through "shaky times." (Gotta always said he was afraid to cut Duron from the squad because God might strike him dead.)

After the World Bowl, Birmingham fullback Charley Harraway, president of the WFL players association, said he hoped to announce "in a few short weeks" a game pitting the Americans against the National League champions or an NFL all-star team. "The WFL players association has been negotiating with the NFL players association for a game," Harraway said. "We've also been negotiating with a major TV network to carry the game. It would be played in Birmingham, and we won't be playing for nothing. I can't say there definitely will be a game, but we're pretty sure. It might make us up our back salaries." What pitiful words. Did Harraway really believe the NFL would help bail out a rival league or had the WFL experience been so surreal that he had lost touch with reality? I never did know, but I felt so sorry for the Birmingham players who had conjured up their competitive spirits and gone to war without paychecks.

The league reorganized for 1975. Putnam was out, and local owners fielded a Birmingham franchise called the Vulcans. Gotta devoted his time to a front office job, putting his pro football savvy to work to try to salvage what could be salvaged, and Marvin Bass became head coach. The WFL folded on October 22, 1975. The Vulcans had the league's best record, 9–3, so I suppose you could say Birmingham was champion both seasons. "I've been coaching thirty-three years," Bass said, "but what I had to do thirty minutes ago makes this the saddest day of my life. I had to tell my football team they are unemployed."

Captain John Matlock, a veteran of the NFL, was crestfallen. "What can you say? What can you possibly say? I'm just sorry to see it happen this way. It's a shame." The competitor in Matlock rose up. "We have a good football team," he declared. "I guarantee you we could beat six or seven NFL clubs. I've been there; I know." Some young Vulcans might catch on in the NFL, the big lineman said, adding: "John Matlock, he's through. I'm thirty-one years old. I've been through the mill."

My colleague Jimmy Bryan said it well in his story in the *News*: "A part of Birmingham died Wednesday.

"The professional football team the city had come to love had a knife stuck in its heart when the World Football League collapsed and breathed its last shortly after noon.

"There was nothing the WFL's most solid franchise could do. It was pulled down by the hopeless ineptness of its feeble brethren."

Some good football players wore Birmingham livery in the WFL—Larry Willingham, Paul Costa, Dennis Homan, Johnny Musso, Alfred Jenkins, Art Cantrelle, Ross Brubaker, Paul Robinson, Harraway, Matlock, Mira, and Reed among them. Reed had the strongest arm I ever saw. One day Jimmy Bryan asked him, "Matthew, just how far can you throw a football?" Reed answered: "As far as I need to."

Willingham and I were reminiscing about the WFL just the other day. "Birmingham was the most fun I ever had playing ball," the former Auburn all-American and St. Louis Cardinals defensive back said. "I was in my hometown, and we were winning and having a ball." Willingham smiled when he remembered Billy Tohill, Birmingham's fiery assistant coach who lost a leg in an automobile accident. "He was asleep one night after curfew, and he had left his door cracked. Me and Steve Williams, who played at Alabama, got down and crawled into his room to steal his leg. There it was, propped against the bed, with a sock and coaching shoe on it. We started crawling out with it, but he woke up and yelled, 'What are you doing?' We left the leg and escaped. He never mentioned it, so I don't guess he knew who did it."

There was never a dull moment with Willingham around. Once at practice he hopped on policeman Bobby Hayes's motorcycle and began racing it up and down the gridiron in Legion Field. Hayes screamed for him to park the thing, but Willingham yelled, "It's all right, Bobby, I've got on a helmet." Willingham's only regret: "I never figured how to turn the siren on."

I mourned the loss of Birmingham's franchise and the World Football League. I mourned the loss of innocence that went with them, the town's and mine. There are no second first times.

I wish I could say I mourned the loss of the Stallions and the USFL, but I didn't. Oh, I hated to see the players and others lose their jobs, but I wasn't sorry to see the franchise evaporate. I didn't like Dotsch—who was certainly no Jack Gotta—and I thought the team's owner, Marvin Warner, was amusingly pompous, whereas the American's Bill Putnam was a good old boy who seemed to enjoy the ride, even though it was bumpy.

And sometimes little things mean a lot. I flew with the Stallions to a game in New York or Chicago or somewhere, and we arrived back in Birmingham in the wee hours of the morning. Members of the team's fan club were at the airport to greet the returning warriors, cheering or waving signs or whatever. I was walking behind a couple of players in an airport corridor, and one of them muttered to the other, "Can you believe these silly bastards?" That struck me as awfully bush league. Fans are the foundation of professional sports. If no one cared to watch a fellow throw a football, then throwing a football would be as useless a skill as I can imagine. (I've long believed it would have a cleansing effect if all the fans of big-time pro sports would go on strike for a year and refuse to attend any event or watch on TV.)

Of all our leagues, I think the USFL played the highest caliber of football, with the WFL a close second. I'd make the WLAF a distant third, followed by the CFL, and the XFL. The Stallions had some superb football players, men such as Tom Banks, Buddy Aydelette, Joe Cribbs, Darryl Mason, Chuck Clanton, Mike Raines, Jim Smith, Cliff Stoudt, Joey Jones, Pat Phenix, Jackie Cline, and Scott Norwood—yep, the Scott Norwood who missed on a forty-seven-yard field goal attempt at the end of the 1991 Super Bowl as his Buffalo Bills lost to the New York Giants 20–19. They didn't win any USFL championships—Michigan, Philadelphia, and Baltimore did—but the Stallions had a couple of strong teams. Their records were 9–9, 14–4, and 13–5.

The USFL began play in 1983 with teams in Birmingham, New York, Los Angeles, Chicago, Detroit, Boston, Tampa, Oakland, Denver, Washington, Philadelphia, and Phoenix. The player whose name was on everyone's lips was Herschel Walker of the New Jersey Generals (New York). The Heisman Trophy winner had left Georgia a year early to play in the USFL. He signed a $5 million, three-year contract. Forsaking college eligibility for pro football is commonplace now, but it was unusual then.

A relative of mine worked for a doctor in Atlanta who was a Georgia fan. Photographs of Herschel were on the walls of his office. He came to work in the morning after Walker made his decision to leave Athens and ripped the pictures down and stuffed them into a wastebasket. Tacky, tacky, tacky. I thought colleges were supposed to prepare students to make a good living, and Georgia did a remarkable job of it with Herschel.

Walker played in the Stallions game that I remember best. It was in Giants Stadium in the Meadowlands, and the evening was surreal, to say the least. Birmingham won 22–7 and Walker gained just twenty-eight yards rushing. The reason was because he had nothing to rush with. The Stallions' time of possession, 43:28. The Generals' time of possession, 16:32. That's one of the stranger statistics I've ever seen. But that wasn't the oddest aspect of the night. Fans decided to act as a perverse chamber of commerce and validate everything bad you ever heard about New York. Fights broke out in the stands. I wondered if I was at a European soccer match. I don't mean a couple of fights. I mean ten, twelve, maybe fifteen fights erupted among the spectators, ranging from two-man encounters to some that required a dozen or more security officers to quell.

A plague spread through that handsome stadium that is within sight of the skyscrapers of Manhattan. A fight would detonate, and spectators would stand and cheer. They booed the yellow-jacketed security men, throwing soft drinks and beer on them. One thug punched out two or three of them before an army finally downed him. Fans in the upper deck began throwing liquids on those below. Those in the lower seats tossed liquids at the television cameraman. With about ten minutes to go, hordes of decent fans gave up and left the stadium to the scum.

On the way to the dressing rooms just before the end of the game, I hustled off the sidelines as quickly as possible. I knew my bald head would make an inviting target. (An Auburn fan who threw a liquor bottle at me when I was on the sidelines in Jordan-Hare Stadium demonstrated as much. He missed. It was cheap whiskey, too. I thought I would have rated Jack Daniel's.) "They were animals tonight," said a Generals employee as he trotted off the field and under the protection of the grandstand. "There are some sick people out there."

"The trouble is they won't do anything to them," said a security guard. "They'll just slap them on the hand and tell them they can't come back into the stadium."

Herschel Walker had strung together five straight 100-yard games before that one, but his team was dead in the water that night. "I reckon we should have watched the fights instead of playing football," he offered in the dressing room. Maybe I shouldn't have been shocked by the eruption of fights. After all, this was New York. A few years before, walking through busy Times Square, I came face to face with a man leading a llama on the sidewalk. I was the only person who gave the animal a second look, the only person surprised by a llama strolling down a street in Manhattan.

The USFL planned to switch to a fall schedule in 1986, but there was no 1986 season. The league was said to be more than $160 million in debt when it died. The good news for the USFL was that, just before it folded, it won an antitrust suit against the National Football League. The bad news was that it was awarded one dollar (but hey, it was trebled to three bucks under antitrust law!) and the USFL is still referred to as the one-dollar league.

The Fire and the WLAF followed in 1991. The Fire's chief accomplishment was its owner, Gavin Maloof, being named *Cosmopolitan* magazine's bachelor of the month, or some such nonsense. Appropriately, he drove a Ferrari. Gavin could eat more than any normal-size person I've ever known. Local restaurateurs loved to see him coming, for he might order two entrées, say chicken and steak. I enjoyed having lunch with him, enjoyed watching him eat.

The Barracudas, an expansion franchise of the CFL, arrived in 1995. The owner was Art Williams, a former Georgia high school coach who made a fortune in insurance. There was a packed house for the team's first press conference. Many of Williams's insurance apostles were in the audience, and he was delivering a presentation that sounded like something straight out of an infomercial. My friend Jimmy Bryan simply cannot whisper. His voice carries like a Tiger Woods tee shot. In the midst of Williams's talk, Jimmy leaned over to me and said, "This guy is the biggest huckster to hit town yet." Half the heads in the room turned toward us. I shook my head innocently and pointed to Jimmy as the culprit.

But I came to like Williams, and so did Jimmy. It was just that the guy was a motivational speaker and author, and while that rah-rah approach might fire up insurance salesmen, it wasn't likely to move members of the press who had suffered through the WFL, USFL, and WLAF debacles, who knew the Barracudas had little chance of succeeding. Art was always going to do something that would "knock your socks off." His announcement of a coach, he promised, would knock your socks off. The coach turned out to be Jack Pardee, who had won one game with the Houston Oilers the year before. But I admired Williams for his generous support of the Reverend Jerry Falwell's Liberty University. Liberty's football stadium is named for him. Falwell was in the Legion Field press box for a Barracudas game, and I enjoyed meeting him and chatting with him.

I miss the LPGA golf tournament that was played at Green Valley. I've always believed the average male golfer can learn more by watching a female pro than a male pro, because he is more likely to duplicate a woman's less explosive swing.

Nancy Lopez was the shining star of the LPGA tour, and I followed her for nine holes. (Her radiant, athletic good looks made that a pleasure.) I watched as she hit a ball into a sand trap. She swung again and it was still in the trap. She swung again and it was still in the trap. She swung again and it escaped the trap by just six inches. I've always remembered that. It was vivid evidence that there are no locks in golf, and I've resisted the temptation, in print, to award any tournament to any individual before it is played, even an individual named Tiger.

The All American Bowl was fun, but it had to depend on corporate generosity. The local public wouldn't support it. Originally it was called the Hall of Fame Bowl, but when its connection to the National Football Foundation Hall of Fame was severed the name was changed. I tried to get the powers that be to rename it the Hospitality Bowl, to trade on its excellent reputation for making teams and fans feel welcome, but they settled on the hackneyed name All American Bowl.

It was gratifying to watch fans from schools that didn't go to a lot of bowls, such as Vanderbilt, Tulane, Kentucky, Texas Tech, and Indiana, enjoying themselves in my city. My niece Chris Massey and her husband, Brant, came to Birmingham in 1989 when Duke played Texas Tech. They lived in Durham, and Duke's appearing in a bowl was a big deal to them. They bought a new Oldsmobile and drove it to town. I got them a parking pass in the officials' lot at Legion Field. Their festive spirit was dampened when Texas Tech beat their team 49–21, and it was extinguished when they reached their new car after the game and found some scumbag had walked down the side of it with a broken beer bottle. So much for the Hospitality Bowl. I've never understood why people want to be sorry as hell just for the sake of being sorry.

The Birmingham Turf Club opened in 1987, and I learned to like horse racing, but it was doomed by lack of interest. The horse racing folks are the nearest to stock car racing people that I've met—unpretentious, salt-of-the-earth types. I spent a lot of time in the barns and in the backside restaurant chatting with jockeys and trainers and stable hands. They were a welcome relief from the stick-and-ball phonies a sportswriter deals with. I've never been much of a gambler, but I'd risk twenty or thirty bucks on the horses and simply count it as the cost of an evening out. I've never been under the illusion that they build lavish casinos because they think I'm going to win.

A nationally famous handicapper named Gary Johnson haunted the Turf Club press box for a while. He had been featured in racing publications for picking an incredible number of winners in a row and making a fortune for a syndicate of bettors. One night he told me: "I know you just bet for fun, but this next race is one I've been waiting on for a month. Bet all you can stand on so-and-so." So instead of two bucks I bet a hundred dollars on so-and-so. I'm still waiting for my horse—and my ship—to come in.

But let me add that the Boltons actually came out ahead on the horses—because one night my wife, Sandra, miraculously hit a trifecta that paid twenty-eight hundred dollars. "And I don't know a horse from a dog," she says. Sandra did the smart thing. She went home immediately after that race, refusing to risk a penny of her windfall. She used the money to remodel a bathroom in our home.

Chapter 9

Ah, the wonderful world of sports—as viewed by one who is still trying to figure out why baseball managers dress like the players and why you score at your goal in basketball but the opponent's goal in football . . .

When UAB decided to field a football team I became an enthusiastic supporter. I knew the program would never reach the level of Alabama's or Auburn's and that the Blazers would never claim first or second place in the hearts of Alabamians, or even Birminghamians, but I thought UAB could be another Southern Mississippi and draw a steady thirty thousand to home games.

I was delighted that a close friend, Jim Hilyer, would be the coach. Our friendship dated back to the days when he was an Auburn assistant under Shug Jordan. I used to go to his home to chow down after games in Auburn. I suggested to Coach Rollie Dotsch that he hire Hilyer for his Birmingham Stallions staff, and he did. Now, more than a decade after the University of Alabama at Birmingham inflated its first football, I detect little interest in the program. Crowds are small, and I rarely hear UAB football mentioned in conversations. The Auburn-Alabama passion is simply so intense and pervasive that UAB hasn't been able to wedge in, as I originally thought it could. I wonder if UAB football will survive.

The school's shabby treatment of Hilyer reduced my enthusiasm for the program. He was there for UAB football when it needed him but out the door of the coach's office when it decided it didn't. Hilyer is that rare combination of scholar and football coach. He is smart enough to have a doctorate in educational psychology and in exercise physiology and a postdoctorate in clinical psychology; he is a capable enough coach to have been on George Allen's Washington Redskins staff. He was and is a faculty member in the UAB School of Medicine, and his availability led to his becoming UAB's first coach. Gene Bartow, the director of athletics, asked Hilyer if he knew who might coach an informal club team wearing UAB colors, and Hilyer volunteered. Then, when the school fielded an NCAA Division III team in 1981, Hilyer coached it to a 4–3–2 record. UAB football was an instant winner.

Hilyer's 1992 Division III squad went 7–3. The program was elevated to Division I-AA in 1993, and the record was 9–2. UAB had a 7–4 record in I-AA in 1994. Hilyer was telling me over lunch the other day that the first I-AA squad had no scholarships; the second, just ten scholarships, which he split up among thirty-five players.

Hilyer told me that Bartow informed him that Claude Bennett, the UAB president, wanted to hire a "name" coach as the program eyed advancement to Division I-A, that Bennett didn't believe it could get sufficient donations without a name coach. Hilyer was to go ahead and coach the 1994 season, and then the name coach would step in. Hilyer said he told Bartow he had no interest in coaching the 1994 season if he wasn't going to be the coach in 1995. Besides, he said, replacing him after 1994 would violate a verbal agreement he had with Bartow. (I am reminded of the old saying: a verbal agreement isn't worth the paper it's written on.) Hilyer said Bartow countered with: "Oh, we'll get the president to change his mind. You just have a winning season." Hilyer had a winning season, but he was shoved out of the plane anyway. His parachute was a job as an assistant AD. On December 13, 1994, he announced his resignation as head football coach.

And what "name" coach did UAB have in mind? "I heard from Bartow that they thought there was a chance they could get Bobby Bowden," Hilyer told me. Well, at least they got a fellow whose last name stated with B: Watson Brown, a journeyman whose most recent job had been that of offensive coordinator at Oklahoma. His record as a head coach at Austin Peay, Cincinnati, Rice, and Vanderbilt was 32–77–1. In ten years as a head man, he'd had two winning seasons.

I first knew Brown when he was an assistant at Jacksonville State, and I like him. But replacing Jim Hilyer with Watson Brown was no more than a sideways move. Hilyer never had a losing season of NCAA football at UAB. His record over four years was 27–12–2. Brown's first five seasons (one in Division I-AA, four in I-A) were losers. As I write this, before the 2005 season, just three of his ten campaigns at UAB have been winners, and his record at the Southside school is 54–58.

"More than pissed off, I was hurt," Hilyer said of his being jilted. UAB is prominent in medicine, and its treatment of Hilyer reminds me of the clichéd medical school scenario: a young fellow's wife works hard to support him while he attends med school; then, when he becomes a doctor, he divorces the faithful wife and marries someone else. I think UAB's treatment of Hilyer bothers Bartow. He has mentioned it to me several times. If he had it to do over, he said, he'd fight a better battle to retain Hilyer as coach. "But I didn't, and life goes on."

Most coaches probably dream of someday having a Heisman Trophy–quality player—but there can be nightmare aspects of the experience, too. Jack Crowe, the head man at Jacksonville State, was offensive coordinator when Bo Jackson played at Auburn. It is common knowledge that Jackson got preferential treatment. As we ate lunch one day I asked Crowe to ruminate on the adventure of coaching the 1985 Heisman winner.

"We made him into something he didn't want to be, . . . " Crowe said. "He sat at my desk and said he didn't want to play football. He did not like football. He told me that when he was nineteen."

So, why did he play? "For what it did for him."

How could Jackson play so well if he didn't like it? "Because he's a phenomenal talent."

Crowe continued: "He was arrogant, aloof, late to meetings, a no-show at practice." Crowe said Jackson was lacking in values when he came to Auburn, "but now he's a man full of values. I'm proud I coached him. I'm proud I watched him grow." Crowe compared Jackson to "the superstar on a movie set" and said his slacking affected his Auburn teammates. "It was a morale issue. We'd literally have everybody at practice but Bo."

Jackson suffered an injury in the second game of 1984 that sidelined him for six games, all of which Auburn won. The team "went on a tear," Crowe said. Bo returned in a loss against Florida, and in the final regular season game, against Alabama, he ran the wrong way when he was supposed to block for Brent Fullwood near the goal line, and the Tide won 17–15. "The team would have been better if he hadn't come back," Crowe said. But, referring to Coach Pat Dye's using Jackson in those games, Crowe added, "I would have done the same thing. If I knew he could possibly play, and he was on our team right now—yeah."

Crowe told a strange story. "His freshman year he wasn't practicing well. I said, 'You don't look like you like football.' He said, 'I don't.' He said he'd rather be just running track and playing baseball. I said, 'Well, maybe that's what you need to do.' He said, 'Maybe you're right.' He started down the hall to Pat's office, and I went and got him. He was holding us hostage. He knew then he had me hostage. And this was when he was young, just a kid."

There was admiration in his voice when Crowe recalled a Bo Jackson that even Nolan Ryan couldn't intimidate. When Crowe was coach at Arkansas and Jackson was playing with the Kansas City Royals, Crowe was in Arlington, Texas, and he attended a game between Texas and the Royals. Ryan was pitching for the Rangers. "Tonight's the night," Jackson told Crowe in a phone conversation before the game. "He put Bo on the ground," Crowe recalled. "It was an intimidation. But the third at-bat, Bo hit it into the parking lot. The ball is still rolling. Nolan Ryan tipped his hat to Bo."

Several years ago the *Birmingham News* got on one of its money-saving kicks and said it would no longer pay the motel bills for its reporters who covered basketball games at Auburn. That meant a long day of doing whatever had to be done in the office, driving to Auburn, covering the game, interviewing players and coaches, writing a story, and driving back to Birmingham. We got home in the wee hours of the morning.

There have been improvements on Highway 280 over the years, but at that time the treacherous route between Auburn and Birmingham was still known as Bloody 280. I used to drive home from Auburn in the dead of winter with the car window down and wind blowing in my face. The radio was blaring and I was singing. All to try to keep awake. I told my wife, Sandra, if they ever found my car upside down in a ditch with the window open and Hank Williams wailing from the radio and the words "poor old Kaw-liga" formed on my dead lips, she should get the best lawyer she could find. I was only half kidding.

But at least I know my pain was not in vain. *Forbes* magazine's richest Americans issue of 2004 estimated the worth of the owners of the *News,* S. I. Newhouse Jr. and Donald Newhouse, at $7 billion apiece. Me and Hank helped them accumulate those fantastic fortunes with our dark, lonesome rides up Bloody 280.

Television biographies of Burt Reynolds, the actor and former Florida State running back, frequently show tape of him making a long run against Auburn. I wondered about his football career, and in 1981 I phoned his former coach, Tom Nugent. Buddy (as he was known then) Reynolds was one of the top high school prospects in the Palm Beach area, Nugent told me.

The coach used the right bait in recruiting him. "He visited the campus and was introduced to a lot of good-looking girls. I think that sold him on Florida State as much as anything. We had a redhead meet him at the plane. A blond had lunch with him. A brunette had dinner with him. We gave him a steady diet of that for the two days he was allowed by NCAA rules to stay. Every meal he had with a different girl. When he was returning home he was climbing the steps to the plane and what he saw was all these good-looking girls yelling, 'Come back, come back,' and me standing there waving a scholarship and saying, 'Sign it, sign it.' "

Like many athletes, Reynolds has become a much better player over the years than he actually was. I heard a TV biographer say he was an "all-conference" back. That would have been a good trick since FSU wasn't in a conference at that time. Reynolds played two seasons at FSU but an injury in a car crash that was later aggravated on the field ended his career. His freshman season, 1954, he played running back behind Lee Corso, who is now a football commentator on TV. Reynolds carried the ball just sixteen times.

"We went up to play Auburn," Nugent said. "Fob James, your governor, played on that team. For awhile we were playing over our heads, and it was close, but Auburn started taking charge, and we started to fade. "Reynolds had been at my elbow all the game. Finally, he tapped me on the shoulder and said, 'Put me in.' You didn't do that in those days. We really stressed discipline back then. I told him to go sit down. Auburn scored, and I was on the sidelines on one knee, and he tapped me on the shoulder again and said, 'I think I can help.' I sent him in, hoping he would get knocked on his butt, but on the first play he ran fifty-three yards, his longest run ever for us. He got to the four-yard line, but we never scored."

Nugent shifted Reynolds to defense the next season, and he became a starter, but injuries sabotaged his career. "I considered him a good player," Nugent said, "with the emphasis on his being courageous and a good, tough kid. He would hit you."

The University of Alabama had new football practice fields, and they were as gorgeously green as the countryside of Ireland, so it was no wonder Bobby Rice, the school's director of athletic facilities, went ballistic when he saw a golfer hitting practice balls and excavating divots from his pride and joy.

But things aren't always what they seem. Gene Stallings, the coach, cooked up a practical joke, and he enlisted Kirk McNair, editor of *'Bama* magazine, to play the villain. McNair went to his golf course and got a bucket of driving range balls. He borrowed a flagstick and flag. He got a couple of yards of sod. McNair arrived at the Alabama practice fields and sent an accomplice out to hold the target flag. He dumped the range balls on the ground. He placed one segment of sod with the dirt side up. He tore the other one into bits and scattered them around the area. He pulled his hat down so Rice wouldn't recognize him and began swinging his golf club.

Stallings summoned Rice to a window and demanded to know why some idiot was hacking up the new practice field. Rice dashed out the door, screaming at the intruding golfer. Stallings ran behind. Before Rice could murder him, McNair raised his hat and grinned. Rice realized he had been suckered and said, "That was a good one." Stallings, the mastermind, adjusted his halo and said, "Bobby, I begged him not to do it."

Nick Carter, "the Oneonta mailman," was a popular good guy (or babyface, as they say in rasslin') during the heyday of weekly professional shows. Carter, a former Birmingham-Southern football player, and Tarzan White, an ex-Alabama all-American, were a formidable tag team that always emerged victorious over the forces of evil.

Nick and I were pals, and I used to visit him at his home in Oneonta. He showed me how the wrestling tricks were done, and when I asked him if there'd ever been a "real" professional match he answered, "If there was, the fans all got up and left after five minutes." Carter recalled a night when one fellow who should have been in on the act wasn't. "Tarzan and I were wrestling in Columbus, Georgia," Nick told me, "and the regular ring announcer was sick, so they brought in a local radio man to take his place. Trouble was, this guy didn't know it was an act. I got in an 'argument' with him during the match, and his eyes got big as saucers. I kicked at him, and damned if I didn't accidentally hit his microphone with my foot and drive it against his mouth, and his lip started bleeding.

"When the match was over, the Columbus police were waiting for me. The ring announcer had called the cops, and they were going to take me in! I asked them if I could go to the dressing room and change clothes before they arrested me, and they said okay. They'd wait at the dressing room door. I whispered to Tarzan to have the car out back of the dressing room. I went inside and quickly pulled on my shirt and pants over my tights and crawled out the back window. I jumped in the car with Tarzan, and we took off home. And I never went back to Columbus, Georgia, again."

Another Nick Carter anecdote: Nick, as I said, was a hero in Alabama, but one day he told me, "I've been wrestling in Atlanta as a villain. I had a skeleton suit made, complete with a mask, and it cost me ninety dollars. In Atlanta I'm 'the Skeleton,' and the fans go crazy when I do dirty things to the babyfaces." A few days later I visited my grandmother Netta Bolton in Lawrenceville, Georgia, near Atlanta. She believed wrestling was on the level as surely as she believed Tuesday followed Monday. She loved to tell me about the matches she'd seen on TV, and I never had the heart to tell her it was fiction. I'd barely entered the door of her house when she said, "Oh, son, We've got a wrestler in Atlanta who's the meanest one yet. I hate him. He's just awful."

I asked her who this monster was. "The Skeleton," she said. Good old Nick got a belly laugh when I told him that story.

The gutsiest act I've ever seen in sports? That's easy. It was Joel Eaves's hiring of Vince Dooley to be head football coach at Georgia shortly after Eaves had been named director of athletics. Dooley, of course, coached the Bulldogs twenty-five seasons and became the school's winningest coach, so it's difficult now to perceive what a huge chance Eaves was taking in hiring him.

Let's set the scene: Johnny Griffith, who had been Georgia's freshman coach, succeeded the legendary Wally Butts as head coach before the 1961 season. Griffith's team went 3–7–0, 3–4–3, and 4–5–1, and he was out. Eaves left his post as Auburn's basketball coach to become Georgia's AD—and he promptly hired the Auburn freshman coach to be head coach of the Bulldogs. Eaves was saying he believed the freshman coach from Georgia's arch rival would succeed where the man who had been UGA's freshman coach had not. I've reflected many times on the courage required to hire the unproven thirty-two-year-old Dooley. When Eaves offered him the job, Vince said, "Well, if you're fool enough to hire me, I'm fool enough to accept." Dooley is one of my half-dozen favorite coaches, all sports. He's a delightful, intelligent conversationalist with broad interests. We share a passion for history.

Golf is not his sport. I was playing with him once when he hit a tee shot between his legs. I have never seen any other person accomplish that. (Cleanly, I mean; I have bounced one or two or three off my ankles and through my legs.) Football is his sport. As much as anyone I know, Dooley confirms my conviction that football is a coach's game. Dooley rescued Georgia. I once chatted with Wayne Swinford, who played for both Griffith and Dooley. "Very few of the players knew who he was," Swinford said of the new coach. "We were skeptical. But after the first meal we had with him we felt at ease. After that it got better every day. Georgia had had good players, but the winning attitude wasn't there. That changed when Dooley came.

"I don't remember what Coach Dooley said during our first meeting with him, but he instilled in us the idea that we were going to put a winning program together. It got everybody thinking winning instead of biding your time. He brought new coaches in, and it seemed like the whole philosophy of coaching changed. From day one you could almost feel it. The biggest impression on me was that we didn't go out and practice from two o'clock until seven o'clock like we had. I think maybe two hours or two and a half hours was it. Practice was better organized. In a five-hour practice you're going to find ways to loaf anyway. It's humanly impossible to go wide open for five hours. That was the biggest impression me, that you didn't have to slave all afternoon."

John Drew of Beatrice, Alabama, was starring for the Atlanta Hawks, and I drove over to Atlanta to interview him for a feature story on his fine career. The Hawks were having a shoot-around in their arena, the Omni. I introduced myself to Drew and told him what I wanted, and he said that would be nice. He pointed to a grandstand seat near the dressing room and said, "Sit there, and when we get through I'll get a shower and dress and come out and talk to you."

The Hawks finished their shoot-around and went to the dressing room.

I waited. And waited. Finally, I entered the dressing room. A trainer was the only person in there. I told him I had been in the arena, waiting for Drew. "He's gone," the trainer said. "He went out the back door. Everybody's gone but me."

Eddie Johnson was having a nice stint with the Hawks, and I called him about an interview. I had known him and written about him when he played at Auburn, and he was cordial and said, sure, he'd meet me for a story. He lived in one of the Atlanta suburbs. He said I'd have difficulty locating his house, but there was a railroad depot in the heart of town. "The depot is easy to find, and I'll meet you there," Johnson said, designating a time. The depot was easy to find, but the player wasn't. I waited an hour and five minutes, and no Eddie Johnson.

Bobby and Judy Allison and their son Davey came to our house for supper years ago. Bobby was a short track driver; Judy was pregnant; and Davey was a toddler. Davey sat in my children's high chair. My wife, Sandra, had prepared fried shrimp. Davey kept throwing his shrimp on the floor. Judy got up and popped him on the butt. Davey stopped throwing shrimp on the floor. After Davey became a star in big-time racing, I enjoyed relating that story to anyone who would listen. "Don't tell that shrimp story again," he would plead when I started.

Life is strange. I couldn't have dreamed that night that the man and child would be the principals in the most memorable sports event I would ever cover—the 1988 Daytona 500. Bobby won it, with Davey finishing second on his bumper. I interviewed Judy that day, and she said she was for Bobby because he paid the bills at her house.

I played golf in Athens with Georgia coach Ray Goff before the 1991 football season. I teed up an orange ball on the first hole, and Goff said, "I wish you wouldn't use that ball. We play Clemson, Florida, and Auburn, and orange is their color."

I thought he was kidding, and I laughed and proceeded to address the ball. "I'm serious," Goff said. "I wish you wouldn't play with an orange ball." So I played with a white ball. In the third game of the season, Alabama shut out Georgia 10–0. I couldn't resist it. I dropped Goff a note that said: "Dear Ray, you forgot that white is one of Alabama's colors."

I flew to State College, Pennsylvania, to cover an Alabama–Penn State football game. Some other writers and photographers were with me. We caught a Delta flight to Pittsburgh, but then we flew an Allegheny Airlines plane to State College. It was about as large as your living room sofa; the weather was stormy; and the plane was rocking and rolling. The fellow in front of me vomited in a paper bag, and if we had been aloft five more minutes I would have joined him in that indignity. When we landed I kissed the ground—literally.

Came Sunday, and the weather was just as violent for the return trip. I called Allegheny Airlines and asked if the flight to Pittsburgh was still scheduled. "Yeah, we're flying to Pittsburgh," the voice on the phone said. "Well, we still have our rental car," I said, "and we thought we'd drive it to Pittsburgh if the flight was grounded." "Hell, if I still had my rental car I'd drive it to Pittsburgh," the fellow with Allegheny Airlines said. That was all we needed to know. We drove to Pittsburgh.

When Alf Van Hoose was sports editor of the *Birmingham News* he got mad at me about something or other and told the executive sports editor not to send me to an Auburn or Alabama football game that Saturday. Being excluded from the coverage, he said, would teach me "some humility."

So, with no assignment that weekend in 1979, I proposed to my friend John Logue of *Southern Living* magazine that I do a story on the historic football program at the University of the South. "Good," he said. "I'll pay you a thousand bucks." So I spent a pleasant couple of days in one of the most gorgeous spots of the nation, Sewanee, Tennessee, watched amateur athletes play football, wrote a magazine piece, and made a grand. Alas, I did not acquire any humility.

Van Hoose was a good golfer, and a purist where the game was concerned. He and I were playing at the Roebuck municipal course in Birmingham one day. We reached the par-three, 137-yard seventeenth hole. It was in the heart of summer; there had been no rain in a couple of weeks; and the downhill fairway was as hard as a sidewalk. Van Hoose hit an iron and missed the green. I was playing like a dog anyway, so I dropped a ball onto the ground of the tee box and swatted it with my putter. The ball rolled onto the green, within eight feet of the hole.

"What the hell was that?" Van Hoose bellowed.

"That was my tee shot," I said.

"That ain't golf," he protested.

"I thought golf was trying to get near the hole," I said, "and I got a lot nearer the hole than you did."

"I don't give a damn," he railed. "That ain't golf."

My two beat his four. I'm pretty sure that's what golf is about.

I was sad, but I was also honored to have been chosen to carry precious cargo. On an August day in 1998, I was one of Fred Sington's pallbearers.

When Alabama fans picked the school's all-star football team of the century in 1992, they didn't select an all-time top player. I took it upon myself to do so in a column, and my choice was Sington, a sixty-minute all-American lineman of 1929 and 1930 and a major league baseball player with the Washington Senators and the Brooklyn Dodgers.

Sington was a role model for adults. His nickname was Mr. Birmingham, and the city never had a better citizen than this sporting goods salesman. On a summer's day in 1989 I asked him how many civic and charitable committees he had served on. "Without counting, I'd say at least 190," he answered. "Every time I turn around there's a different one." My lead on the story of his death was: "It is remarkable that Fred Sington found time to die."

He was all man, but he was as sweet as a ripe peach. "It's so easy to be kind to people," he told me many times. He was always baffled when humans weren't kind to each other. Here's what an admirer said outside the church after the extraordinary Alabama athlete's funeral: "Fred Sington was one of the world's great human beings. What he meant to the University of Alabama, the city of Birmingham, and intercollegiate athletics was important, but the manner of man he was is the reason he transcended Auburn-Alabama." The admirer was David Housel, Auburn's director of athletics.

Eddie Martin, one of the old-time drivers, won a race on a dirt track in the 1940s and was arrested for racing on Sunday. The irony is, Eddie liked to say, that the track was just a couple of miles from the present site of Talladega Superspeedway, where 170,000 fans now keep the Sabbath unholy. Martin was acquitted, and here's another irony: "Later I was a judge in that same courtroom. I was appointed after I retired."

Eddie had a way with words. Once he was stopped by a policeman who was irate because he was doing 100 miles an hour through this 50-mph town, race car in tow. "But I'm driving one car and pulling another," Martin reasoned. "That's just 50 miles an hour each." The officer let him go.

Chapter 10

The end of Eddie Crawford's tenure as Mississippi's basketball coach was announced in a news release that became legendary among SEC sportswriters. At least one old scribe still has a copy, and I'm sorry I didn't save mine. The release, issued after the 1967–68 season, said Crawford was being promoted from head varsity basketball coach to freshman football coach. That was the word it used: "promoted."

Soon afterward I was at a party in Oxford, Mississippi, that Eddie attended. "Did you hear about Adolph Rupp?" I asked him.

"No, what?" Crawford bit.

"Kentucky promoted him to freshman football coach."

Crawford, weary of the whole thing, groaned and walked away.

Referring to such a job change as a promotion was a tad strong even in those days, but the mere fact it could happen spoke volumes about the lowly status of basketball in the SEC—excluding Kentucky, of course. Kentucky hoops has always been exceptional.

An old anecdote still pops up occasionally. Years ago, at a meeting of

SEC athletics directors—most of whom were head football coaches—someone mentioned the upcoming basketball season. An AD–football coach grimaced and said, "Basketball? Are we going to have that crap again this year?"

During my time at the *Birmingham News* I was pleased to see basketball rise to a new level of importance in the SEC. Coliseums replaced gymnasiums. No longer did head basketball coaches double as assistant football coaches. (Even Johnny Dee, who coached Alabama's Rocket 8 in the 1950s, was a football backfield coach, and his most famous product wasn't a basketball player but Green Bay Packers quarterback Bart Starr.)

When I arrived at the *News* in 1961 neither Alabama nor Auburn gave much thought to basketball. Auburn's gym was extravagantly named the Sports Arena, but it really was just a Quonset hut, and Alabama's Foster Auditorium, with its windows open on warm nights late in the season, featured the sulphuric fragrance of Tuscaloosa's paper mill. I used to wonder how panting players kept from throwing up.

But there's something worse than a paper mill. Jim Homer, who played under Coach Hank Crisp (who was better known as a football assistant) at Alabama in the 1940s, told me this story: "We were playing at Mississippi State, and they had an old Quonset hut gym. At halftime we had to go outside to use the bathroom. What we didn't know was that there was an open sewer line out there. Three of us fell into that thing. Well, we came back into the gym just covered. We didn't know what to do. Coach Hank saw us and yelled, 'Get them into the shower!' We got in, shoes and all. I'll never forget playing that entire second half soaking wet."

Fast forward to March 18, 1976. Alabama fell, but not into a sewer. Coach C. M. Newton's Tide fell to Indiana 74–69 in the second round of the thirty-two-team NCAA Tournament. The Hoosiers went on to beat Michigan and win the national championship in Philadelphia's Spectrum. Bobby Knight, the Indiana coach, spotted Charley Thornton, an Alabama assistant AD, after the championship game, and he said, "Tell C. M. that he had the best damn team we played."

That season was heady stuff for a reporter who had cut his teeth at the *News* on mediocre, unemphasized basketball. Alabama went 23–5 to become the winningest Tide in history. A 15–3 SEC count gave Bama its first outright conference title since 1956. Mercy, how that team played defense. It ranked sixth in scoring in the SEC, ninth in field goal percentage, and ninth in free throw percentage, but its defensive average of 69.0 points was a full six points better than the number two club's. Its feat of holding the foes to 43.7 percent of their field goal attempts was the league's best effort.

Center Leon Douglas blocked 77 shots in twenty-eight games. The Tide, incredibly, blocked 148 to its opponents' 48. Anthony Murray, just a sophomore, was the best defensive guard in the conference. Guard T. R. Dunn was laying the foundation for a long NBA career. Rickey Brown and Mule King were tough forwards. Tommy Bonds, Keith McCord, Greg McElveen, and Don Bowerman could come off the bench and keep the gears meshing.

The Tide ripped North Carolina 79–64 in the first round of the NCAA, in Dayton, Ohio, and then it faced undefeated Indiana, winner of twenty-eight straight games, in the Mideast Regional in Baton Rouge. I had never been so excited before a basketball game. I admired Newton as the man who had given muscle to UA basketball. ("C. M. has done as fine a job of taking over a program that was down and making it a national power as any I've ever heard of," Knight said.) I knew the Crimson Tide had a strong chance to win the national title, and in later years Newton would say it was the only team he ever coached that was good enough to be champion of all the land.

"I'm not saying we're going to beat Indiana," Newton cautioned, "but I'm saying we *can* beat them. We're going against a team that obviously is the best in the country. We'd have to play a super game to win—but we're capable of doing it."

But Alabama didn't score in the first 4:52 of the game, and Alabama didn't score in the last 3:58 of the game. It led 69–68 at that juncture, but the Tide didn't make another point.

Now, let me tell you something about sportswriting. The easiest thing in the world is describing a runaway game. Give me a thirty-point victory and I'll write you a fifteen-minute story. But the hardest thing is writing about a great game, and that one was a great game.

The *News* was an afternoon paper then, and there was no deadline pressure. I was rooming with my friend George Smith of the *Anniston Star,* and we set up our portable typewriters in our motel room and began to write. George would type a lead, frown at it, rip the copy paper from his typewriter, wad it up, and throw it on the floor. I'd do the same. The pile grew and grew.

Finally, George said, "I'll tell you what let's do. I'll write a lead and give it to you, and you write a lead and give it to me, and we'll each develop our story from the other one's lead."

We did. George wrote the lead that appeared in the *Birmingham News* under my byline, and I wrote the lead that appeared in the *Anniston Star* under his byline. And to this day George says he got the short end of the stick.

No doubt my excitement about the Alabama-Indiana game sounds unprofessional, but this was high cotton for the basketball writer of the *Birmingham News.* Appearances by our teams in the NCAA tournament weren't commonplace, as they are now. Alabama had reached the NCAA tournament just one other time—the season before—and Auburn wouldn't get there until 1983–84, under Coach Sonny Smith.

Wimp Sanderson arrived at Alabama in 1960 as a graduate assistant coach. He became a full-fledged assistant and eventually the winningest head coach of the Crimson Tide. He once told me: "I remember when we'd travel in what I called hearse cars. There were two old limousines. I think they belonged to the university. We'd take two of them to games with peanut butter sandwiches that we'd eat on the way back. So I've seen the program go from hearses to planes."

Hayden Riley (102–104) head-coached the Tide for eight years during the 1960s. He played in the first game held in Foster Auditorium and coached in the last one. "It was in December 1939, and I was playing for Marion County High of Guin, and we went to Tuscaloosa to play the Alabama freshmen in the first game," he said. "The first time they fired up the furnace it burned the paint off the heating system, and we had to get out of the dressing room at the half because of the smoke." But the new had truly burned off by January 13, 1968, when Alabama played its final game in Foster Auditorium. "It was hard to recruit in Foster," Riley told me. "We'd get people out of Southern Illinois down here, and they'd have a bigger high school gym than ours."

Foster Auditorium and the other gyms of the SEC would heat up when Kentucky came to town. They might not be full for other SEC games, but the home team vs. the Wildcats was marquee stuff. Alabama fans used to throw coins from the balcony onto the playing court when officials' calls didn't please them. They had a stuffed owl, and when the officials fired a gun to end the half or the game, they'd toss the owl from the balcony, as if it had been shot. Adolph Rupp didn't want his men distracted by the sideshow, and in the dressing room before one game he warned them, "Now, I don't want to see a damned one of you paying any attention to that crowd. When they throw that money on the floor, you ignore it." Sure enough, a decision went against the Crimson Tide, and there was a shower of coins, mostly pennies and nickels and dimes. Bernie Shively, the Kentucky athletics director, was sitting at the edge of the bench. A shiny half-dollar rolled along the floor and stopped at his feet. Shively couldn't resist. He picked it up and stuck it in his pocket. Rupp looked at him from the other end of the bench and said, "Well, Shive, I see they met your price."

Riley never had a team that finished higher than fifth in the SEC, but three times—in 1964, 1965, and 1967—his Tidesmen beat Tennessee and Kentucky back to back in Foster Auditorium. The 1963–64 Tide came from eight points behind at halftime to stop Ray Mears's Vols. Two nights later, Rupp brought his league-leading Wildcats to Foster to meet seventh-place Alabama.

The Wildcats were ranked second in the nation and were seeking their twenty-first SEC championship. Kentucky got the title—but not that night, for Alabama scored a stunning 65–59 victory. Cotton Nash, the nation's number one player, made just one field goal and seven free throws, stymied by a 1–2–2 zone that Riley had decided upon a half hour before the tipoff. Bob Andrews and J. W. Berry led the Tide with twenty-two and seventeen points, but it was really defense that won the game. Rupp's growling review: "They outhustled us on offense. They outhustled us on defense. They outhustled us on the boards. They grabbed every loose ball. How do you win from a team playing like that?"

My favorite Alabama player of the Riley era—and, I believe, the best one—was Mike Nordholz, a six-foot-one left-handed guard. He was a driving contortionist who seemed to hang in the air, to defy the law of gravity. "He was an extremely aggressive offensive player," Riley said years later. "He had more moves than any small boy I saw during his time. He was a great competitor." Nordholz's hell-for-leather approach made him susceptible to injury. He suffered a broken wrist each of his three varsity seasons, but the fifty points he scored against Southern Mississippi during the 1966–67 season remains the school record. In fact, he joined LSU's Bob Pettit and Kentucky's Cliff Hagan as the only SEC players to make fifty points at the time.

(Time out for a Cliff Hagan story. The Kentucky great went on to become a five-time all-star in the National Basketball Association. One doesn't do that without having a keen eye. Shortly after Coleman Coliseum opened in 1968, Hagan eyed one of the goals and said, "The basket is a half-inch too low." A measurement followed—and the basket was found to be a half-inch too low.)

Auburn dominated Alabama just before and during my early years at the *Birmingham News.* During a thirty-game stretch that began in the 1957–58 season and ended in the 1970–71 season, the Tigers beat the Tide twenty-six times.

I was sorry our paths crossed for just two seasons before he became AD at Georgia, because Joel Eaves (213–100) was an interesting, cerebral coach of the Plainsmen. His assistant, Bill Lynn, succeeded Eaves as boss Tiger, and though his ten-year record was just 130–124, Lynn continued the mastery of Alabama that Eaves had forged, going 13–3 against the Tide before losing his last four games to Bama.

On February 14, 1970, Lynn's Tigers set a school scoring record by waxing the Crimson Tide 121–78 on the Plain. That record has since been broken, but the sixty points that John Mengelt scored for the Tigers that night remains the Auburn standard. “I don’t think an Auburn team ever played that well before, any time,” Lynn said.

Alabama Coach C. M. Newton saw it differently. “I’m not going to do that to anybody,” he said. Auburn substituted little until the closing minutes. With 4:09 to play, Mengelt had fifty-eight points, and Lynn sat him on the bench for the first time. But fans began chanting, “We want John, we want John.”

Mengelt asked Lynn for the opportunity to score an even sixty. “I told him he could have one more shot, and he’d better hit it,” Lynn explained after the game. It took Mengelt just twenty seconds to make the shot, and then he retired for the night.

Mengelt, who became an NBA fixture, is my all-time favorite Auburn basketball player. In all the years I wrote sports, of all the thousands of college athletes I covered, he is the only one who, when his career ended, wrote me a letter thanking me for writing about him.

There were some dramatic moments in Auburn’s Sports Arena—but none so dramatic as the old Quonset hut’s final moment. On September 21, 1996, fans attending a nighttime Auburn-LSU football game in Jordan-Hare Stadium and those watching the game on TV were transfixed by the sight of the building being destroyed by fire. Spectators elbowed for position on ramps in the stadium to watch the death throes of the Sports Arena, which was just across the street. It was scary, and it was surreal. The Sports Arena was tiny as college basketball gyms go, but it made a huge fire. The destruction was accidentally caused by fans cooking on a grill.

It was a small arena that had been home to small-town players, guys such as Bill McGriff and the Tinker brothers, Wallace and Billy, of Pisgah; Bobby Tucker of New Market; Porter Gilbert of Geraldine; Rex Frederick of Corner; Bill Alexander of Cherokee; Henry Hart of Eufaula; and Layton Johns of Nahunta, Georgia. It was a more innocent time, those days when the Sports Arena hosted Auburn basketball. I am reminded of something Abe Lemmons, the former Texas coach, once said: “Coaches whose teams play in gymnasiums don’t get fired; coaches whose teams play in coliseums do.”

Owen Davis, who became a Detroit sportswriter, grew up in Auburn. He recalled local boys chasing loose balls during the Tigers' practices in the Sports Arena, interacting with the players, who let the kids shoot occasionally. The only time he ever dunked a basketball, Davis said in a story in the *Detroit Free Press,* was when Layton Johns hoisted him to his shoulders.

Joel Eaves's Auburn squad upset Kentucky 61–60 in the Sports Arena on February 20, 1960, in the first basketball game ever televised on the Plain. The team was called Snow White and the Seven Dwarfs because of Eaves's white hair and the players' lack of height. Jimmy Fibbe hit the winning free throw, but moments later Kentucky's Allen Feldhaus had a clear path to the basket, and it appeared Auburn might lose after all. But John Helmlinger reached from behind Feldhaus and blocked the shot on what Davis reckons was "the most memorable defensive play ever made at the Sports Arena."

Eaves's Shuffle Offense featured patience, passing, and layups, which led to high field goal percentages but not high-scoring games. In 313 games, his teams scored 100 points just six times, and five of those games were against Samford, Jacksonville State, and the University of North Alabama.

After one game—perhaps an 89–68 pasting of Vanderbilt in 1962—I was standing beside the radio table, listening in on Eaves's postgame chat. "Clyde Bolton wrote that we can't score," Eaves told the audience. "Well, we scored tonight." Ah, well, everybody loves to stick it to sportswriters when they're wrong.

Eaves and I were friends, though, and we remained so long after he left Auburn to be director of athletics at Georgia. Anytime I was in Athens I'd drop by his office in the athletics department or by his box at Sanford Stadium. I always thought his wife had the neatest name. Her name was Wealthy.

Eaves was preparing for Auburn's 1963–64 basketball season when Georgia gave him the AD's job. The Tigers were to open on December 3, and Eaves was named director of athletics on November 22, 1963. His appointment was lost in the news of the day, though. An hour after Eaves was named AD, President John Kennedy was assassinated.

Eaves's assistant coach, Bill Lynn, was promoted to the head job at Auburn. The best he could muster over ten seasons was a couple of ties for third place in the SEC. Mengelt was his best player, and Joe Newton ranked fourth nationally in the field goal percentage (.606) as a senior in 1963–64. Bob Davis (70–61) succeeded Lynn. He is a great storyteller, but he wasn't a great coach. Stan Pietkiewicz, Mike Mitchell, and Eddie Johnson, future NBA players, spiced his teams, but there were just five editions of Davis Tigers. Mitchell was the first Auburn guy ever selected in the first round.

Speaking of storytelling, I have one about Davis. Auburn was playing at Tennessee, and George Smith of the *Anniston Star* and I dropped by the office of Ray Mears, the eccentric coach of the Vols. Mears was sitting at his desk, throwing darts at the dartboard. Taped to the dartboard was a photograph of Davis. Poor Bob, he had holes in his forehead, cheeks, nose, chin, and eyes. Maybe it was the coaching equivalent of a voodoo priestess sticking pins in a doll. Anyway, Davis lost that game, and his record against Tennessee was 3–7.

Alabama hired C. M. Newton (211–123) before the 1968–69 season, and against Lynn and Davis UA began its push toward becoming the state's premier baskets school. Auburn won twenty-six of thirty games against Alabama during a period that began in 1957–58 and ended in 1970–71. Newton's Tide took off at that point, and he beat Auburn seventeen times over an eighteen-game stretch. His successor, Wimp Sanderson (267–119), went 20–7 against the Tigers during his dozen years as head coach. David Hobbs (110–76), the man who followed Sanderson, lost to the Tigers just four times in fifteen games over six seasons. The worm that Joel Eaves nourished had turned dramatically.

Newton is my favorite basketball coach. I won't go so far as to say what AD Paul Bryant said, but his equanimity was a major factor in my regard for him. Bryant told a reporter he hired Newton "because he's the only basketball coach I've ever known who isn't crazy."

I've always regarded the basketball scene as a weird one. Coaches constantly berate the officials. Fans get lost in mass paranoia, screaming at the zebras until they are hoarse. They believe every call goes against their team, that the other side never gets shafted. You don't see that in other sports. Football coaches and fans are passionate, but they don't yell at the officials throughout the game. A baseball equivalent would be the manager and spectators contesting the umpire's call on every pitch.

The filthy language that boils out from student sections at basketball games pollutes the air. I'll never forget a game being stopped at Auburn because a student threw a piece of ice that struck an official in the eye. If that had happened on the street the punk would have been arrested because witnesses would have turned him in. They didn't at Auburn, of course. I'm always vaguely uncomfortable at basketball games, half expecting some idiot to go postal and shoot everybody.

It was a pleasure to cover Newton. "I made the judgment years ago to worry only about the things I can do something about," he said. "There are a lot of things you can do something about and a lot of things you can't do anything about. Officiating is one thing you can't do anything about. I never worry about officiating." He rarely caught a technical foul. "I think it hurts you," Newton said. "I read that coaches say it helps fire up the team, but I can't recall witnessing many that did the team any good."

Newton, who played for Adolph Rupp at Kentucky, came to Alabama from Transylvania College in Lexington, Kentucky. His won-lost record of 169–138 at the little school was hardly impressive, but Bear Bryant liked his style and hired him. To horror movie fans, Transylvania (the one in Romania) was the home of Dracula. "Maybe he can give the opponents a bad case of anemia," one reporter wrote of Alabama's new coach.

Newton took a cut in pay of three thousand dollars to come to Alabama. He asked Bryant for assurance that he could recruit blacks, because he knew the state's high schools were integrating, and he wanted the best players. And no longer did an Alabama coach have to make excuses for the school's playhouse. Coleman Coliseum, with its 15,043 seats, hosted its first game on January 30, 1968, Hayden Riley's final year as coach. Newton had a talent pool and a decent building in which to house it. Auburn's Beard-Eaves-Memorial Coliseum, which seated 12,500, opened on January 11, 1969. The two buildings lifted basketball to new prominence in the state.

Foster Auditorium had been the scene of the "stand in the schoolhouse door," during which George Wallace, Alabama's racist governor, had dramatically championed segregation. Newton's strong teams, featuring black players, performed in the new coliseum. I always thought it symbolic that Wallace's bankrupt philosophy would be associated with the old gym that had housed all-white Tides while Newton's progressive outlook would bloom in the new coliseum.

In the opening game of the 1970–71 season, Alabama defeated Sewanee 97–58. With the game one minute and thirty-six seconds old, Wendell Hudson made a layup and set three Alabama scoring records: most game, season, and career points by a black man—two. Hudson, a six-foot-five, 175-pound forward from Birmingham's Parker High, was the first black to play in a varsity basketball game for the Crimson Tide. He was the first black scholarship athlete at the Capstone. (Henry Harris integrated Auburn basketball a year earlier.) Incidentally, if you're looking for a trivia question that won't merely win you a few drinks but a distillery, here's one: Who was the first black athlete to participate in a varsity sport for Alabama? The answer is Bill Adams, a walk-on (swim on?) swimmer from Birmingham, in 1970.

Hudson would become my all-time favorite Alabama basketball player. He was a quality athlete, and he is a quality person. Hudson handled a difficult situation with class and courage and aplomb. I was delighted when he was inducted into the state's sports hall of fame in 2001, and I told him so.

Freshmen weren't eligible for the varsity in Wendell's day, and there were some nasty incidents when the Tide frosh played on the road. Some Auburn football players sat behind the Alabama bench and insulted Hudson. Newton protested to Lee Hayley, the Auburn AD, and Hayley put a stop to the nonsense. Hudson got the treatment from bigots at Ole Miss, and when the bus crossed the state line on the trip home, Wendell asked the driver to stop. Newton thought he had become ill—but Wendell simply got out and kissed the ground and said, "I've never been as happy to be back in Alabama."

Hudson—who would become the SEC Player of the Year, an all-

American, and a Crimson Tide assistant coach—was the first in a line of black players Newton would use to energize Alabama basketball. In 1972–73 Alabama started four blacks. In his biography, *Newton's Laws,* the coach said it had never been done in the SEC before, that there was an unwritten rule that no one in the conference would start more than two.

Leon Douglas, Reggie King, T. R. Dunn, Eddie Phillips, Charles Cleveland, Ernest Odom, Robert Scott, Anthony Murray, Rickey Brown, Ray Odums, and other black players had me covering excellent basketball teams instead of the mediocre ones I had grown accustomed to following, and I enjoyed the experience. Douglas was the first Tidesman ever chosen in the first round of the NBA draft. King and Phillips were Newton's other first-rounders.

Newton won three SEC titles and sent two teams to the NCAA tournament—and several other Tides would have played in the tournament if the field had been as large as it is now. Making a sixty-five-team field is one thing: making a twenty-five-team field quite another. The National Invitation Tournament was still important in those days. The entire tournament was played in New York, and Alabama's first appearance in 1972–73 provided me with my first exposure to the Big Apple. I was captivated by the place. I loved it then and I still do.

I wanted to stay awhile, explore New York, but the prospects appeared dire in the Tide's first game. Manhattan led Alabama 86–85 in Madison Square Garden. With eleven seconds to play, the Crimsons had the length of the floor to travel. Alabama in-bounded the ball, and Paul Ellis brought it down court, under terrific pressure from the Jaspers. He passed it to Goober Garrett, and old Goober—the number six scorer on the squad—hit a twenty-two-foot jumper at the buzzer to win 87–86 and buy us several more days in New York. I never covered any other play in any sport that delighted me as much as that one did.

I took an excursion to the Statue of Liberty with the wives of C. M. Newton and assistant coaches John Bostick and Wimp Sanderson. I've always been hot natured and rarely wear a coat, but I was just plain stupid this time. I was freezing as winds raked the boat that was taking us to Liberty Island. Evelyn Newton, Betty Bostick, and Annette Sanderson—

who were dressed in heavy coats, as sensible persons would be—squeezed me in among them and kept me from freezing to death.

Twenty-seven years later I would remember that day as Betty and Annette and I stood in a cemetery in Lexington, Kentucky, and heard a minister say all the good that we already knew about Evelyn.

This photo ran with my column heading when I was the nineteen-year-old sports editor of the *LaGrange Daily News.* Already the hair was disappearing. Courtesy of the Bolton collection.

The young *Gadsden Times* reporter. I couldn't tie a bow tie, so I wore a clip-on. Courtesy of the Bolton collection.

I dedicated my 1973 book, *War Eagle,* to Shug Jordan (*right*), one of the good guys. Courtesy of the Bolton collection.

Chatting with diver Jennifer Chandler, who became a Heart of Dixie princess by winning a gold medal in the 1976 Montreal Olympics. Courtesy of the Bolton collection.

Fred Sington (*right*), a role model for adults, was my choice as Alabama's football player of the century. Courtesy of the Bolton collection.

Thank goodness for a warm press box. Texas beat Alabama 17–13 on a frigid day in the 1973 Cotton Bowl. Courtesy of the Bolton collection.

One of the countless times I interviewed Bobby Allison, leader of the Alabama Gang. Courtesy of Buster Walker.

Left to right: I pose for a picture with *Birmingham News* ace Jimmy Bryan, former Alabama fullback Tommy Lewis, and golf executive Buford McCarty at a party at my home. Courtesy of the Bolton collection.

I never could beat racing's B. J. Parker (*center*) or Al Muskewitz (*right*) of the *Anniston Star* on the golf course. Courtesy of the Bolton collection.

With Vince Dooley at his 2004 Bulldog Invitational golf tournament. Neither of us is a threat to par. Courtesy of the Bolton collection.

Gene Bartow's midwifing UAB hoops in the 1980s was one of the state's all-time great sports stories. I don't remember what we were so excited about in this photo. Courtesy of the Bolton collection.

Ronnie White (*right*) of the *Huntsville Times* and I interview Indy 500 winner Johnny Rutherford. Courtesy of Buster Walker.

The great Auburn quarterback Pat Sullivan and his wife, Jean, attended my 2001 retirement party. Courtesy of the Bolton collection.

Old pal George "Goober" Lindsey joined me in the Legion Field press box in 2000. Courtesy of the Bolton collection.

Left to right: Alabama radiomen Bert Bank and Kenny "Snake" Stabler with me at a Tide game in 1998. I think Kenny was Bama's greatest QB. Courtesy of the Bolton collection.

Serenading my wife, Sandra, in Ryman Auditorium, former home of the Grand Ole Opry. Thank goodness there was no audience. Courtesy of the Bolton collection.

Chapter 11

Alabama's success under C. M. Newton moved me to write my fifth book, *The Basketball Tide,* which was published in 1977. It was a history of Alabama hoops. A photo on the back of the dust jacket is one of my favorites. It pictures our son Mitch, who was a little boy then, jumping and shooting a ball at an outdoor goal while I lean on the post. My wife, Sandra, snapped the photo of the Norman Rockwell scene. Mitch, our third and last boy, was born in Birmingham. We never had a daughter.

Unfortunately, I would come to include *The Basketball Tide* among the evidence that Alabama isn't a basketball state. I've written sixteen books besides the one you're reading, and I've had many autograph parties—and the only time I failed to sell a single copy was at an autograph party for *The Basketball Tide.* I think it was my best sports book, and no history of Crimson Tide baskets had ever been written—but it sold like cold cakes. A well-meaning Auburn fan phoned me and said, "I saw your book on Alabama basketball. Now you must write one on Auburn basketball." I told her, "The only thing that would sell fewer copies than a book on Alabama basketball is a book on Auburn basketball. Count me out."

It was this apathy toward basketball that led to Newton's resigning as Alabama's coach. His last Bama team was the 1979–80 Tide. It got off to a 5–6 start but finished 18–12. For the first time, he heard complaints from people he thought were supporters that he had too many black players. Fans in this state will back a program that's winning big, but interest dwindles when a team slips, and interest in the Tide declined that year. Alabama beat LSU and Kentucky on the road, and the players were excited to return home and play Georgia. But Newton watched the excitement drain from their faces when they saw the small crowd of some six thousand. Bama lost 68–65.

That night Newton used his postgame radio show to express his disappointment in the sparseness of the audience and to offer the bitter opinion that the program was appreciated more away from home than it was at home. He told Evelyn he thought it was time for him to leave the Capstone. "It's always best to leave while you're still in love," she offered. He was still in love with Alabama, but the romance was waning. Newton resigned after the season and accepted—at less than half the pay—a job as associate commissioner of the Southeastern Conference. He recommended that Wimp Sanderson be named his successor, and AD Paul Bryant agreed. You know what they say about being the coach who succeeds the legend. Well, in Wimp's case, forget it. All Sanderson did in a dozen seasons was become the winningest coach in Alabama history (267–119). He took ten Tides to the NCAA Tournament and advanced to the Sweet Sixteen six times. His teams reached the final of the Southeastern Conference Tournament nine times, winning it five times.

I admired Newton for his equanimity and rational approach to the game. Sanderson's methods were quite different, and I was turned off by them. I saw in his twisted facial expressions genuine hatred for the refs. Plenty of folks were delighted by his screaming and contortions, but I wasn't one of them. I stopped being the paper's primary basketball writer and became the featured sports columnist during Sanderson's tenure. Naturally, I didn't attend nearly as many games, but I wrote a fair amount of columns about the sport.

One day I phoned Sanderson; his secretary told him I was on the line and the first words out of his mouth, delivered angrily, were, "Goddamn it, why don't you write more about basketball?" Now, the *Birmingham News* overplays basketball to the point of being ridiculous. I told Wimp: "There's so much basketball in the paper now that when the paperboy delivers my copy I dribble it back up the driveway. I called to invite you to lunch. We're still going to lunch—but now you're going to pick up the check."

"Aw, I know I'm paranoid," Sanderson said.

"Damn right you're paranoid," I agreed.

We enjoyed a nice lunch at Michael's, Birmingham's late great sports restaurant, and Wimp told me some stories, and I wrote a column about him. And he picked up the check.

I thought it amusing that Sanderson would concern himself with my supposed lack of promotion of basketball while he refused to do something that would have been of more promotional value to basketball in this state than anything I could have ever done—namely, play UAB. It's ridiculous that the Blazers and Crimson Tide don't meet. Of course, in 1992–93 UAB earned the right to be smug. The National Invitation Tournament arranged the first and only meeting of the two clubs, in Tuscaloosa, and the representatives of Birmingham campus won 58–56. The general attitude of UAB partisans since then has been: "We whupped 'em on their home floor, and they ain't asking for a rematch. What more could we want?" The evening could have been sweeter for UAB only if Sanderson had been the coach, but it was David Hobbs's first season as boss at the Capstone.

But, all that said, I once again return to my premise that Alabama isn't a basketball state. That Tide-Blazers game was ridiculously ballyhooed by the press—but it didn't even draw a capacity crowd. In a basketball state, they would have been scalping tickets for such a matchup.

Before the historic night, C. M. Newton, then Kentucky's director of athletics, said, "If you can't sell that game out, there's not any interest in basketball." It didn't sell out. The game pulled 13,496 spectators into

15,043-seat Coleman Coliseum. I signed off my column that night with these two paragraphs:

> Some have suggested that the state Legislature should force Alabama and UAB to play, as the Kentucky Legislature mated Louisville and Kentucky. But that's nonsense.
>
> In the first place, there are a lot more Alabama grads than UAB grads in the Legislature. In the second place, when our inept Legislature got through, both schools would be located in South Dakota and playing in the Continental Basketball Association.

But Sanderson's wild man antics and refusal to play UAB notwithstanding, he was a superb coach, and Alabama was fortunate it promoted the longtime assistant after Newton resigned instead of seeking a "name" coach. C. M. lifted Tide hoops from an exercise merely bracketed between football season and spring practice to prominence, and Sanderson not only kept it there, he improved the product.

I'll admit Wimp was fascinating. Of course, so is a race car when it's flipping end over end. How could you not be fascinated by a man who, when the buzzer sounded on a close loss to Vanderbilt, fell face down on the floor in front of the bench, as if a sniper had shot him?

How could you not be fascinated by a man who, at halftime of a game against Georgia, roared into the dressing room and kicked a Gatorade bucket, severely spraining his big toe? The next day he limped to practice and watched with his leg propped up and his toe bandaged.

How could you not be fascinated by a man who, after a road game, angrily kicked a container that held the players' boxed lunches and then bounced around the dressing room with a boxed lunch stuck on his foot?

His friend Sonny Smith, the former Auburn coach, described the supercharged Sanderson as a man who needs a passing lane in a car wash. His friend Hugh Durham, the former Georgia coach, described him as "a pessimist who believes he's going to win." I think I know what Durham meant. It's simply Wimp's nature to agonize, to fear the sky is falling, before every game, though he believes in his coaching abilities. Durham recalled a round of golf when Wimp knocked in a 140-yard fairway shot for an eagle and immediately saw the glass half empty, remarking that he probably wouldn't hit another good shot all day.

Every coach wants to recruit talented players and then make them better. Wimp could do that. Nine men who played for him when he was Bama's head coach were first-round choices in the National Basketball Association draft: Eddie Phillips, Ennis Whatley, Buck Johnson, Derrick McKey, Jim Farmer, Robert Horry, Latrell Sprewell, Jason Caffey, and James Robinson. Some of the other outstanding players were Michael Ansley, Keith Askins, David Benoit, Eric Richardson, Terry Coner, Mike Davis, Bobby Lee Hurt, Gary Waites, and the present Tide coach, Mark Gottfried.

Unfortunately, Sanderson's career at Alabama ended in 1992 on a sour note. He was ousted after problems involving a female employee of the university. A couple of years or so later we were having lunch, and Sanderson told me, "People respect you and pay attention to what you write. If you would write a column saying I should be allowed back into coaching it might help me." I told him that, indeed, I thought he should be back in coaching, and I would write a column saying so. I did, and Arkansas–Little Rock hired him. I have no idea whether the column was a factor in his return to coaching, but if it was I am pleased. Wimp, by the way, never mentioned the column to me.

David Hobbs succeeded Sanderson as coach of the Crimson Tide. His record was 95–60. He had a couple of twenty-win seasons and two NCAA Tournament teams, but he was out after six years. Antonio McDyess, Roy Rogers, Jason Caffey, and James Robinson were first-round picks who played for Hobbs.

Mark Gottfried was the popular choice to succeed Hobbs before the 1998–99 season. He was the fifth and last Alabama basketball coach I covered for the *Birmingham News.* Since he and his wife, Elizabeth, have five children, he announced when he accepted the job that the university had immediately reached two of its goals: raising the attendance and the noise level in Coleman Coliseum. Gottfried's celebrated young star Gerald Wallace was an NBA first-round selection.

Auburn reached the NCAA Tournament for the first time in the 1983–84 season. The Tigers must have liked the newly discovered tune, for they paid five straight visits to the Big Dance, reaching the Sweet Sixteen in 1984–85 and the Elite Eight in 1985–86.

Sonny Smith, my all-time favorite Auburn basketball coach, was a comedian. Still is. The rostrum for his down-home humor these days is a Birmingham radio talk show that he and Wimp Sanderson host. As unlikely as it seems to those who believe hatred is the natural order between Auburn and Alabama, they are old friends.

I'm no psychiatrist, but I suspect Smith's cracking of jokes springs from a painful upbringing. As Smith himself said, "Sonny grew up tough." Home was Roan Mountain in the Tennessee hills, and his father was a bootlegger. "There were about 300 or 400 people in town," Smith told me. "The first time my family went out of town, we drove to Roanoke, Virginia, in a dump truck. My brother and I were in the back. We were poor.

"My dad was a bootlegger and also a deputy sheriff. I tell that as a joke, but it's true. He had a heck of a job. He wasn't about to get caught."

The authorities did descend on the Smith place one memorable time, though. "They raided our house," Sonny said. "My mother hid the liquor in the bed with her. She was known to be sickly, and they thought she was sick. They patted her on the head and said, 'Irmie, we're going to get old Grigg one of these days, but we hate to bother you because we know how sick you are.' When they left we threw the cover back, and my mother got out of bed, and we were right back in the liquor business."

He loved his mother, Irma, dearly. "I had a great mother. She was one of those people who could rub salve on a wound. She was the best."

Paul Lambert succeeded Bob Davis as Auburn's coach, but he was killed in a motel fire and never coached a game. Smith left the head coaching job at East Tennessee State to succeed Lambert. "I basically turned down the Auburn job the first time, and they hired Paul Lambert," Smith said. He was going to tell Art Derozier, the president of East Tennessee State, that he was turning it down again when his mission took a strange turn. Before Smith could say anything, Derozier said, "Sonny, I wish you'd stay, but I know you're going to take the Auburn job." The president cataloged all the advantages of a bigger school and added that he would certainly accept the presidency of a larger school if it were offered. He understood perfectly.

But he didn't understand at all. "I came in to tell him I was going to stay, and he came on with all this negative stuff and talked me out of it," Smith said. "It wasn't that he didn't like me. We were friends. He wanted me to stay."

Smith immediately learned basketball's place in the pecking order at Auburn. Lee Hayley, the director of athletics, told him that on rainy days the football team would have first refusal on the arena for practice purposes. But Doug Barfield, the football coach, never pushed it. "There were times when he could have, too," Smith said. "Doug was a great guy."

Smith coached the man who would become the most famous basketball player the state ever produced, Charles Barkley. When Barkley became an NBA first-round draft choice after his junior season of 1983–84, he had averaged 14.1 points and 9.6 rebounds during his Auburn career. He played for Philadelphia, Phoenix, and Houston, retiring after the 1999–2000 season, most of which he missed with an injury. He was named one of the top fifty players in NBA history.

I remember covering the Gator Bowl tournament in Jacksonville, Florida, when Barkley was an undergraduate. Barkley was alone on one end of the court when a teammate fired a long pass. Rather than snatching the ball and dribbling for an easy layup, Barkley ran alongside the bouncing ball, intending to dramatically scoop it up at the last second. But he slipped and fell on his fat butt.

At halftime the public address announcer called for a doctor to go to the Auburn dressing room to see Coach Smith. As I recall, Smith had a virus or something else that wasn't serious, but when I asked him after the game why he required a doctor, he cracked, "Too much Charles Barkley."

Smith and I chatted recently, and I asked him what it was like coaching Barkley. "It was like having a root canal," he said. "Actually, Charles was the kind of guy who wanted to be at practice—he just didn't want to be at practice and practice hard.

"I don't coach anything like my personality. I was real hard on kids. The football team used to gather up to hear me get on them. Instead of hammering Charles and running him and cussing him and hitting him—I hit him twice with my fist—if I had coached him a little differently I think he would have been a more productive player. I think if I had treated him a little more like pro coaches treat some players, treated him like a star, it would have been better."

Barkley wasn't a national recruit, but Smith knew he was special. "Nobody knew he would be as good as he became," Smith said, "but I knew he would be a pro, and when I signed him I told him he could leave Auburn after his junior season. He played hard and practiced hard for me his junior season because he was playing for a contract. He could take over a game and dominate it. I tried to talk him out of going pro when he did, but he said, 'Wait a minute. When you were trying to talk me into coming to Auburn you said I could do it.'"

Barkley was a fat guy who was called the Round Mound of Rebound when he played at Auburn. He didn't look like a basketball player then, though he would trim down as a professional. "The thing people don't know is that we pushed the fat thing because it got us publicity," Smith revealed. "It got us publicity with ESPN." Part of the problem was a back injury that limited Barkley's practicing and led to his putting on weight, Smith said, "but he never was as heavy as we said he was."

Barkley was inducted into the Alabama Sports Hall of Fame in 2001. He was a nationally famous figure, not only for his basketball ability but for his big mouth, but I got the impression the fellow from little Leeds, Alabama, was deeply moved by the honor. "I've had an unbelievable life," he told me before the induction ceremony. "It has exceeded all expectations. Even if you're the cockiest guy in the world you couldn't sit down and say this is how I want my life to turn out. I had the greatest job in the world, and the other was gravy. I met presidents. I played in two Olympics. That's not stuff you ever think about." The Phoenix resident was still living the good life, as a national TV commentator. "I'm enjoying playing golf every day and working two days a week," he said.

Barkley has become a noted philanthropist. He gave a million dollars to fuel the Charles Barkley Education Foundation so that students of his alma mater, Leeds High School, might have college scholarships. "I've lived the American dream," he told me. "I believe I was sent here by the Lord to make the world a better place. If a person doesn't get inspiration from my life, they're an idiot. When I speak to kids I tell them there's not a person living who thought my life would be like this.

"Things have worked out for me. The only reason I went to Auburn was because they weren't any good. If Alabama or UAB hadn't been any good I would have gone to one of them. It's amazing how things work out. I didn't think I could play with those players at Alabama and UAB."

Sonny Smith coached Auburn's all-time leading scorer, Chuck Person, who also went on to a long career in the NBA. Person poured in 2,311 points in four years for the Tigers. "He was the hardest working player I ever coached," Smith said. "He was the only one who would practice the two and a half hours and keep you there another hour and a half. He'd come to your office and break down films and ask questions. I thought he'd be a real good coach, and he is coaching in the NBA now.

"I remember one game against Vanderbilt, he was scoring at such a rate—everything was going in, no matter how he shot it—that the fans of the other team booed him when he passed the ball instead of shooting. I've never seen that before or since."

It's interesting to note that Frank Ford and Gerald White were starting guards on the first four of Smith's five straight NCAA Tournament teams. "They were leaders as freshmen," he said. Jeff Moore was the starting center and Chris Morris a starting forward on the second, third, fourth, and fifth Big Dance squads. Chuck Person started on four teams, including three NCAA Tournament clubs. Smith not only surrounded himself with talent, he surrounded himself with young talent. Chuck Person and Morris were selected in the first round of the NBA draft.

Tommy Joe Eagles flopped as Smith's successor, despite the presence of Wesley Person, who became one of Auburn's finest before being drafted in the NBA's first round.

What's in a name? Maybe more than you'd think. Pat Dye, who was Auburn's director of athletics, asked Sonny to furnish him a list of names of men who might succeed Smith as head coach when Smith left. Smith got up a list, and John Lewandowski of the sports information department suggested he add Tommy Joe Eagles of Louisiana Tech. He did. As Smith tells it, Dye came to Eagles's name and said, "Tommy Joe Eagles. Eagles. War Eagle. We're going to interview that boy."

Cliff Ellis followed Eagles before the 1994–95 season to become the sixth and last Auburn basketball coach I would cover for the *Birmingham News.* The Tigers, led by star Chris Porter, returned to the NCAA Tournament after a ten-season absence. Ellis was just about everybody's national coach of the year as those 1998–99 SEC champions went 29–4 and reached the Sweet Sixteen of the NCAA Tournament. I wrote about the 1999–2000 squad that shook a leg in the Big Dance, too. Mamadou N'diaye was an Ellis product who was picked in the first round of the NBA draft.

But Auburn fired Ellis after the 2003–4 season and hired Jeff Lebo, a fellow I'd never even met.

I don't know for a fact that this occurred, but it was told to me on good authority, so I believe it did. A Birmingham sportswriter missed out on the biggest exclusive of his life because he simply refused to believe the tipster who gave him the information. It was so preposterous he didn't even bother to check it.

Gene Bartow, the coach at UCLA, was going to leave one of the great powers of college hoops to head up the program at UAB, which didn't even own a basketball? Sure, and I've got some nice oceanfront property in Remlap I'd like to sell you. Yet it did happen. UAB fielded its first basketball team in the 1978–79 season, and sitting on the end of the bench was Gene Bartow, who had led two other teams, Memphis State and UCLA, to the Final Four. In two seasons at UCLA, where he succeeded John Wooden, winner of ten national titles, Bartow had compiled a 52–9 record, and now here he was coaching at a school most folks in Los Angeles had never heard of. He also was its director of athletics.

Bartow coached eighteen years at UAB, compiling a record of 365–204. That's the most victories by any Division I coach in the state's history. His third squad of Blazers reached the Sweet Sixteen in the NCAA Tournament, and his fourth one made the Elite Eight. Seven others played in the tournament. The UAB arena is named for him. Dick Vitale, the prominent TV basketball commentator, once said Bartow's success at UAB and the job Bobby Cremins did at Georgia Tech were the two greatest college basketball stories of the 1980s. I think he was correct.

Bartow retired as the Blazers' coach after the 1995–96 season. His record in thirty-four seasons as a head coach (Central Missouri State, Valparaiso, Memphis State, Illinois, UCLA, UAB) was 647–353. He retired as director of athletics in 2000.

Bartow and I chatted recently about his strange move from UCLA to UAB and about his years at the Southside school. "It was a very difficult decision," he said. "I started in May 1977 serving Jerry Young, the vice president for finance, as a consultant. They were going to start a Division I basketball program. I told them all I knew that they needed to do to start up a Division I program. I recommended they take a look at Kermit Davis, who had coached at Mississippi State, and at Bob Polk, who had coached at Vanderbilt. A couple of weeks went by and Jerry asked me to meet them again. I met them in Kansas City. That's when they approached me about coming here. My first impulse was there's no way I'd do it." But Young was "a great salesman who had great vision, and Dick Hill, the president, was a wonderful person." And, lo, they sold Bartow on a move that shocked the basketball world.

At UCLA he had been the proverbial guy who succeeded the legend—and you know what they say about that. At UAB he wouldn't be succeeding anyone. "I wasn't having fun at UCLA," Bartow said. "Succeeding Coach Wooden was like succeeding Coach Bryant at Alabama or Coach Rupp at Kentucky."

Three factors ultimately sold him on coming to UAB, Bartow said. "I had never made any money in coaching. UAB offered about three times more than I was making at UCLA. That was a factor. Then there was the nut element at UCLA, pressures to win the national championship. Nothing was satisfactory to them but winning the national championship. A third factor was that it appealed to me to be director of athletics, along with coaching."

In 1980–81, UAB basketball's third season of existence, one of the truly amazing stories of sports in our state was written. Bartow's Blazers won the Sun Belt Conference Championship and reached the Sweet Sixteen in the NCAA Tournament. They beat Kentucky before losing to Indiana. UAB's fourth squad trumped that one. It repeated as Sun Belt king and then made the Elite Eight of the NCAA Tournament, knocking off Bobby Knight's Indiana as well as Virginia, which was led by its celebrated giant, Ralph Sampson.

Those early teams featured two of Bartow's finest stars. "Oliver Robinson turned into an all-American," he said. "Chris Giles was one of the great defensive players I've ever been around. They were our leaders, and we had a lot of other really good players. Steve Mitchell and Jerome Mincy followed them, and for seven or eight years we had some pretty good basketball teams."

I asked Bartow to name his top five UAB players. He readily mentioned Robinson, Giles, Mitchell, and Mincy. "Those four for sure," he said. "There were so many others. Andy Kennedy holds a lot of records. You'd have to consider him. We had Robert Shannon for two years. We had Carlos Williams."

The UAB game that is closest to his heart? "My favorite game of all time has to be the win over Virginia that propelled us into the final eight. Anytime you reach the final eight you've created a milestone because there are only eight teams left in the country. A lot of good coaches around the country have had some awfully good teams that never got there. It was my third one. I had one at Memphis and one at UCLA.

"We had a lot of great wins. The one over Indiana to get us to Virginia was a big win. We had two wins over ranked Michigan State teams. We had some great games over the years with South Alabama and Auburn and got more than our share of wins in those games."

Bartow has fond memories of his years at UAB—but they aren't all fond. "My first twenty years there were really great," he said. "I worked for four great presidents—Dick Hill, Scotty McCallum, Claude Bennett, and Paul Hardin. My last three years were not all that much fun, so I retired as director of athletics after twenty-three years." W. Ann Reynolds was Bartow's fifth president at UAB.

Bartow experienced stunning early success, and he averaged twenty wins a season over his entire run, but only one of his final half-dozen squads reached the NCAA Tournament. His last two teams went 14–16 and 16–14. His son Murry Bartow succeeded him as head coach (and became the second and final UAB basketball coach I covered for the *Birmingham News*). Murry's 1998–99 team played in the NCAA Tournament, but he was unable to rekindle the old magic, and the school called on Mike Anderson, a Birmingham product who was an assistant at Arkansas, to lead the Blazers.

Chapter 12

I COVERED THE TWO MEN whose careers were the most instrumental in the promotion of Southeastern Conference basketball, Kentucky coach Adolph Rupp and Louisiana State star Pete Maravich. I rank them in that order as generators of interest in hoops in SEC land, but I'll discuss Maravich first.

Pistol Pete's three varsity seasons at LSU (1967–68, 1968–69, 1969–70) not only saw him rewrite the conference record book, but all these years later his name still leads all the rest. He holds the SEC record for points in a career (3,667), in a season (1,381 in 1969–70), and in a game (69 vs. Alabama in 1969–70). The first two figures also are NCAA records. Maravich averaged 44.2 points a game during his three years and 44.5 points in 1970, still conference and NCAA records for a career and a season. The list goes on and on, but those are the most important statistics. I don't want this story to turn into something best read by a CPA.

Maravich, a loose-jointed six-foot-five guard, was a long-range gunner, and if the three-point shot had been in the rules in those days there's no telling how many points he would have scored. And it's interesting to note he holds the NCAA career record for total points even though freshmen weren't eligible for varsity play then. As a matter of fact, when Maravich first burst onto the scene at LSU, some fans would watch the freshman preliminary game and go home before the varsity game began.

I think Pete Maravich was the greatest player in the history of the SEC. Yet, there was an odor of the counterfeit about the records he set. His father, Press Maravich, was his coach, and Press made sure the ball was in Pete's hand, that his boy was the one taking the shots. It's strange what sticks in the mind. I've seen a million basketball plays, but I vividly remember LSU's Apple Sanders catching a rebound against Alabama and, instead of making the easy put-back, turning to look for Maravich so he could get the points.

Pete was the one who brought the ball downcourt, but his role wasn't that of the typical point guard. He wasn't looking to feed a teammate. His aim was to free himself for the shot, and his incredible dribbling ability facilitated it. He wasn't called "the white Globetrotter" without reason. Maravich holds the SEC record for career field goal attempts, 3,166. In three years he shot 1,205 times more than the second-place man, Tennessee's Alan Houston, did in four years. Maravich's total also is the NCAA record. His shooting percentage, though, is an unremarkable .438.

Yet, even while Press Maravich's methods turned me off, I was captivated when I watched Pete play, and I realized there were some benefits beyond the obvious ones to him and his son. LSU's record was a modest 49–35 during Pete's years, and only one of his three squads had a winning record, but the Pistol filled arenas wherever he suited up. He raised the excitement level of SEC basketball dramatically. Even today, LSU plays in the Pete Maravich Assembly Center. How many gyms do you know of that are named for players?

The Maravich-Maravich show also provided some comic relief. During one game, when a team was giving his son a hard time, Press kept screaming to an official, "Get 'em off Pete! Get 'em off Pete!" Finally, the ref stopped the game, walked over to the LSU bench, and deadpanned, "Coach, which one is Pete?"

C. M. Newton's first Alabama team, the pathetic 4–20 squad of 1968–

69, was in Knoxville for a Saturday game against Tennessee. The Volunteers were to host LSU on Monday. Alabama's manager accidentally walked into a Tennessee practice on Friday. He came out and, embarrassed, said to Newton, "I hate to tell you this, Coach, but they're working on a drill to stop Pete Maravich." Yet, the only SEC game the Crimson Tide won that season was against LSU. Maravich scored forty-two points. He made nineteen field goals, but he shot forty-nine times. In fact, when Pistol Pete set the conference record of sixty-nine points against Alabama in 1969–70, the Tide won the game 106–104.

Maravich played against Kentucky six times. He averaged fifty-two points a game against the Wildcats. The sixty-four points he made in 1969–70 is the third highest figure in SEC history and still the most ever scored against Kentucky. Yet, UK won all six games. Adolph Rupp's policy was to let Pete have his fifty-two points and shut down his teammates. And so it went during the Maravich years. The Pistol fired and fired and fired, but it was the opposing team that so frequently was the last one standing.

I delighted in covering Adolph Rupp because I have a keen appreciation of history, and in the presence of Rupp I was barely removed from the origins of basketball. Rupp played at Kansas for Phog Allen who played at Kansas for James Naismith who invented the sport. Rupp himself had some college classes under Naismith, who used to tell him he didn't believe basketball ever would attract national attention or reach the status of a sport to which admission could be charged.

Rupp did as much as anyone to assure that Naismith was a bust as a prophet. He became Kentucky's coach before the 1930–31 season and his final season was 1971–72. His record over forty-one years was 876–190, a percentage of .822. (Okay, that's a span of forty-two years, but one is missing; we'll deal with it later.) He was the winningest coach in college basketball history when he hung up his whistle. His Wildcats won four national championships and twenty-seven Southeastern Conference titles.

Rupp was coaching high school ball in Freeport, Illinois, when he applied for the Kentucky job. When the athletics board asked why it should hire him, he answered: "I'm the best basketball coach there is." The Baron of the Bluegrass was an acerbic, droll, witty, sarcastic, complicated character. He loved being on stage, loved putting people on. Rupp, an advocate of man-to-man defense, surprised Tennessee coach Ray Mears with a 1–3–1 zone in 1963–64, and Kentucky won 66–57. In his postgame press conference Rupp explained the defense: "It was a transitional and stratified man-to-man backed by a hyperbolic paraboloid between the ball and the basket."

"What's that?" a writer asked.

"You know what a paraboloid is, don't you?" Rupp said. "It is a sort of a cone. And a hyperboloid is one with one of the points cut off it. Stratified means in layers, and transitional means changing. So that should explain it."

I liked to situate myself near Rupp and Kentucky announcer Cawood Ledford and listen to their dissection of the action on the postgame radio show. During commercial breaks, Rupp would chat with the press. He seemed to especially enjoy entertaining the opponent's writers after Kentucky had beaten their teams. Once he got in a dig about Alabama or Auburn on the air then told me, "That's for the folks in Kentucky. I hope you won't write it for the folks in Alabama." He knew, of course, that I would.

One guy who could get his goat was Babe McCarthy, the Mississippi State coach who was as eccentric a character as Rupp was. Kentucky was playing in the little gym in Starkville, and State fans were ringing those infernal cowbells when Kentucky players went to the foul line. Officials told them they didn't have to shoot as long as the cowbells were ringing. John Cox walked to the line and just stood there as the fans shook their cowbells. He stood and stood and they shook and shook. Finally, McCarthy went to the microphone and told the Mississippi State students, "Please be quiet." Then he added: "They're gonna miss anyway." Mississippi State won, and the students carried Babe off the floor.

McCarthy's Bulldogs won the SEC title outright in 1958–59, 1960–61, and 1962–63 and shared it with Kentucky in 1961–62. One of the memorable games I covered was Mississippi State–Kentucky during the 1961–62 season. McCarthy's Bulldogs came to Lexington with an 18–1 record, ranked ninth in the land. They had lost only to Vandy in eight SEC games. Rupp's Wildcats had a 17–1 record, were ranked second in the nation, and were undefeated in conference play.

Heck, I was impressed before the game ever started. The 11,500-seat Memorial Coliseum was the biggest arena I'd ever seen. Frankly, I was awed by the sight of that many seats under a roof—and I would feel the same way some fifteen years later when I first saw the 23,000-seat Rupp Arena. (You want to talk basketball states? Kentucky still practices in Memorial Coliseum, and the first workout of the season—Midnight Madness—draws a capacity crowd and a statewide television audience. Now, that's a basketball state.) Anyway, Babe's Bulldogs and the Baron's Wildcats squared off in Memorial Coliseum in a game I'll never forget. The *News* had a Mississippi edition in those days, and I spent a lot of time in Starkville, and McCarthy had charmed me. I considered State a local team, and I wanted the Bulldogs to win.

Kentucky featured Cotton Nash, a six-foot-five blond sophomore forward from Lake Charles, Louisiana, who looked like a movie star. LSU and Tulane and other colleges had wanted him to play football. A host of schools had wanted him to play basketball. UCLA promised him a date with Jane Fonda. He passed on Fonda and Los Angeles and chose Rupp and Lexington.

I don't know that I have ever seen another basketball player who made it look as easy as Nash did. After Kentucky played Georgia Tech, Atlanta sportswriter Furman Bisher wrote: "You will seldom, if ever, see a boy so big with so much grace, so much agility, so much maneuverability and with so soft and velvety a touch as Nash. There were times when Rupp was using his versatile young man to bring the ball downcourt when Georgia Tech pressed its defense. With his size and his massive hands, Nash gave the impression of a circus giant dribbling an orange."

Kentucky fans wouldn't even entertain the notion that the drawling, insulting McCarthy and his Mississippians could beat Kentucky and Nash on their hallowed home floor. Yet, it happened. State won 49–44. McCarthy's method made it even more infuriating. There was no shot clock in those days, and his Bulldogs played slowdown basketball. "I remember their stalling tactics," Nash said years later. "They got ahead and put a man in each corner. They would dribble and dribble and work for the crip shot." State made eleven of eighteen shots in the first half to take a 28–22 lead. "Dribble for fifteen minutes and play defense for five," McCarthy told his men at halftime. They shot eight times and made seven in the second half.

The year before, when Kentucky beat State 68–62 in Starkville, someone placed a wreath on the doorknob of the Bulldogs' dressing room. The ribbon bore the words: "Rest in Peace." (I've always suspected Babe had it done.) "Put it away," McCarthy told the student manager. "Next year we'll take it to Kentucky." With two seconds to play in Lexington, Babe pulled the wreath from under his coat and handed it to a student manger, who tossed it onto Kentucky's goal as the game ended. A weeping Kentucky cheerleader pulled down the wreath and tore it to pieces. (The wreath story didn't end there. After Kentucky beat State 65–59 in Lexington during the 1963–63 season, Kentucky football players stuck a wreath on McCarthy's head.)

Babe was at his best in the press conference after the 1961–62 upset of the Wildcats. "I was hoping one of you fellows would ask me how we handled Nash," he said. "I was going to tell you my daddy had a cotton gin, and I was always good at handling Cotton." Actually, Nash scored twenty-three points that night—but Babe wasn't one to let facts get in the way of a good line. That was one of just forty home games that Rupp would lose in forty-one seasons. Eighteen of his clubs were undefeated at home. During one streak the Wildcats didn't lose at home for ten years.

Rupp was superstitious. He was known as the Man in the Brown Suit. It wasn't merely a matter of preference in fashion, though. During his second year as a high school coach in Freeport, Illinois, he bought a new blue suit to replace a worn brown one. His team lost that night, and from then on he wore brown. On the afternoon or night of a game he looked for hairpins that had fallen on the sidewalk or in the arena. A good haul of hairpins meant a good night on the court.

Rupp picked up a bobby pin as the team was entering Florida's gym for a practice, and he told player Brad Bounds, "This means we're going to have good luck, Brad."

"Coach, you're not superstitious, are you?" Bounds asked.

"No," Rupp said. "I learned a long time ago, when I first started coaching in Illinois, that it's bad luck to be superstitious."

Rupp was approaching his 800th victory in 1968. The Wildcats were in Tuscaloosa, and before the game Rupp made an unscheduled visit to his motel suite where he found a huge cake lettered in icing that read, "800th Victory!"

"My God!" he bellowed." Who put that here? You'll get us beat as sure as hell!"

That superstition was unfounded. Kentucky beat Alabama 84–76.

Rupp could sting his players with his vitriolic, rhetorical tongue. Ed Beck, who later became a minister, recalled a game in which the Wildcats were trailing Ole Miss at halftime. In the dressing room he sliced the players one by one, saving Beck for last because he was the only one from out of state. Said Rupp: "Ed, I want you to go to the hotel right now and write me a letter. No, write me a theme. No, you'd better make that a doctoral dissertation on this subject: why Adolph Rupp was crazy enough to go to the state of Georgia after the likes of you.

"Ed, you have eaten well at the university over the last two or three years, and I am going to let you play the whole second half no matter how poorly you do—and I know it will be poor—but before we go out on the court, do you see the corner over there? I want you to go over to that corner and puke up everything you have eaten at the University of Kentucky over the last three years because you have never earned it, and at the end of this game I want you to go into the dressing room, look me straight in the eye, and say, 'Coach, I did something in this coliseum tonight, even if it was only over there in the corner.' "

Or he could make his point with amiable brevity. Once Rupp stopped a wishy-washy practice, stood in the middle of the court, raised his arms to the heavens, and pleaded, "Dear God, would you please send me someone who is worth a damn?" At that moment Gov. A. B. Chandler appeared at practice. "Thank you, God," Rupp said.

Rupp's caustic sarcasm could take strange turns that left players scratching their heads. Vince Splane asked for permission to attend his grandmother's funeral out of town, and Rupp granted it. A few days later the Wildcats were practicing poorly, and he blew his whistle and called them into a circle. "My God, boys, we're not going to continue playing like this," he railed. "We're not playing girls' rules. This is war!" Then he singled out Splane and said, "And another thing, boys, we're not going to have any-more of this grandmother-dying business."

Before a game with the Volunteers, Rupp told his team, "All those Tennessee players are SOBs!" Several Wildcats glanced at Wallace Jones, a Kentucky star. One got up nerve enough to remind Rupp, "Er, Coach, Jones's brother plays for Tennessee." Without hesitation, Rupp said, "I mean all of their players except Jones's brother."

File this in the Athlete I'd Least Like to Be category: After a key Saturday night victory, Rupp presented the game ball to Lee Huber. But on Monday he called Huber into his office and said he'd heard Huber had been out on the town on Friday night, breaking training, and he didn't deserve the game ball. Rupp wanted it back. Whereupon Huber had to confess he had sold the ball to a fraternity. Ouch!

Rupp couldn't stand for a guard to walk the ball up the floor. One night a guard was doing exactly that. Rupp leaped to his feet—and, wouldn't you know it, in that precise moment the arena got quiet—and the coach screamed, "Quit that (bleeping) around out there!" A woman sitting behind the Kentucky bench didn't appreciate the language. She stood up and hit him across the back with an umbrella. Rupp's only acknowledgment was to turn to assistant Harry Lancaster and say, "See who hit me."

One night Kentucky was stomping Arkansas State 34–4 at halftime. In the dressing room Rupp looked over the score book and a frown creased his face. His players wondered how he could possibly be angry about anything. He noted that one Arkansas State man had all four of his team's points. "Who is guarding number twelve!" he demanded.

Jack Parkinson confessed: "Coach, I am."

"Well, get on him," Rupp demanded, "because he is absolutely running wild!" Parkinson and the rest of the Wildcats evidently straightened up, for Kentucky won 75–6.

Rupp remains the most important figure in the history of Southeastern Conference basketball. But his career at Kentucky was tainted. The NCAA gave his program the death penalty, and the Wildcats wouldn't be playing any basketball during the 1952–53 season. Rupp's players had been involved in college hoops' notorious points-shaving scandal of the late '40s and early '50s. That revelation led to an in-depth investigation of the Kentucky program, and other irregularities were found. In fact, Judge Saul S. Streit of the general sessions court, County of New York, ripped Kentucky's athletic policy as "the acme of commercialism and overemphasis."

Kentucky's getting into NCAA trouble over basketball may have been a stroke of luck for its football coach, a fellow named Paul Bryant. In his book *Unsportsmanlike Conduct,* Walter Byers, the longtime executive director of the NCAA, wrote that there was evidence of NCAA rules violations by Bryant at the same time as Rupp's. Ohio State coaches complained that Bryant's representatives tried to buy a high school star who lived in Conneaut, Ohio. The report said Kentucky recruiters left a thousand dollars at the boy's home. Byers pointed out that Bryant left Kentucky "relatively unscathed" because of the NCAA's and the public's preoccupation with the basketball mess. Bryant departed Kentucky to coach in the Lone Star State, and his new school, Texas A&M, was put on probation.

One of the irrepressible characters I covered was Dale Brown, the LSU basketball coach of twenty-five years whose final season was 1996–97. He is the second winningest coach in SEC history (448–301), trailing only Adolph Rupp. Brown, appropriately, was born on Halloween. He was, er, different.

The 1987 SEC Tournament was played at the Omni in Atlanta. Brown vowed not to sleep until his Bengals won the thing. He stayed awake sixty hours, passing the time by watching television, phoning sportswriters who were in town to cover the tournament, and jogging in downtown Atlanta in the middle of the night (which should have won him a medal for bravery). LSU reached the final game, but it lost to Wimp Sanderson's Alabama 69–62. In the postgame press conference Wimp quipped, "I went by the LSU bench to shake hands with Dale before the game, but he was sound asleep."

Brown laughed at Sanderson's line, but there was another line he didn't find amusing. It was during SEC Media Days, when Shaquille O'Neal was playing. Wimp, just trying to be funny and entertain the press, said, "Dale's team is so good even he can't screw it up." The press laughed, but Brown wrote Sanderson a letter saying he didn't appreciate the remark. Wimp wrote him a letter saying he meant no harm, even telephoned him to apologize. Brown kept mentioning it every time he'd see Sanderson. Once he even said, "Wimp, you know I beat you five straight games after you made that statement."

As I have said, C. M. Newton was not a demonstrative basketball coach. It took a lot to infuriate him—but Brown managed it. Alabama and LSU met in Baton Rouge during the 1978–79 season. The Bengals had the game locked up with thirty-eight seconds to play. Brown called a timeout, and a purple and gold banner was unfurled from the ceiling. It proclaimed LSU the SEC's regular season champion. The crowd went wild. Newton thought the show was totally out of line. He had won three SEC titles without any such shenanigans. He told Burl Crowell, one of the officials, "If you don't get this game started before I get back to the bench, we're leaving the floor and you'll have to finish the game without us. We're not going to participate in their damn celebration." Crowell got the game rolling again. Newton just got madder when Brown later told him displaying the banner "was not in poor taste."

Brown wore his emotions on his sleeve. He once called the NCAA "Gestapo bastards." If he wasn't afraid of the NCAA he wasn't likely to be afraid of Bobby Knight, whose Indiana Hoosiers destroyed Brown's two best chances of winning the national title and then went on to win it themselves—once in nearby New Orleans.

In a *Sport* magazine article, Brown called Knight "a despicable human being who has everyone—the NCAA, the referees, the media, other coaches—intimidated out of their pants by calling people cheaters and deciding who can and can't coach. Well, I defy intimidation." He accused Knight of robbing his players of the enjoyment of their college careers, of bullying the zebras, and of using his influence to get players on the Olympic and Pan Am squads. "Some smart man once said, 'Be proud of your enemies.' Well, I'm extremely proud to know that Bobby Knight can't stand me."

Knight, of course, responded. "As long as the Dale Browns of the world are in disagreement with me, then I think I'm in pretty good shape." Later, Knight spoke of his team trailing and how he began to fear Indiana might lose the 1987 regional title to LSU—but "then I looked down the floor and saw Dale Brown, and I knew, well, we had a chance." When reporters tried to get Knight to talk about Brown at the 1988 regional, Knight responded, "When you ask questions about him, you should direct them to a psychiatrist, not me."

Brown, in his own inimitable style, once said: "The way to settle this would be to put me and Coach Knight in a wrestling room naked and whoever came out first would be the best man. I'm sick of him bullying and kicking people around." In a restaurant Brown stuck out his leg and tried to trip Knight. Brown said his leg was extended so far he looked like the comic book character Plastic Man. Knight ignored him and stepped over his leg.

Ray Mears was a bombastic basketball coach and an ardent promoter. I'll admit fifteen years of Mears were great fun for an SEC basketball writer, even one who preferred his coaches more modulated. Of course, I only caught him two or three times a season.

I once asked Bob Davis, the Auburn coach, to contrast Mears and C. M. Newton. They certainly were at opposite ends of the spectrum in the SEC. "They're completely different," Davis said. "C. M. is the ideal type of coach when it comes to control and calmness. He goes at it in a businesslike way. He doesn't use the crowd and things like that. Ray has a style all his own. Don't get me wrong—I'm not knocking it. He's a wild person who believes in using the crowd. He uses anything—posters, signs, write-ups, anything you say. He uses anything to stimulate his squad—that big T they run through before the game, the unicycles, the loud music in the locker room.

"Each has his own way. They're just different, that's all. That's the nice thing about this game—everybody has to do it his own way. And each would be a failure if he tried to copy the other. C. M. would fail if he tried to coach like Ray does, and Ray would fail if he tried to coach like C. M. does."

In 1969 Mears's Volunteers were playing at Vanderbilt, where the team benches are at the end of the court. Near the finish of the freshman game, during a timeout, Mears, wearing his bright orange blazer, walked the length of the floor to Tennessee's bench. He knew the Vandy students would boo him, but he hadn't expected the violent reaction and screaming and profanity that occurred.

It backfired. The inspired Tennessee freshmen beat the Vandy frosh, and then the riled-up Vols' varsity won 70–60 in a game it was expected to lose. "Vanderbilt's crowd helped us win," Mears said. So he took the Nashville Walk in 1970 and 1971, and each time the Vanderbilt students' reaction was more vociferous—and each time Tennessee won.

Bill Skinner, Tennessee's six-foot-seven, 250-pound javelin champion, accompanied Mears on his 1970 Nashville Walk. Vanderbilt students swiped Tennessee's orange and white warmup ball and were tossing it around in the stands. Skinner waded in among the kidnapers of the ball, and a normal-size student gulped and returned it to Skinner without protest.

The Tennessee-Vandy scene grew nastier and nastier (with Vanderbilt students even throwing oranges at the Vols), and in 1972 SEC commissioner Tonto Coleman requested that Mears not take his Nashville Walk and also that his unicycle rider, Bill Seale, not perform his pregame act. Mears complied—but Tennessee nevertheless won its fourth straight over the Commodores in Music City.

My favorite basketball story: On January 12, 1992, Troy State set an NCAA record by scoring 258 points against DeVry. After the game a young reporter asked Troy coach Don Maestri, "Coach, did you in your wildest dreams ever imagine that you'd score 258 points in a basketball game?"

Maestri smiled and answered, "Son, my wildest dreams don't have anything to do with basketball."

Chapter 13

I USED TO OCCASIONALLY DRIVE out to Memorial Park in Auburn and stand at Shug Jordan's grave and remember the good times. I haven't done that in awhile. I should do it again next time I'm in Auburn.

Jordan's death on July 17, 1980, wasn't unexpected. He had suffered acute leukemia for four months. Four football seasons had passed since he had coached Auburn, so his name had long been absent from the daily sports news. The word that he had died at his home did not come as a numbing, surreal thunderbolt, as would the announcement of Paul Bryant's death from a heart attack on January 26, 1983, less than a month after he had retired as Alabama's coach.

Bryant attended Jordan's funeral service at Holy Trinity Episcopal Church in Auburn. A seat was reserved for him at the front, but he said he'd just stand at the back. Bryant didn't want to be the center of attention, walking down an aisle. "What should I do?" a perplexed undertaker asked the Reverend Bill McLemore, who was conducting the service.

"You let Bear Bryant do whatever he wants to do," McLemore answered.

The service lasted just fifteen minutes. Before it began, reporters asked McLemore for a copy of his sermon. There wouldn't be a sermon, he said. "The people gathered here are the sermon for Coach Jordan," he told the audience.

It's better to die like Bryant did than like Jordan did, though both left this earth prematurely, at the age of sixty-nine, which doesn't seem nearly as old to me as it once did. Jordan was terribly thin at the end. Terry Beasley spoke with him on the phone three days before he died. He asked Beasley not to visit him, because he preferred that Beasley remember him as the strong, energetic man who had coached Terry when he was Auburn's magical receiver.

When I heard of Jordan's death I recalled one of the great adventures of my writing career. In 1970 I suggested to Jordan that I move into the athletic dorm for three days during preseason workouts, that I live and practice with the players and write a series of articles about the experience. He loved the idea and said come ahead. The plan was for another *Birmingham News* writer, Jimmy Bryan, to do the same at Alabama, but Bryant wouldn't permit it.

I didn't scrimmage (I didn't have a death wish) but I took part in the other drills. I was thirty-four years old and in decent physical condition. The practice field incident I remember most vividly occurred during a passing drill. We were running crossing patterns. Pat Sullivan, realizing I wasn't exactly Terry Beasley, tossed me soft passes that I easily caught. Dieter Brock (who would later transfer to Jacksonville State and become a great pro in the Canadian Football League) burned one in there that I barely saw. I didn't catch it, but it caught me—on the end of a finger. It felt like it drove my finger back into the general area of my collarbone.

"You okay?" big Gene Lorendo, the offensive coordinator, asked. Okay? I was trying to keep from crying in front of an entire football team. I mentioned that to Brock years later when he was coaching at UAB. He didn't remember it. "Well, there's the evidence," I said, showing him a finger that was still a little bent.

(I never quite got over football. In 1974, when I was thirty-eight years old, my son Mike talked me into playing in a game with him and some other nineteen- and twenty-year-olds. They had an organized league with sponsors, and it was real tackle football except for one minor difference—they didn't have uniforms or pads or helmets. The good news was that I actually scored a touchdown. The bad news was that one of those young broncos caught me with a blind side block and broke two of my ribs.)

Lights-out in the Auburn athletic dorm, Sewell Hall, was at 10:30. I was snoozing away at 1 A.M. when there was a loud knock. I stumbled to the door in my underwear, and there stood Brownie Flournoy, the resident counselor. "I just wanted to be sure you weren't breaking curfew," he said. Funny, funny.

Spending twenty-four hours a day with Auburn players impressed upon me just what a fellow goes through to play big-time college basketball.

Larry Willingham sat on the blue carpet in the lobby of the athletic dorm, motionless, his back against the wall. He had just come in from morning practice. Afternoon practice was ahead. Someone yelled "lunch." "I don't want to get up," Willingham said. "You get in a position like this, you don't want to move. You get molded to the floor."

James Owens left the lunch table, and he was already thinking about the afternoon drills. "You can hardly rest waiting for what's going to happen this afternoon," he said. "Everybody eats real fast so they'll have a lot of time to rest."

There were some laughs, too. During one meal on an August evening the freshmen sang Christmas carols and danced together, to the unrelenting boos of the upperclassmen. I gulped when some of the players called me "our freshman" and ominously mentioned a friend who owned a boa constrictor. They demanded to know my room number. I gave them the wrong number.

When they learned it was my birthday, Pat Sullivan said menacingly, "Birthday, huh? You ever heard of the board?" I wasn't crushed by a snake or blistered by a board, though. Indeed, there came a moment on the night of August 31, 1970, that I'll always remember fondly. We were eating the evening meal when Betsy Dunbar, the assistant dietician, walked out of the kitchen with a birthday cake. The freshman stood in their chairs and serenaded me with "Happy Birthday." I blew out all the candles and silently wished Auburn a memorable football season.

Shug Jordan didn't have to permit me to live and practice with his team for three days, but he did. That's the kind of person he was. I wasn't a distraction for the players. They had a few harmless laughs and so did I. My presence must not have poisoned the well, for those Tigers of 1970 went 9–2, conquering Alabama in the Iron Bowl and Archie Manning's Ole Miss in the Gator Bowl.

Jordan's death brought back another memory that wasn't pleasant, a recollection of a few words I wished I had never spoken. Several years before he died I took a week off from my regular duties and wrote the obituaries of four men, all of whom were living, Jordan, Bryant, former Alabama football coach Red Drew, and former Auburn track coach and director of athletics Wilbur Hutsell. Newspapers routinely prepare obits of well-known persons in advance. When death comes, the research is done and the story written, and a quick update renders it ready for publication.

I dropped by Jordan's office and told him, "You'll never guess what I did last week. I wrote your obituary." Jordan had a wonderful sense of humor, and I expected the remark to provoke some wisecrack. But he didn't respond, didn't say a word, didn't smile. I was embarrassed, and I changed the subject. Later I learned there had been a downturn in his health. I would have given a week's pay to have had those words back.

Jordan coached his final game on November 29, 1975. He had a poor team that would finish 4–6–1, and Bryant had a superb one that would go 11–1. There was no reason to think the Tide wouldn't win. It did, by a score of 28–0. But even that morning, in that setting, Jordan could find a spot of humor and share it with friends. The team was staying at the Sheraton in Birmingham, and the telephone instructions said that if a guest wanted coffee brought to his room he should punch 3. Jordan said he did, but nothing happened. So he punched it twice more. A voice came on the line, and Shug said, "This is room 128, and I'd like some coffee."

The voice on the other end said, "This is room 333, and I'd like some, too."

Jordan retired with a record of 176–83–6. Doug Barfield, who was his offensive coordinator, succeeded him as head coach of the Auburn Tigers. I would cover Barfield, Pat Dye, Terry Bowden, Bill Oliver, and Tommy Tuberville on the AU football throne before I retired in 2001.

Barfield was the classic example of the unfortunate coach who follows the legend. Some Auburn supporters wanted Barfield in the big office and others wanted Paul Davis, the assistant head coach, to get the job. It's tough enough to win when you're everyone's choice.

It became a cliché: "Doug Barfield is too nice a guy to be a college head football coach." Well, a lot worse things can be said about a fellow. Gene Lorendo, a member of Jordan's original staff, told me a story. He said Barfield, trying to decide whether to retain Lorendo, called him into his office and asked him his thoughts about the situation. "Doug," Lorendo said, "I don't think you've got the balls to be a head coach." Lorendo told me Barfield thanked him for his candor, and big Gene became an ex-Auburn assistant coach.

Barfield's record in five seasons was 29–25–1. He never beat Alabama. The 1979 Tigers climbed to 8–3, but in 1980 a Tennessee team that would have a losing season destroyed Auburn 42–0 in Jordan-Hare Stadium. It was a defining moment, and Barfield's support all but evaporated. His club finished 5–6, and he was gone.

Amid the frustration of his stint as Auburn's head coach, Barfield got off a funny line that I still remember. It was Auburn-Alabama week one of those seasons, and I went to Tuscaloosa. I asked Bryant when he was going to retire. "When we block two damned punts against Auburn, that's when!" he shot back. He was, of course, remembering two that the Tigers blocked to win the Punt, Bama, Punt game of 1972. Later in the week I went to Auburn, and Barfield asked me, "How long is Bryant going to coach? Do you have any idea when he'll retire?"

"He told me this week that he won't retire until Alabama blocks two punts against Auburn," I answered.

"Well," Barfield said, "tell him we'll let him block two Saturday if he'll retire."

Pat Dye succeeded Barfield before the 1981 season. He restored Auburn football to respectability, winning four SEC championships, forging a record of 99–39–4, and beating Alabama six times in twelve years. Nobody ever said Dye was too nice a guy to be a head coach. He had played for Wally Butts at Georgia, coached under Bryant at Alabama, and learned from both that football is largely a matter of assault and battery. Those professors were never accused of being too nice, either. Pat Dye wasn't old school; he went to the school they tore down to build the old school.

Dye was a Georgia country boy, and I could relate to that. How country was he? Well, a hog bit the end of his toe off. Is that country enough for you?

Of all the head coaches I've known, Dye was the most like Bryant, which is ironic considering he coached Alabama's number one rival. Of course, he spent nine years as Bryant's assistant at the Capstone, so he had ample time to observe the master. Dye, like Bryant, stressed the physical side of football. Dye decries today's rules that allow offensive linemen to use their hands. What did Bryant think? Bear walked into the office one day and told his assistants, "Men, they just took the first step in ruining football when they permitted offensive linemen to hold. They just took the fun out of defensive football." What should be a blocking contest has become a pushing and shoving activity, and it's conducted not by quick, scientific players but by 325-pounders whose principal role seems to be taking up a lot of space. Dye and Bryant, of course, were "real" linemen when they played.

Neither Dye nor Bryant ever found a substitute for hard work. They believed they could and would outwork the opposition and benefit from the labor, and they did. Both talked about work a lot. They learned hard work as farm boys, though Dye didn't grow up in poverty as Bryant did.

Dye played at Georgia, in the Canadian Football League, and in the military. He decided he wanted to coach, and he petitioned Bryant for a job. Bryant phoned Wally Butts, who had coached Dye at Georgia. "Can Pat Dye coach for me?" he asked.

"I don't know whether he can coach for you, but he could have damn sure played for you," Butts said.

Dye had just gotten out of the service, so he had no civilian clothes. He bought some suits, and he was wearing new duds when he drove from Atlanta to Tuscaloosa to interview for a job. "I had heard about Coach Bryant getting to work early, and I wanted to impress him," Dye told me. "I decided I'd be there when he got to work at 6:30 in the morning. I said,

'Well, it's four and a half hours over there, so I'll leave at two o'clock and be sure to get there. I was so excited I didn't sleep anyway. I got up and dressed and took off.

"I got to Birmingham and it was still dark. I got to Tuscaloosa and it hadn't even begun to break day. I looked around and there wasn't anything open. I finally found a service station and pulled up and looked at my clock and it was 6:30. I looked at their clock and it was 5:30. I had forgotten the time change."

Dye drove to the athletic offices and made small talk for an hour with the only person on the premises, the janitor. Eventually Jimmy Sharpe and Richard Williamson, a couple of assistants, arrived. Bryant showed up at 7:30 and told them to get a cup of coffee while he opened his mail, and he'd talk to Dye later. "We were walking back from the Student Union, me in my new pin-striped seersucker suit," Dye remembered. "I was walking beside Jim, and Richard was behind us, and I heard him laughing. He said, 'Boy, how long have you had that suit?' I said, 'I just bought it. This is the first time I've had it on.' He said, 'I figured that.' I said, 'Why?' He said, 'You haven't cut the tags off of it.' I still had the pockets sewed up and tags on both sleeves and on the back pocket and everywhere else and was fixing to go in there and talk to Coach Bryant about a job."

Sharpe and Williamson snipped the tags off and Dye was saved from that embarrassment. He approached Bryant with the confession that he knew nothing about coaching but wanted to learn. Bryant hired him, and a coaching career was born.

Dye became head coach at East Carolina and then Wyoming and then Auburn. He compiled a 99–39–4 record during his years (1981–92) on the Plain. His coaching career ended in the storm of an NCAA investigation and probation.

It appeared that Vince Dooley, the Georgia coach, a former AU player and assistant, would succeed Doug Barfield at Auburn. Don Leeburn, one of Dye's old teammates at Georgia, phoned Dye in Wyoming and asked if he'd be interested in the Georgia job. "I think Vince Dooley is going to Auburn," Leeburn said. Of course, Dye was interested.

Just as Bryant had, Dooley heard Mama's call, and he seriously considered taking the Auburn job. He'd had solid success at Georgia, and his 1980 squad was headed for a Sugar Bowl victory over Notre Dame and a national championship, but he was flattered that his old school was beckoning. Dooley's wife, Barbara, a Birmingham girl who had met Vince when she was an Auburn student and he was an assistant coach, knew there are no second first times, that if her husband returned to Auburn the situation would be different from what it was when Vince was a quarterback and later an assistant coach on the Plain. Sweet memories are wonderful—but that's all they are, memories. She thought Auburn wanted a savior, and she doubted her husband should be attempting such a role at that stage of life. She told Dooley to coach where he would be the happiest, but she added: "Whatever you decide, I just want you to know that it's only a four-hour drive, and you can visit us on your off weekends." That night Vince told Barbara he had decided to stay in Athens.

So Pat Dye changed gears and went after the Auburn job. He pointed out to the selection committee that if Auburn was to prosper on the football field it must compete with its two biggest rivals, Georgia and Alabama. He had played for one and coached for the other, and he knew the inner workings of both. The selection committee asked Dye how long it would take him to beat Alabama. "Sixty minutes," he said. He simply meant the Tigers must play well for an entire game, but the answer struck a chord and it was widely repeated by Auburn folks.

Dye couldn't get an answer from Auburn—but Wyoming wanted one from him. He had coached there just one year and hadn't actually signed a contract. He could sign a binding contract immediately or quit his job, Wyoming said. He quit, gambling that Auburn would hire him. He was relieved when it did.

A reporter asked him if it bothered him that Auburn clearly wanted Dooley. "I was the third son, and my mother and daddy wanted a little girl, so I've been living with that all my life. I was supposed to be named Patricia," Dye said. "That doesn't bother me at all. What is important is that they ended up with the best coach."

Auburn knew it had hired the right man when Patricia's—I mean

Pat's—second edition of Tigers went 9–3 and beat Alabama 23–22. The Tide had downed Auburn nine straight years before Dye's boys ended the string in 1982. That was Bryant's final season. Dye was fortunate in that Alabama football would be in turmoil for much of his time at Auburn. He would coach against Ray Perkins, Bill Curry, and Gene Stallings.

Dye once told me that Bryant liked him because he couldn't intimidate Pat as he did other assistant coaches. I don't know, but what happened before their first meeting as head coaches of Auburn and Alabama, in 1981, is vintage Dye. Bryant liked to walk onto the field before a game, his houndstooth hat pulled down, like a carving come to life off Mount Rushmore, Alabama fans cheering. It was high theater, and he figured to intimidate the opposing coach. Dye met him at the middle of the field and announced, "Coach, before you say a word, you ain't going to intimidate me. We're fixing to get after your ass." Bryant just laughed. Alabama won 28–17, but it had to come from behind in the fourth period to do it. A year later, Pat Dye handed Bear Bryant the final defeat of his coaching career.

Dye said he and Bryant were as close as could be expected, considering they head-coached such serious rivals. Pat remembered when they both played in a charity golf affair in Memphis during that summer of 1982. He told Bryant his plane was flying right over Tuscaloosa on the way home and asked Bryant if he'd like a lift. Bryant answered, "Yes, if you won't tell anybody I got in that damn Auburn plane."

I covered Dye when he was an assistant coach at Alabama and head coach at Auburn, and I tended to think of him in dual terms. I liked to needle him, as one old country boy might needle another one. He might get pissed, but he didn't stay pissed. I saw an opportunity over lunch one day when it appeared Curry would leave Alabama for Kentucky, and Dye asked if I knew who might succeed him.

"I don't know," I said, "but I know who I would hire if I were Alabama."

"Who?" Dye asked.

"Pat Dye," I said.

"Aw, shit. Crap."

"Don't tell me," I insisted. "You'd walk to Tuscaloosa for that job. You've beaten Alabama the last four years. It would be the ultimate flattery for them to say, 'We can't beat you, so we want you to come coach us.'"

"Aw, bullshit," Dye said. "Crap."

Dye, of course, did something at Auburn that Bryant never did at Alabama. He fielded a Heisman Trophy winner, Bo Jackson. Yet, Jackson would be instrumental in one of Alabama's victories over Auburn. He became Wrong Way Bo in the 1984 Iron Bowl.

Trailing 17–15 with 3:27 to play, Auburn had fourth and goal at Alabama's one-yard line. Dye decided to skip the field goal and go for the TD. Brent Fullwood would run to the right, with Jackson leading as a blocker. Only trouble, Bo went left instead of right, and Rory Turner dropped the unprotected Fullwood for a three-yard loss. Turner's famous quote: "I just waxed the dude."

At least the play produced a memorable joke. Before the down, Dye sought the help of the Almighty. Looking skyward, he asked, "Lord, which way should we run, left or right?"

After a moment, God said, "Run right."

The play failed, and Dye pleaded, "Why did you tell us to run right, Lord?"

God turned to the entity at his side and said, "I don't know. Hey, Bear, why did we tell them to run right?"

Terry Bowden succeeded Dye, making NCAA history by becoming the first coach to begin a Division I career with twenty straight victories. It was all the more remarkable because he inherited a program that was on NCAA probation. He led Auburn to its first 11–0 season in 1993. In five-plus years his record was 47–17–1. He was 3–2 vs. Alabama.

I rarely hear Auburn fans say anything good about Bowden. Dye's last two teams went 5–6 and 5–5–1, and then Terry won twenty in a row. Bowden's next-to-last club compiled a 10–3 record, won the Peach Bowl, and lost by a single point to Tennessee in the SEC championship game—but his strange departure during the 1998 season seemed to negate, in the minds of the fans, the good things. After six games, with the record at 1–5, Bowden resigned. Many fans saw it as a coach quitting on his players. I think there was another side. I think Bowden knew he was going to be ousted, and he chose to leave on his own schedule.

I hated to see Bowden leave—and one reason was selfish. Bowden was a good interview. Get him talking, and he'd go on and on and on. Some writers made fun, in print, of his loquaciousness. That was dumb. I thought newspaper reporters wanted subjects to talk to them.

Before the 1995 football season, Kent Partridge, Auburn's sports information director, told me AU was going to push Bowden's senior runner Stephen Davis for the Heisman Trophy. Partridge said we could make the announcement through my column. He would get Davis and me together in his office for an interview, and I would have an exclusive. Sounded good to me. Partridge and I waited for Davis. And waited. Stephen finally showed up twenty minutes late for his first interview as a Heisman candidate. Now there's a sure way not to win friends and influence people and get votes.

I'm not a conspiracy nut, but I've always wondered if there was more to Davis's "candidacy" than met the eye. Auburn opened the season with a 46–13 stomping of Ole Miss. Mississippi coach Tommy Tuberville apparently came to the Plain believing Bowden would attempt to get Davis's Heisman campaign off to an impressive start by constantly feeding him the ball. Ole Miss put eight and nine defenders on the line. Davis ran just fourteen times, for 70 yards. Quarterback Patrick Nix completed twenty-eight of thirty-nine passes for 372 yards. In my more suspicious moments I've wondered if Bowden suckered Tuberville. Was there really any intent to push Davis for the Heisman?

Davis finished the season with 1,068 rushing yards, a nice total but hardly Heisman numbers. He ran the ball forty-one fewer times than he had the season before. When the votes were tabulated, Ohio State runner Eddie George won the Heisman and Davis wasn't even in the hunt.

Bill Oliver, the defensive coordinator, became the interim head coach when Bowden left after six games in 1998. He won two and lost three in an impossible situation, and Auburn hired Tommy Tuberville to be its boss man.

Tuberville is a pleasant, cordial fellow, and I found working with him to be easy. When I started writing sports at the *Birmingham News* in 1961 all the college head coaches were older than me. Before I retired in 2001 all the college coaches were younger than me, a situation that always hit home when Tuberville would address me as "Mr. Clyde." But, what the heck, time marches on, and I thought it was attractively quaint.

Tuberville was defensive coordinator at Miami. The most famous fellow he coached was Dwayne Johnson. Johnson was a member of the Hurricanes squad that lost to Alabama in the Sugar Bowl showdown for the 1992 national championship. Gino Toretta, the Miami quarterback, won the Heisman Trophy, and both of Alabama's defensive ends, Eric Curry and John Copeland, were consensus all-Americans, but it was Johnson, a substitute defensive tackle, who gained more fame than anyone else on either team.

Johnson went on to become the top celebrity in another "sport," professional wrestling, and an action movie star. Fans know him as the Rock. Tuberville recalls a young man who was quite different from the strutting wrestler of today. "He was one of the most mild-mannered kids I ever coached," Tuberville told me. "He probably didn't say fifty words the whole time. He was real laid back, kinda shy. He didn't have the defensive mentality at all. We were a real aggressive team, but he wasn't a real aggressive person. He played quite a bit, but he was never a true starter. He was a super guy, though. He was polite and well-mannered."

Tuberville isn't a wrestling fan, and he didn't realize Johnson had become a wrestler until one night in the late 1990s when he happened to recognize the fellow the television announcers were calling the Rock. Tuberville called his wife, Suzanne, into the room and said, "Look. That's Dwayne Johnson."

You never know, do you?

Chapter 14

I WAS DRIVING TO TUSCALOOSA to begin an assignment that I dreaded more than any I had ever undertaken in my newspaper career. It was the night of Wednesday, January 26, 1983. Bear Bryant had died of a heart attack that afternoon, and my assignment was to go to his home and write an "atmosphere" story.

I had known the coach's wife, Mary Harmon Bryant, for years. I liked her and she seemed to like me. I had met some other members of the family. I hoped they regarded me as a writer who was sincere and fair, who didn't follow the path of phony sensationalism that some others walked. But I didn't know. Would their eyes narrow when they opened the front door and saw me standing there? Would they think I was a journalistic vulture who had come to intrude in their time of grief? Would they dismiss me with a rebuke and a slam of the door?

The death of Paul Bryant had saddened me as it had saddened millions of other Alabamians. I brushed back tears, as they did. I was made acutely aware of my own mortality. Shug Jordan, whom I covered for fifteen football seasons, was gone, and now Bryant, whom I covered for twenty-two seasons, was too. All of us, the mighty and the meek, have a rendezvous with death.

I made myself a promise as I drove to Tuscaloosa. I would write a tasteful, dignified, straight-up story that would honor the greatest college football coach who ever lived. The state was awash in tears, but I would not write a cheap tearjerker. I owed Bryant and his family and myself and (so I thought) my newspaper that. Whatever powers of writing I had, I would summon them on this night.

I needn't have worried about my reception. I was welcomed into the Bryant residence, thanked for coming. This family was accustomed to the attention of the press and the public. It fully realized the unique place the head of the household occupied in the hearts and minds of Alabamians and that his death was a story of surpassing importance. I was relieved.

Bryant's son-in-law, John Tyson, a judge on the Alabama Court of Appeals, was particularly attentive to me, telling me he would help me get whatever I needed. That made me feel better about taking out my pad and making notes. It's impossible to make notes unobtrusively. "Joe Namath was sitting there, and Sonny Werblin was sitting there," the judge said, recalling a day from the past. "Joe said he wanted to stay over and take all the little ladies to dinner who were good to him when he was here. He spent two days doing that."

Jim Beech, one of Bryant's old friends, was paying his respects. He touched a stationary bicycle behind the sofa. "We were talking about exercise, and I told him I had the answer, a bicycle," Beech said. "I carried it to him. I had put the first 100 miles on it, and I see he put 224 more on it."

Jeff Coleman, whose service to the University of Alabama dated back to his days as Wallace Wade's secretary, remembered one of Bryant's kindnesses. "When I retired he wanted to be sure I still felt part of the university. He took me to all the out-of-state games. I'm probably the only person who saw every Alabama game he coached, and I probably couldn't have done that without his help."

Tyson told me a story, and I felt comfortable laughing, even in that setting. The judge was asked to be a member of the athletic committee of Auburn University–Montgomery and, being the Bear's son-in-law, he naturally felt uneasy. "I told them I'd better call Coach Bryant before I accepted," he said. "I did, and he said, 'You have to pay your civic rent, John.'"

The *Birmingham News* was still an afternoon paper, so I had plenty of time to devote to crafting a story. I worked on it much of the night. It began:

> TUSCALOOSA—Two lights glowed in the cold and rain beside the double front doors at 77 High Forest Wednesday night, not to welcome home the man of the house as they had for years, but as beacons for his friends who came to offer condolences to his family.
>
> Inside the handsome brick house of Paul William Bryant and Mary Harmon Bryant unfolded a tableau familiar to most American homes visited by the great mystery.
>
> There were tears and sorrow, but also there were acceptance of death and resolve that the living must live. And Bryant's family members and friends whispered fond memories of the Alabama football coach who died of a heart attack Wednesday afternoon.
>
> "I think he's in heaven, and he's got Pat Trammell and Jim McKenzie, and he's getting up 11 good ones," Bryant's daughter, Mrs. Mae Martin Tyson, said. Her swollen eyes smiled faintly when she mentioned her daddy and an Alabama player and a Kentucky player who preceded him in death.
>
> She was tired, but she shook hands with visitors at the door, and she answered the phone. "This is Mae Martin," she told a caller. "Mama can't come. She's been doing great, but she needs rest right now."
>
> Her husband, Judge John Tyson, was there, and the Tyson children, Mary Harmon, who is named for her grandmother, and Marc, who delighted his grandpa by making all-city of Montgomery in football, basketball and baseball.

> So were Bryant's other child, Paul Jr., and wife, Cherry, and their three daughters, Stella Gray, Mae Martin, who is named for her aunt, and Anna Laurie.
>
> Visitors went to the den and, inevitably, gazed at the portrait of Bryant that looked down on them from over the mantel. It was painted during his early years as head coach of the Crimson Tide, and he wore a cap with crimson bill and white crown.

The story continued in that vein. I knew I had aced it. I went to the office the next day and, frankly, expected to be commended for the tone and content of the story. Instead, Neal Sims, the executive sports editor, said, "Your story didn't make me cry."

In other words, I should have written a tearjerker.

I bit my tongue and said, "Good. It wasn't supposed to make you cry. This is an intelligent, upper-class American family that is grieving but bearing up in the way I hope my family would under the same circumstances. They aren't a bunch of hillbillies screaming and hollering and jumping in the casket."

The only other thing I ever covered that approached the death of Paul Bryant as a generator of mass emotion was the death of Davey Allison in 1993. Bryant was an old Caesar who had conquered the football world and thus delighted his subjects. Allison was a young man who was stricken in the prime of life, robbed of future conquests by a helicopter crash. His mourners were confident he would have conquered the racing world, too. I believe Davey would have won several championships if he had lived.

The *Birmingham News* responded to Bryant's death and funeral and the massive outpouring of love with excellent blanket coverage. It was one of the paper's high points during my forty years on the staff.

Bryant's death shocked the football-speaking world. He had retired as Alabama's coach less than a month before. He was still its director of athletics. Something he had once said was recalled and repeated from Hickory Flat to Beaver Town, from Veto to Canoe: "Quit coaching? I'd croak in a week." Bryant coached his last game on December 29, 1982. He died on January 26, 1983.

I had grown accustomed to Auburn football being in the hands of someone other than Shug Jordan, and now I would have to get used to someone besides Bryant coaching Alabama. A clearly defined segment of my career, the era of Shug and Bear, had passed. I would cover Ray Perkins, Bill Curry, Gene Stallings, Mike DuBose, and Dennis Franchione at Alabama.

Bryant's last Alabama team went 8–4. After that 1982 squad lost to Southern Mississippi in Tuscaloosa, I wrote in a column that, after Bryant retired, Crimson Tide football wouldn't be the overwhelming force it had been under him. In the first place, the effect of scholarship limits was kicking in, and every team had some good players. Alabama could no longer stockpile athletes. Talents who would have been playing for the Tide would be playing against the Tide. In the second place, simple common sense said that if Bryant was the best college coach who ever lived (as I believed), the program wouldn't be the same under someone who wasn't. Alabama couldn't have it both ways.

The column, of course, provoked a knee-jerk reaction among many Alabama fans. "You're nuts," an irate letter writer informed me. "You'll never live to see the day Alabama football skips a beat." Sure I would, and I didn't have to live long. In 1984, his second year as Bryant's successor, Ray Perkins coached a 5–6 team. It was the first losing season at the Capstone since Ears Whitworth's 1957 club stumbled in at 2–7–1. The most ignominious of Alabama's beatings in 1984 was administered by Vanderbilt at homecoming. It was the first time since 1957 that a Tide team had lost a homecoming game. Alabama football had begun a roller-coaster ride that would continue for years.

Many fans assumed that Perkins, who played for Bryant in the 1960s, was Bear's handpicked successor, and that since Bryant couldn't be wrong the good times would surely continue forever. "It Takes a Giant to Replace a Bear" a popular bumper sticker of the day assured them (though Perkins had a losing record as coach of the New York Giants.)

Joab Thomas was Alabama's president when Perkins was hired. I recently asked him about the process. "We had a search committee," he said. "We had a couple of trustees on it, a couple of deans, two or three faculty members, and some former football players. We got nominees from Coach

Bryant. I think he gave us two nominees, and Ray was one of them. He definitely did not give a priority. I asked Coach Bryant pointedly about that." Thomas wouldn't name Bryant's other nominee.

I checked into a Tuscaloosa motel the night before Bryant's funeral. The door of a room across the hall from mine was open, and I heard some of Bryant's former players reminiscing. I joined them. I knew two or three of them and some I didn't know. Perkins was among them. I had never met him. I introduced myself and wished him success as the new coach of the Crimson Tide.

Without responding to my greeting, he turned to the others and asked, "Is this guy good press or bad press?"

I said, "Damn, man, you've been in New York too long."

My image of Perkins had always been a pleasant one. I remembered him as one of the stars of Alabama's 39–28 Orange Bowl victory over Nebraska that delivered an improbable 1965 national championship to the Crimson Tide. Perkins caught two touchdown passes from Steve Sloan as Bama rolled up 518 yards that night. "This is the greatest offensive team I've ever been around," Bryant said, and his talented receiver was a key ingredient in the formula.

But when I had to deal with Perkins the coach, I forgot about Perkins the player. I found him to be a cold, abrasive, strange person. He seemed to find satisfaction in being disliked. He would have pissed off Will Rogers. (For the younger folks in my audience, Will Rogers was a humorist of bygone years who said, "I never met a man I didn't like.") Perkins's press conferences were like dental appointments. You were relieved when the ordeal ended. Now, I'll admit members of the press can ask dumb questions, but even a good, logical question could incite Perkins's trademark icy reply: "Are you a coach?"

Ron Grillo, a Birmingham TV reporter, had coached John Cappelletti at Monsignor Bronner High School in Upper Darby, Pennsylvania. Cappelletti won the 1973 Heisman Trophy as a runner for Penn State. Grillo hoped Perkins would ask him, "Are you a coach?" He planned to answer: "I coached a Heisman Trophy winner. Have you ever coached a Heisman Trophy winner?" Alas, Grillo was never targeted.

Jokes seemed to fly right over Perkins's head. One day he was giving the press a tour of the university's new football building, and I was walking ahead of the group. I looked into a room and saw one of the most impressive pieces of furniture I've ever laid eyes on. It was a huge, gorgeous conference table that must have cost a fortune. "Well, I'll be darned," I said. "Some assistant coach has already carved his initial in this table."

"Where? Where?" an agitated Perkins demanded.

"Ray, I was just kidding," I said.

Helmets and jerseys and pads were hung on the wall at the door of the new equipment room downstairs. It was merely an instructional display of just how much armor the Tidesmen wore into battle. A reporter reached for his billfold and asked, tongue in cheek, "How much are the helmets? Maybe I can buy one." No, no, the stuff wasn't for sale, Perkins hastened to explain. It was merely displayed for the press. Oh.

I dropped by to see Perkins one day, and as I entered his office he said, "Come on, we're going somewhere." We drove to the Tuscaloosa airport, boarded a private plane, and flew to Huntsville. An assistant coach met us and drove us to a nearby high school. Perkins was recruiting a player. "Come in with me," he said. "I want you to meet this boy." I had thought it odd that he sought my company on the trip to Huntsville, and now I figured Perkins wanted the boy to infer that the *Birmingham News* hoped he'd choose Alabama. "I'll just stay in the car," I told Perkins. He kept asking me to come in, and I kept saying I wouldn't. So he went inside and I waited in the car. The boy signed with Auburn.

A 14–14 tie with LSU in 1985 produced a funny story, though it's probably apocryphal. Alabama scored a touchdown with 1:23 to play, and instead of going for two points and the victory, Perkins ordered a PAT kick for a tie. A shocked Alabama fan turned to the fan sitting next to him in the stadium and said, "Coach Bryant would have gone for two."

"No, he wouldn't have," the other said. "He would have gone for one, just like Perkins did." Then he added, "Of course, Coach Bryant would have been ahead 34–0."

Perkins stayed just four seasons before returning to the NFL as Tampa Bay's coach. His record at Alabama was 32–15–1. A New Orleans newspaper quoted me as saying, "Getting rid of Ray Perkins and the Birmingham Stallions in the same year is better than curing world hunger." The quote was accurate.

I was delighted when I learned that Bill Curry would succeed Perkins. I knew Curry and considered him a man of integrity, the kind that college football needed. Curry was an interesting blend. He had been a center in Vince Lombardi's Green Bay Packers dynasty, so he was plenty tough. He had attended seminary, so he was an intelligent, caring person. He had a magnetic personality that was as different from Perkins's as light from dark. I looked forward to covering his stay in Tuscaloosa.

That's because I didn't foresee the distress that Curry's hiring would provoke in many Alabama fans. Good gosh, there were death threats against Curry and Joab Thomas, the school president who hired him, and security measures were implemented at the press conference officially introducing him as the new coach.

There had been bad blood between Alabama and Georgia Tech years before, when Bryant was the coach, and some Tide fans recoiled at the notion of having as the Alabama coach a man who had played at Tech and coached the Yellow Jackets. They noted that Curry brought a losing career record as a head coach (as Perkins had) and that he had never beaten Auburn. Tech had been tied by Furman the year before. (The Furman debacle would be recalled when, in Curry's sixth start at the Capstone, the Tide fell to Memphis State.)

A lot of Alabama folks wanted a member of the "Alabama family" to coach Alabama's football team. Curry, at Bryant's urging, had gotten the Bear and Bryant's old friend Tech coach Bobby Dodd back together, and I had been surprised to find a framed, personalized photograph of Bryant on the wall of Curry's office at Tech. But, no, Curry certainly wasn't "family."

Curry's years at Alabama constituted the strangest phenomenon I ever covered. Bryant had repeatedly stressed the necessity of everyone pulling together. I knew he would have supported whoever coached the Crimson Tide if he had been alive. I assumed Alabama folks believed in and thus would honor the old master's bedrock philosophy, but a significant number didn't. They didn't want Curry as coach, and no matter what happened they by gosh weren't going to change. Termites among the fans and former players and in the athletic department were gnawing away.

After Alabama won a 17–16 thriller at Penn State in 1989, one fan said he was sorry the Tide blocked an 18-yard field goal attempt at the end to preserve the victory because that would make it more difficult to get rid of Curry. Alabama "supporters" actually were pulling against Alabama. Some advised recruits to go elsewhere. "I can recruit against Auburn," Curry told me, "but I can't recruit against Alabama." After one loss, some redneck threw a brick through Curry's office window.

More than once I wrote that Bryant must be turning over in his grave because of the treatment Curry was receiving from Alabama people. I pointed out that many coaching luminaries had built their reputations at schools other than their alma maters, men such as Wallace Wade, Frank Thomas, Joe Paterno, Woody Hayes, Darrel Royal, Robert Neyland, Bob Devaney, Bud Wilkinson, Tom Osborne, and Johnny Vaught. Pat Dye was head-coaching Auburn, and it didn't bother AU folks that he had been an assistant for Auburn's number-one rival, Alabama, and had played for Auburn's number-two rival, Georgia.

Curry's 1989 club went 10–2, won the SEC championship, and played number-one Miami tough before losing in the Sugar Bowl. He was named SEC Coach of the Year. And he resigned the Alabama job to become head coach at Kentucky. Curry said the terms of the new contract that Alabama offered him would have diminished his power. Kentucky really wanted him, and I think he saw the dawning of a bright new day. I had lunch with Curry and his wife, Carolyn, at their home in Tuscaloosa. As I recall, it was a couple of days before he actually made up his mind. "I hate to see you leave," I told him, "but these people are never going to accept you. You'd better take the Kentucky job."

He left Alabama with a 26–10 record. He was 0–3 against Auburn, but he was 3–0 vs. Tennessee and 3–0 against Penn State. His detractors like to say he couldn't recruit, but he had recruited the core of the 1992 national championship Crimson Tide.

Kentucky is a noted graveyard for coaches, but I hoped Curry would succeed there. It didn't happen. Six of his seven seasons were losers. He became a TV football commentator, a good one. During Curry's stay in Lexington I read a classified ad in the *Birmingham News* for a plot in Elmwood Cemetery. It was "near Bear Bryant's grave," the ad boasted. I clipped it and mailed it to Curry with the notation: "Georgia Tech SOBs need not apply." He framed it and hung it on his wall.

Curry and I still keep in touch by telephone and letter. He keeps the world in perspective. When he was in Rome he sent me a postcard that pictured the Colosseum, noting that the penalty for losing in that stadium was indeed serious.

Gene Stallings was next. His selection was popular with former Alabama players and fans. He had been a member of Bryant's original Crimson Tide coaching staff in 1958 (at a salary of $4,500 a year). He had played for Bryant at Texas A&M, indeed was one of the legendary Junction Boys. He was a member of the "Alabama family." He also brought a losing career record as a head coach, as Perkins and Curry had. Stallings had been on the minus side of Texas A&M and with the St. Louis–Phoenix Cardinals. I always thought it strange that the first three Alabama coaches after Bryant came with losing records.

I liked Stallings tremendously. He was the kind of fellow who, during an interview in his office, would whip out the bread and mayonnaise and salt and pepper and a tomato and craft a tomato sandwich for me and one for himself. I love mater sammiches, and so does he.

Stallings and I shared a common ailment—backache. I was taking pills I had gotten at a holistic medicine store, and I brought him a bottle. After he had retired and returned to his ranch in Paris, Texas, he sent me a belt with copper inside. He had just bought one for himself, and here was one for me, and he hoped they would help both our backs.

Several years after he left the Capstone we were chatting on the phone, and out of the blue Stallings said, "I miss you." I was touched. "I miss you too, Gene," I said. "Come back and coach the Crimson Tide." He chuckled and said, "I don't think so."

Alabama fans were excited to have one of "Bear's boys" on the throne.

Perkins had exiled Bryant's famous coaching tower from the practice field, and Curry had committed the sin of being from Georgia Tech, but Stallings was savvy enough to say the right things. "Alabama people love Coach Bryant, and they tolerate the rest of us," he offered, and a million Tide supporters smiled in unison.

Stallings is a man of great humanity. Raising a Down syndrome child, John Mark, was a challenge but a blessing. Johnny has a free pass to heaven, Gene told me, and what could be better than that? Stallings came to see his boy's handicap as a gift. He once said: "Johnny has given us love—total, unconditional love—and joy. And what we thought was the worst thing that could ever happen to us turned out to be a true blessing for every single person in our family. He's been the cement that's made us so close."

When he was a young assistant at Alabama, Stallings and his wife, Ruth Ann, were the parents of two daughters, Anna Lee and Laurie. Bear Bryant occasionally would kid him, "When are you and Ruthie going to have a little football player?"

"Real soon, I hope, Coach Bryant, real soon," Stallings would answer. They wanted a son. Sports had always been a huge part of Stallings's life, and he naturally hoped for a football-playing son. Perhaps, he thought, he could play for Gene and Bear Bryant. Stallings would even watch an Alabama player in action on the practice field and imagine him as the son he would have some day. Of course, it didn't turn out that way. The realization that Johnny was different was devastating.

Johnny was born on June 11, 1962. Stallings dropped a coin in a hospital pay phone and practically shouted, "We've got the boy, Coach Bryant!" But when the nurses brought the other mothers' babies to them and didn't bring Johnny, Ruth Ann was puzzled and frightened. She asked her husband to quiz the doctor. Stallings told me a chilling story. He located the doctor and asked him if there was a problem. In a matter-of-fact tone the doctor answered, "Yes, we think maybe your baby is a mongoloid."

Stallings said he was so stunned by the news and the doctor's cold-hearted manner of speaking that he drew back his fist to hit him—but Gene fainted dead away before he cold deliver the punch. Stallings told me that off the record. It was such a human story, a story that would touch so many hearts, and I begged him to let me write it, but he wouldn't. I later read it in his book *Another Season: A Coach's Story of Raising an Exceptional Son.*

Some advised Gene and Ruth Ann to put their son in an institution, but they'd have none of that. They raised Johnny at home, and Gene and Johnny together became familiar sights on the various football fronts of Stallings's life. Johnny's influence led Gene to become more tolerant of less-gifted players. Because of Johnny's presence, players on every team Stallings coached got the subtle message that they should do the best they could with whatever they had. I saw Ruth Ann and Johnny in press boxes for years. They inspired me. "As good as we've got it, we should be ashamed to ever complain about anything," I once told my sportswriter friend Al Browning.

I chatted with Stallings by phone in December 2002, and he told me he would soon make a trip to Alabama to help sell special Christmas ornaments to benefit RISE. "I'll let you have one for half price," he joked. Stallings became acquainted with RISE, a program that serves children with disabilities, during his stay in Tuscaloosa, and he has been a supporter for years. In 1993, at a groundbreaking ceremony for a new RISE building, he had to fight back tears when he heard the surprise announcement that the facility would be named the Stallings Center to honor his family's commitment to the less fortunate.

The tough football coach was the kind of guy who, when he was leading the Crimson Tide, would acquire a pet raccoon and get up in the middle of the night to feed him with a bottle. He named the little fellow Gerald Jackoon, after his close friend Gerald Jack.

Shortly after Stallings came to Alabama as head coach, he and I played on a four-man team in a golf scramble. We faced a par-three hole that was guarded by water. I hit my tee shot into the drink. So did the next fellow. And the next one. It was up to Stallings, our A-player, to save the day. He did. For a moment it looked as if his tee shot might kerplunk into the cup. It rolled past the flag by some eight feet, an excellent shot. "I knew you'd choke," I said, feigning disgust that the ball didn't go into the hole. All these years later, while we talked on that cold December day in 2002, he mentioned that remark, and he laughed just as he had in 1990. Stallings is an easy guy to be with.

His career as Alabama's head coach began alarmingly. Southern Mississippi beat him 27–24 in Birmingham; Florida beat him 17–13 in Tuscaloosa; Georgia beat him 17–16 in Athens. He was 0–3. A 7–5 season ended with an embarrassing 34–7 loss to Louisville in the Fiesta Bowl. It was particularly embarrassing for me. The Tide defense had arisen mightily, and in the last seven games before the bowl no opponent had scored in double digits. The seven had managed just thirty-eight points total. I was interviewing Browning Nagle, Louisville's quarterback, and he asked what I thought about the game. "I'm not being a smart ass," I told him, "but I really doubt your team will score a touchdown." During the postgame interview, Nagle spotted me in the press mob and said, "There's the fellow from Birmingham who said we wouldn't score a touchdown. What do you think now?"

"I think you scored a bunch of them," I said.

Stallings had beaten Auburn in his first season, but there were still misgivings. His squad had been shockingly unprepared to play in a bowl game against a football program that was on a level below Alabama's. But in 1991 the Tide won eleven and lost one, and in 1992 Alabama went 13–0 and upset Miami 34–13 in the Sugar Bowl for the national title. Or at least it was an upset if you believed the betting line, which had the Hurricanes favored by eight points. I wrote a column picking Alabama to win: "Miami hasn't seen a defense like Alabama's, and from here it looks like Tide 21, Hurricanes 17." I tried to get up enough guts to pick Alabama by two touchdowns, but I couldn't.

But things turned sour when Alabama went on NCAA probation, and forfeiture amended 1993's record of 9–3–1 to 1–12. Stallings's last three teams went 12–1, 8–3, and 10–3, and he retired with a 62–25 record in seven years in Tuscaloosa. Even the tall man who looked and talked like Bear Bryant had his critics. Alabama fans griped about his conservative coaching style and close scores such as 17–10 over Southern Mississippi, 13–0 over Louisiana Tech, 10–7 over Memphis State, and 21–7 over Bowling Green. As the program unraveled under Stallings's successor, Mike

DuBose, and the Crimson Tide was losing with regularity, I phoned Gene at his home in Texas and said, "Well, there's one good thing—the bitching fans aren't having to watch any more of those boring 14–7 Alabama victories." He chuckled, albeit grimly.

Fans deluged Bob Bockrath, the director of athletics, with phone calls and faxes begging that DuBose be named head coach. He was Stallings's defensive coordinator, and he had played for Bryant. When Stallings resigned I immediately wrote a column saying DuBose should be named his successor. Was he the best man available? I didn't know, but my eyes had been opened wide enough that I realized that wasn't as important to fans as his Capstone pedigree. He was "family," and that was the main thing.

DuBose said it was his dream job, but the experience turned into a nightmare. Revelations of an improper relationship with a female employee of the university hit him broadside. His first squad, the 1997 club, went 4–7. The next two improved, to 7–5 and 10–3, with the 1999 bunch winning the SEC title. But the 2000 team, which had been rated third in the nation before the season, imploded to 3–8, and DuBose was out. His record was 24–23–0.

There was dissension among the coaches and dissension among the players, and 2000 was a surreal disaster. It was topped off by a 9–0 loss to Auburn in the Tigers' first appearance in Tuscaloosa since 1901. DuBose used his position to expound his Christian religion so frequently that it annoyed many and led others to make jokes. I didn't think it was my place to judge him on the matter, and I didn't. I pointed out that fans considered it wonderful when Jay Barker, quarterback of the 1992 national champions, spoke out on religion but improper when Mike DuBose, coach of the 3–8 squad of 2000, did it. But when DuBose addressed the Birmingham Monday Morning Quarterback Club and spoke of the valuable lessons that could be learned from losing, I knew he was the only person in that room of perhaps three hundred, including me, who was on that wave length.

Dennis Franchione came from Texas Christian to succeed DuBose. His 2001 Alabama squad went 7–5 with a 32–7 victory over Auburn on the Plain as the highlight. I retired before Franchione coached a game, but I'd had lunch with him, interviewed him, written about him, found him to be soft spoken and impressive. He had a reputation for organization. A member of the athletics department who had observed the backbiting among DuBose's coaches told me, "It's like walking through corporate offices in the football building now, and I mean that as a compliment." I thought Franchione was the man to lead Alabama through yet another period of NCAA probation.

Franchione invited women to his Football 101 class in the preseason, and they came by the hundreds. They were fascinated by the handsome, gray-haired Coach Fran. I saw it in their eyes. He and his assistants and players taught them about the sport. They loved it. I wrote a feature story about the class, and as we were leaving, a member of the athletics department asked me what I thought. "It's like everything else in college football," I said. "If he wins everyone will talk about how nice he was to consider the ladies. If he loses they'll say he should have been coaching football instead of spending time with women."

Franchione's second Alabama team compiled a 10–3 record, good enough that most fans were willing to overlook an upset loss to Auburn in Tuscaloosa. Then the coach who had praised his players' loyalty for not transferring to other schools because Bama was on probation . . . bolted to Texas A&M. Oh, well, at least a bunch of women learned some football.

Alabama hired Mike Price from Washington State to succeed Franchione. For the first time since I came to the *Birmingham News* in 1961 the school had a head football coach that I didn't know. Accused of being the star in yet another Alabama sex scandal, he was fired before he ever coached a game. Bama selected Mike Shula, an NFL assistant who had played quarterback at the Capstone, to succeed Price. At least I once again knew the man who was bossing Crimson Tide football.

Chapter 15

I've always been bewildered—not to mention amused—by fans who live or die according to the result of the Iron Bowl. Or any football game, for that matter. Gusty Yearout, a star linebacker for Shug Jordan at Auburn in the 1960s, told me a story that lends perspective to a rivalry that creates mass psychosis in our state.

"At Auburn, the coaches hated Alabama more than the players did, and I guess it was the same at Alabama. Back then we had two weeks to get ready for the game, and they'd try to get you so wired up about playing Alabama.

"I was captain of the Auburn team, and before the game I was spitting nails and was so fired up I wanted to kill those guys. I'm walking to the center of the field and here comes Kenny Stabler from the Alabama side.

"I'm giving him this hard-ass look and frowning and slobbering, and he says, 'Gusty, what are y'all doing after the game?' The referee is trying to introduce us, and Stabler says, 'We've got a room at the hotel. Some girls are coming by, and we've got some beer. When this thing is over, get a couple of your buddies and come by.'

"The referee is trying to get Stabler to shut up. The referee is trying to at least flip the coin. I said, 'What room are y'all in?' Kenny had me so laid back. I was ready to bust him in the mouth, but then I'm asking, 'What room are y'all in?'

"And I think some of us did go by after the game."

I have my favorite Auburn and Alabama players. Some are friends of mine years later—Yearout is in that group—and others are just folks I appreciated and wrote about when they played. Yearout is a leading Birmingham lawyer, but he might never have become an attorney except for the farsightedness of Shug Jordan. "I always wanted to be a lawyer," Yearout told me. "But athletes get it in their blood, and I didn't want to give up football. I knew I couldn't play pro, but I went to see Coach Jordan and said, 'What I'm thinking of doing is coaching for a couple of years, and if I don't like it I'll go to law school.'

"He said, 'Coaching appears to be a more glamorous job than it is. I think you'd be a good coach, but you can do better in life in a profession. I want you to go to law school two years and then if you don't like law school you can come back and I'll give you a job.'

"I never went back. Once I got in law school, coaching never crossed my mind again."

Good, for Yearout successfully represented me in a lawsuit against a developer after mudslides poured onto my property.

Jay Barker is one of my favorites. He improved more over the course of his career than any other player I've covered. Occasionally I'll read the phrase: "Jay Barker, who quarterbacked Alabama to the 1992 national championship. . . . " But Barker was far from an accomplished quarterback his sophomore season. The team won with defense. In thirteen games it surrendered a mere 122 points, the fewest for an Alabama squad since the 1980 club's ninety-eight points. And no Tide since 1992 has been that stingy.

When Barker was a freshman his team had first down at the opponent's one-yard line in a Bryant–Denny Stadium scrimmage, but he was flagged for taking too much time. "Jay, you've got to watch the play clock!" Coach Gene Stallings yelled. "You can't get a penalty in that situation!"

"Where is the play clock?" Barker asked sheepishly.

The lad who couldn't find the play clock would become Alabama's all-time winningest quarterback and earn the Johnny Unitas Golden Arm Award as the nation's top senior QB and be named the SEC's offensive player of the year. The fellow who was awarded a scholarship as an afterthought is at or near the top of the popularity chart of Crimson Tide players, all-time. He even had a modest professional football career.

I naturally wished Jay well because he was from Trussville, my town, and he attended Hewitt-Trussville High, my three boys' alma mater, but I appreciated him more because of his Christian witness. In a world in which evil so frequently seems to prosper and goodness go unrewarded, it was nice to see one of the good guys become a star. I've always believed the hand of God was tremendously involved in the development of Barker as a football player because, to me, it seemed the total was greater than the sum of the individual parts, if that makes any sense.

Jay spoke the bravest words I've ever heard a college football player speak. It was more courageous than standing your ground during the most ferocious blitz. He told the press he was a virgin. Suffice it to say that the quarterback of the Crimson Tide—in any year—wouldn't have to be a virgin if he didn't want to be. There's no telling how much good Jay did by speaking those few simple words. One of my wife's friends told her a story. The woman's fourteen-year-old grandson read Barker's statement and told Grandma he was relieved to know he didn't have to have sex as a youngster. Certainly television, with its hedonistic programming is doing its best to influence him otherwise.

Barker, a Birmingham radio talk show host, is one of fifty-nine Alabama players who made first-team all-America during my forty seasons at the *News.* The others are Billy Neighbors, Lee Roy Jordan, Wayne Freeman, Dan Kearley, Joe Namath, David Ray, Paul Crane, Steve Sloan, Richard Cole, Cecil Dowdy, Bobby Johns, Ray Perkins, Dennis Homan, Ken Stabler, Sam Gellerstedt, Mike Hall, Alvin Samples, Johnny Musso,

John Hannah, Jim Krapf, John Mitchell, Buddy Brown, Woodrow Lowe, Wayne Wheeler, Leroy Cook, Sylvester Croom, Mike Washington, Ozzie Newsome, Barry Kraus, Marty Lyons, Jim Bunch, Don McNeal, Dwight Stephenson, Thomas Boyd, Tommy Wilcox, Jeremiah Castille, Mike Pitts, Cornelius Bennett, Jon Hand, Bobby Humphrey, Van Tiffin, Derrick Thomas, Kermit Kendrick, Larry Rose, Keith McCants, John Mangum, Phillip Doyle, Robert Stewart, John Copeland, Eric Curry, Antonio Langham, David Palmer, Michael Proctor, Kevin Jackson, Michael Myers, Dwayne Rudd, Chris Samuels, and Shaun Alexander.

Thirty-seven Auburn players made first-team all-American during my years at the *News*: Jimmy Sidle, Tucker Frederickson, Bill Cody, Jack Thornton, Freddie Hyatt, David Campbell, Buddy McClinton, Larry Willingham, Pat Sullivan, Terry Beasley, Mike Fuller, Ken Bernich, Neil O'Donoghue, Keith Uecker, Bob Harris, Donnie Humphrey, Bo Jackson, Gregg Carr, Lewis Colbert, Ben Tamburello, Brent Fullwood, Aundray Bruce, Kurt Crain, Tracy Rocker, Stacy Searels, Walter Reeves, Benji Roland, Craig Ogletree, Ed King, David Rocker, Terry Daniel, Wayne Gandy, Chris Snelling, Brian Robinson, Frank Sanders, Victor Riley, and Takeo Spikes.

There are some great names among the ninety-six listed above—but I also remember Shug Jordan studying a wall of photos of Auburn all-Americans and remarking, "You know, some of these fellows, I can't remember anything they ever did." Selecting all-star teams is, indeed, an inexact, sometimes ridiculous, science.

I delight in the company of Thom Gossom, who had guts in abundance. We had lunch at John's in Birmingham not long ago, and I urged him to write a book about his experiences. He was the first black football player to graduate from Auburn. Moreover, he was a walk-on who lettered as a split end in 1972, 1973, and 1974. Can you imagine the courage it took for a black athlete to walk on at Auburn in those days? He had some bad experiences, but Thom is a man of goodwill who isn't consumed by the memory of them.

He laughs when he tells this story: "The SEC Skywriters came to Auburn, and someone asked Coach Jordan how many black players he had. He said, 'We don't have black players. We don't have white players. We just have Auburn players.' I was standing behind him, and I held up two fingers, and the writers could read my lips: 'I know. Two.'"

Gossom played at John Carroll High in Birmingham, the same school that produced Pat Sullivan, and then presented himself as a candidate for football on the Plain. "Naïveté is bliss," he told me. "I never thought of it as anything more than playing football at the time. When I was a senior at John Carroll I wrote down that my goal was to play football at Auburn, and I carried that in my billfold until I graduated from college. My dad tells me now that he was afraid for me. He didn't tell anybody I was playing."

He encountered bigotry. "In everything like that you have to prove yourself," Gossom said. "I had to prove myself three or four times over. There was one guy—I won't call his name—and we fought nearly every day. I'd run an out route and he'd tackle me like a torpedo, and I'd stiff-arm him and push his neck back and he'd call me a nigger and we'd go at it. I was a walk-on, and nobody likes walk-ons anyway."

Gossom remembers it as "a heck of a transition period. I'd go to class and there'd be two hundred kids and you're the only black in class. And you're a football player and nobody's expecting you to be bright anyway." Gossom aimed a fun dart at me when he added: "And I was interested in journalism, and that was a double whammy."

Gossom became a television and movie actor. He has appeared on such TV shows as *In the Heat of the Night, West Wing, NYPD Blue, ER, Boston Legal,* and *Providence,* and in the flick *Fight Club.* I talked to Gossom a day or two after Carroll O'Connor died. O'Connor portrayed Chief Gillespie on *In the Heat of the Night* and, more famously, Archie Bunker on *All in the Family.*

"I had a tough night over his death," Gossom told me. "He was an incredible guy. Everyone called him Pops. He gave me my start in television, and I'm indebted to him. He cast me in *In the Heat of the Night.*" Life takes some strange twists, doesn't it? A fellow who encountered bigotry on the Auburn practice field would come to worship the man who played TV's most famous bigot, Archie Bunker. "Carroll played this bigot," Gossom told me, "but there was this huge amount of empathy for him, and you liked him. He said things you couldn't say today. I think in the back of his mind he didn't want to be just remembered as Archie Bunker."

Integration, of course, was the biggest social change in sports during my career. James Owens was the first black football player Auburn signed, and Wilbur Jackson was Alabama's. I felt for the early blacks on both teams because I knew that no matter how the schools tried to spin it, it was no tiptoeing-through-the-tulips situation.

I enjoyed the guys, black and white, who beat the odds to play. They made for good readable stories, and they weren't puffed up with celebrity. Charley Pell, one of Paul Bryant's "itty-bitty boys," a tackle on the national championship team of 1961, was a favorite. Pell never played football until he was a senior at Albertville High School. "Mama and Daddy didn't want me to play," he told me. "I had a brother who was injured one year, and they felt like I'd have the same bad luck.

"Bobby Golden, an Auburn graduate, was the new high school coach. He walked up to me one day in the hall and asked me why I didn't play football. I told him my buddies had come to the house to try to get them to let me play. He asked if Mama would object to him coming by, and I said I wished he would. Coach Golden talked to Mama three and a half hours one day. He was a deacon in the Baptist Church and a Sunday school teacher, so she figured he couldn't be all that bad." So Pell played as a high school senior—in the backfield.

Alabama offered a scholarship to another Albertville player, but he turned it down, and it went to Pell. "It must have been about the last one left," he said. "I didn't know they knew Albertville existed." Pell had seen a grand total of one college football game when he signed his scholarship, and that was because he won a trip to Birmingham to see Alabama-Tennessee. The first time he saw the campus in Tuscaloosa was when he reported for practice as a freshman. He had never met Bryant. "I saw Coach Sam Bailey," Pell recalled, "and I punched one of the boys who had been recruited real heavily and I asked him if that was Coach Bryant. He said hell no, and I told him I just didn't know."

Pell weighed 179 pounds when he reported. Nevertheless, he was immediately moved to the line. He never weighed more than 188. Pell not only played with distinction, he became a head coach, at Jacksonville State, Clemson, and Florida.

In 2001 Pell invited me and a few other friends to dinner at his home in Southside near Gadsden. He was dying of cancer, and he wanted to be with us one more time. Jimmy Bryan was there, and George Smith, and Rudy Abbott, and Cotton Clark. We refer to it as the last supper. Charley laughed at the old stories, and he appeared strong and vital. I suppose one always grasps at straws, and I wondered if perhaps there had been some miracle turnaround. I mentioned to his wife, Ward, that Charley looked good. She smiled and explained that the morphine was working overtime. "Charley's dying," she said.

I remembered another night when I was in the Pells' home in Gainesville, Florida, after Charley's Gators had won a football game, maybe against Auburn. A guest got plastered and disappeared into the kitchen. He ambled out, singing, with a pot on his head, as if it were a hat, and beating another pot with a big spoon, as if it were a drum. He reminded me of a drunk in a comic strip. Ward is a beautiful, classy, sweet woman, and I was surprised when she laughed merrily at the buffoon who was tearing up her kitchen. Then she whispered to me "That (bleep) is one of our biggest boosters," and I knew why she was pretending he was hilarious. I mentioned that episode at the last supper. "I remember it well," Ward said, this time with a sincere laugh. She even told me his name.

Charley Pell died on May 29, 2001, shortly after the last supper. He was just sixty years old.

The greatest group of overachievers I ever covered was the Amazin's. With Pat Sullivan and Terry Beasley gone, Auburn's 1972 squad was picked to flounder in the lower reaches of the SEC, but it went 10–1 and upset the Crimson Tide in the Punt, Bama, Punt game. I was honored when the Amazin's invited me to their thirty-year reunion in 2002.

The mule of that bunch was Terry Henley, a tailback who ran the ball more than any man had ever run it before. The Plainsmen passed just 105 times in1972, a third as much as in 1971, Sullivan's senior season. Henley not only brought determination and toughness to that team, he brought humor. He was—and is—quick witted and a natural comedian. I enjoy his company.

Auburn, of course, blocked two punts and ran them in for touchdowns to beat Alabama 17–16 in 1972 in Legion Field. "When are you folks going to quit talking about those blocked punts?" an Alabama man asked Henley years later. "When you folks stop singing about playing in the Rose Bowl," Henley answered.

Henley, a Birmingham insurance man, told me a funny story from that game. "It was not against the rules for the players to sell tickets. I came up with the ingenious idea of buying all the other players' tickets, and I'd be the only one to have any. The game came around, and I ended up with all the tickets in the XX, YY, and ZZ temporary bleachers at the end of the field. People would call, and I'd tell them I had fifty-yard-line tickets. They'd send me a hundred dollars and I'd send them a couple of end zone tickets. I was making the money.

"We got off the bus at the stadium, and a lot of players walked around the field in their dress clothes to stretch their legs. I never cared about that. I liked to sit in the dressing room and try to find my name in the program.

"Johnny Simmons, our safety, came in the dressing room, and he said, 'Terry, there's a bunch of people out there cussing you and screaming for you.'

"I said, 'Are they Alabama fans?'

"He said, 'No, they're our fans.'

"Well, I had long hair, and I liked to lead the team onto the field with my helmet under my arm, letting my hair blow. But this time I tried to get lost in the middle of the team when we ran out. I could hear the fans yelling, 'Where is he? Where is he?' We were doing our exercises, and they were yelling, 'You scumbag, you put us in the end zone.'

"But you know where all thirty-three points were scored? In that end zone. After the game people were coming up to me and saying, 'Terry, our seats were just great.' They loved me again."

A former player I admire is Bobby Humphrey. I've told him as much. He is a role model for the times in which we live. What I mean by that is that the Alabama and NFL star went down the road none of us should travel, but he returned to God and became a respected member of the community. He is head coach of the Birmingham Steeldogs.

Humphrey was in jail in Columbus, Georgia, in 1993, charged with cocaine possession. As he sat there, in that horrible place, he remembered the youngster who was raised in a Christian home. He remembered the running back who set rushing records for game, season, and career at the Capstone (1985–88). And he contrasted all that with what he had become and uttered the plaint that humans always have spoken when they realize just how far they have strayed: "This ain't me."

I interviewed Bobby in December 1994, and he recalled that demeaning experience in jail in Columbus. "The man came to me and said, 'You want to get out?' I said, 'I think I need to sit here a couple of days and think about it.' I sat in that jail a long time. I never went to sleep. I said, 'I'm going to sit here a couple of days and sort things out.'"

He didn't stay that long, for he was bailed out, but he had time to think about what he had become, and it was a far cry from what he had been. A few days later he was shot, though not seriously wounded, by a friend. "Most people think that's when I turned my life around," he told me. "But I was already in the process. It had already been working on me."

Humphrey was placed on three years' probation for cocaine possession, but it's difficult now to imagine him ever being involved in such a ruinous lifestyle. He is a busy church worker who believes we have a Helper in our battles against our worst natures: "God gave us the Holy Spirit, which is a fighting tool." Humphrey returned to the University of Alabama and got his degree, and I was delighted to write an article about that accomplishment.

Funny story: The Steeldogs were playing poorly in one game, and Humphrey was chewing them out at halftime—but with a sanitized vocabulary. Finally, one of the players interrupted with: "Hey, Coach, do you want us to cuss for you?"

Pat Sullivan is a fast friend. In fact, after Jimmy Bryan and I retired from the *News,* the UAB offensive coordinator called and said he wanted to take us to lunch at Andrew's, a Birmingham barbecue joint we all three favor. He thanked us for writing about him, which is rare treatment by an ex-athlete.

I remember where I was when I learned the Auburn quarterback had won the 1971 Heisman Trophy. I was in a motel room in Norman, Oklahoma, where I had gone to cover one of those games of the century that come along every four or five years. This one was between top-ranked Nebraska and number-two Oklahoma. It was Thanksgiving night, and I was alone, watching on TV, but when they opened the envelope and called Sullivan's name I yelped, "Awright!" I was relieved because I was afraid an injustice might be done, that the eastern press might swing the award to Ed Marinaro, a runner from Cornell. Cornell? Please. Beano Cook, the TV commentator, and I got into a heated argument at a party. "If Marinaro played for Southern Mississippi instead of a New York lightweight he wouldn't even be considered for the Heisman," I said, "and Southern Miss plays a better brand of football than Cornell does."

Nothing was more fun that covering the Pat Sullivan-to-Terry Beasley years. In 1968, when freshmen weren't eligible for the varsity, Pat and Terry led a remarkable comeback that produced a 35–27 victory over the Alabama frosh. The Tide had led 27–0. Sullivan and Beasley had demonstrated that, with Pat throwing and Terry outsprinting cover backs, anything was possible, and that anticipation energized Auburn fans every Saturday. Indeed, in 1970 Auburn beat Alabama 33–28 after trailing 17–0 in the first period. "Get ready, Beez," Sullivan said to Beasley when the Tigers fell behind. "We're going to win it just like when we were freshmen."

Auburn crushed Wake Forest 57–0 in 1969 to usher in the Sullivan-Beasley varsity era. In later years I struck up a friendship with Jeff Byrd, who had been a Wake Forest lineman that day. He told me, "I was playing guard, and Auburn had the ball on its first series. The snap count was three, but on two Mike Kolen, their great linebacker, hit our center and knocked him flying over the fullback. The Auburn fans went crazy, cheering for an off-sides play. I said, 'Uh oh, we're in for a long day.' "

I could relate to something Sullivan said, because when I was a boy living in Statham, Georgia, and we'd get up a football game in Wayne Holliday's backyard we'd each try to be the one to "catch" being Charley Trippi. The consolation prize was being Frank Sinkwich. After those two University of Georgia all-timers, it didn't much matter. What Sullivan said, thirty years after he suited up for Auburn, was this: "There's not a day that goes by that someone doesn't come up and say something like 'when I was a kid I used to be you or I used to be Terry playing football in the backyard.' They'll say, 'I had a number 7 jersey and my buddy had a number 88.'" Sullivan was 7 and Beasley was 88.

I was delighted when Beasley was inducted into the College Football Hall of Fame in 2002, joining Sullivan, who was inducted in 1991. Pat was at the ceremony in New York to applaud his old running mate. "We were a tandem," Beasley said. "We were a team. Now we've both been honored. Finally, the tandem is together again."

When I think of Terry Beasley, I recall the words of F. Scott Fitzgerald: "Show me a hero and I will write you a tragedy." The years have been unkind to Beasley. The first chapter in his 1999 autobiography, *God's Receiver,* is titled "Not Quite Right in the Head." The expression applies to him, Beasley wrote. Blows to his head when he was playing football are exacting their toll. He counted sixteen concussions, including some that left him unconscious. His brain damage is "permanent and is a deteriorating condition," he wrote.

Beasley thinks injuries in college contributed, but he believes "the real everlasting damage to my brain" occurred when he played with San Francisco in the National Football League. In 1997 the NFL granted him line-of-duty disability. The hardest lick he ever took was administered by Dick Butkus, the Chicago linebacker. When Beasley was a rookie, the 49ers ran a power sweep. His job was to block Butkus out of the play, which he did. It gained twenty-seven yards. Later San Francisco ran the same play. According to Beasley, Butkus made no effort to tackle the ball carrier. He wanted revenge. "I went to block him and he nearly took off my head." Beasley, who calls Butkus "a vicious animal on the field," doesn't remember leaving the game or getting dressed.

I interviewed Beasley for a column in 1996. He told me a specialist said his brain "looked like Swiss cheese. I have trouble remembering things," he said. "I'm very forgetful. I'm still okay in certain areas, but the damaged areas won't ever regenerate. They're gone." He added: "I can recall some of the games I played in, but I couldn't tell you what I did last week." Beasley, indeed, was famous for returning to the game after being decked. "When we played and you got knocked out, when you woke up you went back in," he told me.

Beasley, who lives in Moody, Alabama, was a top salesman for a golf cart company. One day he couldn't remember how to get to a course he had called on dozens of times. When he did arrive he couldn't recall the name of the person he was meeting, though they were well acquainted. Then he couldn't remember the terms of the contract. He had to stop working. He'll probably never work again.

Beasley's wife, Marlene, a nurse, said something that everyone who ever saw him play knows to be true. "Terry gave everything he had when he was playing football." If he could relive those young years would be he play football again? I'll never forget his answer. "Yes, but I'd try to do it better. I'd try a little harder."

God's Receiver, written with Rich Donnell, is an excellent, gripping book. Beasley's Christian faith is inspiring. In an epigraph to the first chapter he quotes Philippians 4:13: "I can do all things in him who strengthens me." It's obvious that Auburn's great receiver, though terribly weakened, is remarkably strengthened.

I'll let you in on a secret. Let's say you have a question about the intricacies of football. Would you rather ask a sportswriter or a former college and NFL quarterback? I'd go for the QB, too. In fact, I used to regularly quiz Scott Hunter during and after games. The former Alabama, Green Bay Packers, and Atlanta Falcons quarterback was a Mobile sportscaster, and we covered many of the same games. "What did I just see, Scott?" I'd ask as we broke bread at halftime in the press box or as we waited for a coach to show up for a postgame press conference in the interview room.

Scott has been a friend of mine since he played for the Tide, and he seemed to enjoy our little ritual as much as I did. I didn't go in for a lot of technical stuff in my columns and stories, but sometimes an explanation along those lines was necessary and, thanks to Hunter, my readers would actually think I knew what I was talking about. There, now you know my dirty little secret.

Hunter, who is now a Mobile stockbroker, rewrote the chapter on passing in Alabama's record book during the seasons of 1968, 1969, and 1970—but his last two Tides went 6–5 and 6–5–1. After that, Paul Bryant said Alabama could no longer win with dropback passing. He adopted the wishbone formation, and Alabama dominated college football in the 1970s.

Because of the slippage when he was playing, some fans almost want to stick an asterisk beside Hunter's records. Well, let me tell you, Scott Hunter gets a bum rap. It wasn't his fault that Tennessee scored 41 points, Auburn 49, Southern Cal 42, and Ole Miss 48 during those years—that the 1969 team surrendered 268 points and the 1970 team 264 points. (By way of comparison, let's note that Snake Stabler's undefeated 1966 club gave up 44 points and shut out six foes.)

The blame for those two subpar seasons can be laid at Bryant's feet, not Scott's. Recruiting had suffered. Bryant was, as he admitted, "going off in all directions." He was enjoying his star status, accepting awards, being in TV specials, playing golf with celebrities. In short, he wasn't taking care of business. He had relaxed his famous discipline in dealing with Stabler in 1967, and he believed that lapse subsequently infected other players. In 1969 Bryant agreed to become head coach of the Miami Dolphins, but then he backed out, which might say something about his focus during the bad times.

A drug problem struck the team in1970, and seven players were given the option of withdrawing from school or letting the law handle it. These junction boys faced a real junction, and they chose to leave school. Just don't blame my buddy Scott Hunter for Alabama's puny years of 1969 and 1970.

Bo Jackson, of course, was the finest athlete I ever covered. Four or five years ago I was looking through some old football magazines and found one that purported to list the top one hundred high school prospects in

America during Bo's senior year at McAdory High. His name was not among them, but he won the Heisman Trophy as an Auburn runner in 1985. I frequently cite Jackson as an example of the uncertainty of recruiting. After Georgia's Herschel Walker won the Heisman in 1982, I said I'd never see another running back who was that good. But it didn't take long. Bo was better, I think.

Bo didn't have a football under his arm or a baseball bat in his hand when he provided me with my fondest memory of the Jackson years. He was relatively new at Auburn, just a kid, and I was interviewing him, He had a speech impediment, and he was struggling with almost every sentence. But he hung in there and answered my questions, and I admired him for doing so. I thanked him when we were finished. Then I patted him on the shoulder. It was unspoken assurance that I knew it hadn't been easy for him.

Of the millions of words that the career of Vincent Edward Jackson has produced, something a teammate said testifies as well as any to his greatness. Gregg Carr, the linebacker, offered: "Usually when you come off the field after playing defense you want to sit on the bench and relax. But that wasn't the case when Bo was playing. You wanted to stand up and watch him run."

As a boy, Jackson shared the floor and two beds with nine brothers and sisters in a three-room home on a dirt road in the Raimond community on the outskirts of Bessemer. As a young man, he had a choice of major league baseball or NFL football. And he chose both. I remember so many columnists scolding Bo for trying to play two sports on the highest level. He couldn't do justice to either, they said. I applauded him for his decision, because I thought there was a good chance that he could become what he indeed did become, a star in both.

He played in football's Pro Bowl game and in baseball's All-Star Game, and every sports fan in America knows his name. If he hadn't chosen both, he would have been just another superb player in the one he did choose. And when I see the Chicago businessman on TV and hear him speaking with a flawless tongue, I smile at the memory of the kid who labored through that interview long ago.

For sheer potential to excite a crowd, David Palmer rivaled Bo among the players I covered. He could flit all over the place, and writers described the little fellow as a "water bug" so frequently that it became a cliché. He was officially a receiver, and he could return punts and kickoffs with rare artistry, but I think he could have been one of the finest wishbone quarterbacks ever if that formation had still been in vogue.

One of his greatest plays occurred not in a game but in practice, not on the field but on the sidelines. Alabama's 1992 squad was practicing in New Orleans' Superdome for the Sugar Bowl game with Miami. Palmer ran a sideline route and caught the ball as he went out of bounds. A little boy was standing too close to the field, and a collision seemed unavoidable.

But Palmer dropped the ball, clutched the boy against his body, and rolled forward, shielding the kid with his body. The lad was shaken but uninjured. He probably wanted to cry, but there was nothing to cry about. If the receiver had been anyone but Palmer, the boy might have been hospitalized. "It was unbelievable," Gene Stallings said after he got the kid a hat and a tee shirt. "He hit that boy going full speed, but David wrapped him up so tight the boy never felt a thing."

Gregg Carr is the most atypical ex-football player I've ever known. Try fitting him into any cliché and you'll realize you're dealing with a square peg, round hole problem. In the first place, he doesn't look like a man who backed the line for Auburn and the Pittsburgh Steelers. He's downright slim, and he confesses to having been "the lightest linebacker in the NFL." Not only does he fail in the "big" category of "big, dumb football player," he puts to rout the "dumb" part. Carr graduated in engineering at Auburn and then—in a most curious twist—became an orthopedic surgeon.

Carr was the SEC's most honored athlete in 1984. As an Auburn senior he was a consensus all-American, National Football Foundation Scholar Athlete, and one of the NCAA's Top Five Student Athletes. The future Birmingham doctor played on Pat Dye's first Auburn team, in 1981. By 1983 the Tigers were winning eleven of their dozen games and finishing third in the nation. "My recruiting class was ranked as one of the worst in the SEC," Carr told me, "but from that class six or seven guys played pro football. It was just a matter of hard work and teaching them to believe in themselves."

When he played in the Hula Bowl all-star game after his senior season, he weighed in at 198 pounds. ("Studying engineering, I didn't get much sleep.") At Pittsburgh he weighed 215 pounds. "Of all people, I was the middle linebacker on short yardage situations," he said. Carr was a sixth-round draft choice and one of some twenty-three linebackers in camp that first year. He was one of seven who made the squad. During his five seasons with Pittsburgh, Carr observed an orthopedic surgeon and became interested in medicine. "I thought that was a way I could stay close to athletics when my playing days were over," he said. He accepted the ten-year commitment that was required and enrolled in medical school at UAB. His engineering background has aided him in his role of doctor, "because the body is an engineering marvel."

It was fun watching Barry Smith grow up and then play for Alabama in the late 1970s. He is the son of *Anniston Star* columnist George Smith and his wife, Agnes, two of our close friends. And it struck a note in my topsy-turvy mind that Barry had an upside-down view of the football world. He was a long snapper, the ultimate specialist in specialized football. He was so skillful that he usually delivered the ball so that when the holder touched it down on placements the laces were facing the goal post.

How is it viewing the football world from between your legs? It's fun, Smith told me, but it's difficult to concentrate when some terminator is head on and "fixing to kill you and you can't look at him. I'd at least like to see his face before he kills me."

He weighed just 185 pounds. But Smith probably was the best in America at his job. He got an early start. When he was a little boy playing with the bigger boys, they made him snap. "It's something I started doing in the backyard, and now it's paying for my education," he said. "You can't beat that."

Smith actually worked his way up to second-string defensive back at Alabama, but he suffered a separated shoulder, and after that Bryant wasn't going to risk losing his snapper—especially one who fired the ball fifteen yards in eight-tenths of a second, which was considered excellent. Smith, now an Anniston trucking executive, was one of the first men downfield under a punt. "I have to be fast," he said, "Because it doesn't take much to put a featherweight like me on the ground. I practice my dodge technique often—dodge or die."

He may have set a world's record for the longest snap. When he was a freshman snapping for the junior varsity, the Tide led Georgia Tech 5–0 and decided to surrender an intentional safety. Smith snapped the ball into the fourth row of seats at Bryant–Denny Stadium—and was amazed when uncomprehending thickheads in the crowd booed him.

It's difficult to compare players of different eras in any sport, but the problem is compounded in football because some guys played both offense and defense, while others saw action on just one side of the ball. You probably were sitting there sipping your French roast coffee and wondering who I would choose as the greatest Auburn football player. No? Well, I was. I reasoned that he had to be a two-way man. I mean, I think Bo Jackson would have been good on defense, and I think Mike Fuller would have been good on offense, but I know Tucker Frederickson was good on both. He's my Plainsman among Plainsmen.

Frederickson played halfback, fullback, and safety (1962–64). Twice he won the Jacobs Blocking Trophy as the best blocker in the SEC. "I never saw anybody who hit as hard out of the secondary as he did," his quarterback, Jimmy Sidle, said. His coach, Shug Jordan, described the 220-pound Frederickson as "the most complete player I've seen in the thirty-eight years I've been connected with the game." Later, Jordan would call him "the greatest athlete I ever coached." Tucker ended his Auburn career with 100-yard-plus rushing games against Georgia and Alabama, finished sixth in Heisman Trophy voting, and then became the first player selected in the NFL draft, by the New York Giants. Alas, his pro career was sabotaged by injury.

Frederickson is from Hollywood, Florida. Auburn took him without ever seeing him play. But for a moment Jordan must have wondered if he was seeing proof (86 proof) that he shouldn't sign Tucker. Frederickson made a recruiting visit to Auburn. He flew to Montgomery, and assistant coach Dick McGowen drove him to the campus. He went to a room in Graves Center, where the athletes lived, and Auburn quarterback Bobby Hunt suggested they attend a fraternity party. Frederickson said he'd change his shirt first. He tossed his Samsonite suitcase onto the bed and opened it—and the first things Jordan saw were six bottles of whiskey. "Oh, my gosh," Jordan said. Frederickson was stunned. "Coach, this isn't my suitcase," he pleaded. "I swear it's not."

Somehow, during the trip Tucker's suitcase and another traveler's identical bag had gotten switched. Jordan believed him, and Auburn signed a future all-American. He made Auburn's team of the century as a defensive back—"He was probably the most devastating safetyman that's ever played in the SEC," former Jordan aide Buck Bradberry says—but fans likely remember him best as a mow-'em-down blocker in the Avalanche play. In 1963 Jimmy Sidle became the first quarterback to rush for 1,000 yards. The Avalanche was a simple rollout with Sidle carrying the ball and halfback Frederickson and fullback Larry Rawson blocking.

I wish college football would return to limited substitution. It makes no more sense for football players to play just one way than it would for a baseball team to have a nine-man fielding platoon and a nine-man batting platoon. I'd like to know if some of the part-time stars would be as good if they played twice as much. I know the answer regarding Tucker Frederickson, who is now a real estate developer living in North Palm Beach, Florida.

I interviewed John Croyle when he played defensive end at Alabama in the 1970s, and he told me he planned to found a ranch for abused children after his football career ended. In the story I referred to him as "Deacon John Croyle" because he was a Baptist deacon. It made a good story, but I had no idea whether he would follow up on the plan. He did, and Big Oak Ranch, which has saved so many boys and girls, is the result. I've worked with John almost from the beginning, publicizing the ranch whenever an opportunity arose. And sometimes when it didn't. An editor once sent down word for me to "quit writing about that damn ranch so much."

I included a chapter on Croyle in my book *They Wore Crimson.* Early on, he didn't want to go into detail about some of the horror stories he had encountered. "Just say we're helping abused children," he said. I told Croyle the facts of readership life that any newsperson learns. You can write that twenty people were killed in a tornado in Midland, Texas, and readers will forget it in five minutes, but you can write that a little girl is trapped in a well in Midland, Texas, and they'll follow the story for days. The specific is always better than the general.

I will say, albeit immodestly, that by detailing some of the abuse, I won hearts and donations for Big Oak Ranch, which is headquartered in Springville, Alabama. There were times when I wiped away tears as I made notes. I cannot begin to comprehend a mother putting her little boy into a pot of boiling cooking oil up to his waist. And I cannot comprehend him saying, years later, "I still love my mother." The word "abuse" makes one frown, but this description of the plight of an eight-year-old boy makes one want to fight. "He slept in a cage under the car," Croyle told me. "Both his arms were broken. There were multiple fractures throughout his body. Every inch of his body had been bruised. He had been beaten with golf clubs, sticks, ropes. He told the judge it wasn't so bad one night because he found a plastic bag to cover his face with to keep the ants off."

God bless John Croyle and Big Oak Ranch.

Chapter 16

When Michael Jordan stepped onto the field at Hoover Metropolitan Stadium for the first time, he noticed the basketball goal on a sign in right field that promised five thousand dollars to any batter who knocked a ball into the hoop. "Five thousand to make a three-pointer," Jordan mused. "Now, that's a tough three-pointer." It was April 1994, and the world's best basketball player was playing baseball. Jordan, who had led the University of North Carolina and the Chicago Bulls to hoops championships, shocked the sports-speaking world by announcing his retirement from basketball to give baseball a shot, and here he was in the livery of the Birmingham Barons.

Birmingham sportswriters do rub shoulders with nationally famous folks as well as state celebrities, and in this chapter I'll mention my impressions of some of them. No other scenario was as unforeseen, as strange, as Michael Jordan's manning right field for the Barons. Jordan played one season, batting .202, hitting three homers, driving in fifty-one runs, and stealing thirty bases in 127 games before he gave up baseball and returned to basketball.

The Barons had drawn 277,096 fans to the Met in 1993. They pulled a franchise record 467,867 in 1994. Jordan's final Saturday home game, on August 27, attracted a stadium record audience of 16,247. The Chicago White Sox signed Jordan, used him in an exhibition game against the Chicago Cubs on April 7, and sent him to Birmingham of the Class AA Southern League. He debuted against Chattanooga on Friday night, April 8, as the starting right fielder. He flew out in his first at bat and went 0-for-3 as 130 members of the national and international press looked on. Jordan's stay in Birmingham created a press frenzy. More than 500 journalists from the United States and eight foreign countries covered the club. The Barons played on television three times.

A couple of things stand out in my mind all these years later. One is Jordan's demeanor. He wasn't the big shot playing in a bush league. He was businesslike, but he was friendly enough and quotable and his press conferences were informative. He knew he was a story, and he worked with the press. Early on, I wrote in a column: "I'll tell you one thing. It's been a long time since anyone in sports has impressed me off the field as much as this man has. He has been cooperative with the press, far beyond the call of duty. After dealing with so many jerks and prima donnas, it's impressive to hear the greatest basketball player in history apologizing for being late for a press conference after a minor league baseball game."

The other thing that sticks in my mind is my friend Harry Walker's itching to get at Jordan. Harry the Hat was a noted hitting instructor. Big leaguers still made their way to his home in Leeds to study at his batting cage. The former major league manager and UAB coach led the bigs with an average of .363 in 1947. "Michael Jordan hit .200," Walker told me, "but I could have had him hitting .250. Nobody asked me, and it certainly wasn't my place to horn in." I don't remember the details, but Walker said his White Sox handlers weren't teaching Jordan the proper techniques. Anyway, I thought of Harry as a master house painter observing and shaking his head in amazement as an unskilled neighbor sloshed paint and it ran down the walls of his home.

The no-fun police, of course, criticized Jordan for donning a baseball glove. He was somehow "insulting" the sport, they decided. I applauded him in a column:

> Hey, Michael Jordan isn't trying to be a brain surgeon or an admiral or the head of the department of philosophy at a university. He's just a ballplayer trying to play with a different ball. And he's trying hard. . . .
>
> Spare me all the talk of the purity of baseball. Despite all the lyrical prose written about it, baseball is just a bunch of sweaty guys wanting to hit a ball with a stick and run around some bases like children. Michael Jordan hasn't insulted baseball, as some have written. . . .
>
> I'm all for him. This country needs some pioneers, some mountain climbers. It needs to quit being discontented and negative about everything and to cheer someone who tries.

Jordan's first workout at the Met came on Tuesday night, April 5. The practice was closed to the public, but the press was admitted. Terry Francona, the manager, pitched when Jordan stepped into the batting cage. Michael swung and missed at the first two throws, bunted one, and then started spraying some to the outfield. Some flew close to the fence, but none went over. "I've been off four days," Jordan explained, as the press hung on his every word. "It takes awhile to get your eye back." His knee, slightly injured in spring training, was okay, he said. "It's a beautiful facility," Jordan remarked when asked about the dandy little ballpark. "I wasn't too surprised. I heard a lot about it."

After the workout, the Barons gathered around a TV set to watch a White Sox game. "I watched baseball before, but I watch it with a different eye now," Jordan said. "Now I watch it to learn, to pick things up." The next morning, in his second workout as a Baron, Jordan drove two balls out of the park. "You just need more Wheaties and Gatorade," he teased another player whose best shots fell a little short of home run land.

The Barons opened their season on Thursday night, losing to Chattanooga 10–8 at the Met. Jordan wasn't in a Birmingham uniform, for he had played for the White Sox in the Windy City Classic exhibition against the Cubs in Wrigley Field that afternoon and gone two for five with a double and two RBI. Just as Francona, the manger, walked into his office after the opener, his phone rang. He spoke to the caller and then told the press: "My right fielder is lost." Jordan had flown back to the Magic City from Chicago and gotten confused during his drive from the Birmingham airport.

Birmingham wasn't the only Southern League team that was delighted Jordan was playing. Before the season opened there was an unprecedented demand for tickets in other cities. Some Barons' visits were sold out, and tickets for games against B'ham in June and July were going fast. Even season ticket sales were soaring. Jordan was validating his role not only as the foremost celebrity in basketball but in sports, period. Said Huntsville general manger Don Mincher, "The crush was immediate. We found out Jordan was going to Birmingham around 8 A.M. the day he was assigned, and by 8:30 there was a line for tickets.

Finally, Jordan actually played in a game for the Barons. Chattanooga won 10–3 on April 8, but Jordan's three at-bats were greeted with enthusiastic cheering as were his throws from the outfield. That he went 0-for-3 at the plate seemed incidental. All the hoopla leading up to his first game may have gone against the Barons. The club sold some 9,600 tickets in advance, and it was disappointed when just 10,359 showed up. That was near capacity in the 10,800-seat stadium but fewer than the 14,000 that had been mentioned as possible. "We probably were at fault for speculating on the size of the crowd we expected," Barons president Bill Hardekopf said. "Couple that with the fact it was on television. People just decided not to fight the crowd."

Those who came were revved up. Birmingham's Cindy Brown was among some seventy-five fans who were leaning over the fence along the right field foul line ninety minutes before the 7:10 start, hoping for a close-up view of Jordan. "I love Mike" was painted on her right cheek. "I've been here since 3 P.M.," said Ms. Brown. She explained she was a Rockford, Illinois, native and lifelong Chicago Bulls fan, though she had never seen Jordan play basketball in person. She arrived so early she had to wait in the parking lot two and a half hours before the gates opened at 5:30. "But it's worth it to see Michael," she declared.

Doug Adams and his son Marcus drove over from their home in Fayetteville, Georgia, and arrived at the Met at 2:45. "This is a major experience," said Adams, a high school teacher. "It's one of those things that years from now you can say, 'I was there.'"

Michael Jordan hadn't played baseball since he was in high school, and he wasn't much of a professional player, but the Southern League and its fans loved him. He went 0-for-4 in his final pro game, in Huntsville, and even at the doorway of football season he pulled 7,987 spectators. Jordan's draw for the year, at home and on the road, was 986,185. It wasn't the last time he wore his Barons uniform, though. He donned it again in 1995 to play in a movie, *Space Jam.* It was a combination live action–animated film with Loony Tunes characters. That was fitting, because the world's foremost basketballer playing minor league baseball in Birmingham was pretty loony.

I watched on TV as Muhammad Ali took the torch from swimmer Janet Evans and laboriously ignited the Olympic flame in Atlanta in 1966. The hands that used to confound Sonny Liston and Joe Frazier and George Foreman and Floyd Patterson were shaking pitifully from Parkinson's syndrome, and I was relieved when Ali succeeded in his ceremonial task. I know millions worldwide must have been holding their breath, too.

I thought back to better times, when I had supper with Ali in, of all places, the Lambda Chi Alpha house at Auburn University. He was thirty-one years old and healthy and frisky and full of himself, and the kids loved his appearance at their fraternity and so did I. It was May 15, 1973, and Ali had come to Auburn to lecture in Memorial Coliseum as part of the Horizons III program. Before his talk there was a press conference and supper with the frat boys, and I was invited to break bread with the unlikely group.

Ali looked at the yellow squash on his plate and told how at home his wife liquefied the vegetable in a blender to accommodate the broken jaw Ken Norton had given him in the second round of their fight. He was between bouts with Norton. On March 31 Norton had had the good fortune to crack his jaw and win in twelve rounds. On September 10 Ali beat Norton in twelve.

"This food smells good," Ali said. "The cook must be colored."

He fixed a mock frown on one fellow and said, "He looks like Frazier."

Ali told us how Gorgeous George, the wrestler of bouffant and bobby pins, had been the inspiration for his sideshow approach to the vanilla sport of boxing. "He came down that aisle wearing a robe with diamonds in it," Ali recalled. "He took a fellow's beer away from him and poured it over the man's head. Of course, I found out later that fellow was part of the show.

"Everybody was shouting, 'Kill him, kill him,' and he sprayed deodorant in the opponent's corner. But all those people who were shouting had come to see him. I said, 'This is a good idea.' "

This Cassius Marcellus Clay Jr., who lived in a modest bungalow and who was whipping every amateur, learned a merchandising secret: You don't sell the steak you sell the sizzle. "It worked, didn't it?" Ali reflected that night in Auburn. "Haven't you heard people talk about, 'He needs a whupping'? I want them to boo me. Those seats cost a hundred dollars." I wrote in my column that night: "He isn't the champion, but it is his name that stirs emotion, not the champion's. No one is neutral about Ali. Half the population doesn't know who the champion is."

Ali thought any champ ought to be colorful. "Those fellows have got the title but no imagination," he said over supper. He delighted the frat boys by discussing his phony feud with broadcaster Howard Cosell. "There is a Howard Cosell doll," Ali said. "You don't wind it up, but it talks anyway." And: "Cosell wanted to be a boxer, but they couldn't find a mouthpiece to fit him."

Ali may or may not have been the best fighter of all time, but he certainly was the most outlandish, the most promotional of all time. His boast, "I am the greatest," his poetic predictions regarding his approaching bouts, and his scathing verbal attacks on his upcoming opponents were worthy of his role model, Gorgeous George. He generated a level of interest in boxing that was comparable to that generated by Tiger Woods in golf. Ali was the planet's best-known and best-loved athlete of the twentieth century, and I wouldn't argue with *Time* magazine's deeming him the most instantly recognized human being in the world.

He was controversial. He was the heavyweight champion when he was stripped of his title, blackballed from boxing, and sentenced to prison after declaring he was a conscientious objector and refusing to be inducted into the U.S. Army. He became a hero of the anti–Vietnam war movement. The Supreme Court ordered that all charges against him be dropped, and he was never imprisoned, but he lost three and a half years from his boxing career. He regained the heavyweight title, but many believed he wasn't the same after his return.

The loss to Ken Norton was on Ali's mind at Auburn. He seemed strangely out of character from the bragging, wisecracking Greatest when he said, "I didn't train like I should. I didn't eat like I should. I took it for granted. I believe God has been punishing me for the way I have been acting. I was intoxicated with greatness." Intoxication with life was the subject of his address to the 2,532 students who gathered in the coliseum. It could best be described as a sermon. Don't bank on material stuff, he warned. He left his wit at the press conference and the frat house. He avoided anything controversial.

In my column that night in Auburn I wrote:

> Ali is a natural comic, a man with a feel for what makes others laugh. But he doesn't want to be remembered primarily for the sizzle. He wants to be recalled as one who had the steak, too. He wants to retire as heavyweight champion of the world, defeating along the way the men who defeated him.
>
> His plan is simple in the telling if not in the execution. In a year and a half he proposes to:
>
> 1. Defeat Ken Norton, which shouldn't be difficult unless by some freak of fate Norton should break his jaw again.
> 2. Wrest the championship from George Foreman.
> 3. Destroy Joe Frazier in a vengeful title march.
> 4. Quit.

He did defeat Norton. He did regain the championship from Foreman, on October 30, 1974, a year and a half after he ate with the Lambda Chi Alpha boys at Auburn. He did beat Frazier. He kept fighting.

In 1978 he lost the crown to Leon Spinks. Seven months later, in that same year, he beat Spinks, but that fight was for only the WBA version of the title because Spinks had been stripped by the WBC for failing to meet top contender Ken Norton. Ali "retired" in 1979, but in 1980 he took on WBC titleholder Larry Holmes. Huge mistake. He was a pathetic figure who had lost every round when Holmes was awarded an eleventh-round TKO. Ali didn't want his career to end with his butt on a stool in a corner, so on December 11, 1981, he fought Trevor Berbick, a ham-and-egger, in the Bahamas. The fight was held in a shabby ballpark with seedy dressing rooms. There was no bell or timepiece, but someone finally found a cowbell and a stopwatch.

"Forty is fun, because life has just begun," Ali quipped before the match. "Age is mind over matter. As long as you don't mind, it don't matter." Berbick easily outpointed him. He was through. Like so many athletes, Muhammad Ali had played his sport too long.

Try as it might, major league baseball can't quite seem to commit suicide. It lost me when the players went on strike in 1994 to produce the eighth work stoppage since 1972 and to cancel the World Series, but in the overall picture my opinion matters about as much as what I think about strawberry ice cream.

I was reminded of that on April 3, 1999, when an exhibition game between the Baltimore Orioles and the Philadelphia Phillies pulled 13,384 fans to Hoover Metropolitan Stadium, and the fact was punctuated with an exclamation point when I met Patti Schoenbein of Gardendale, Alabama.

It was midnight before game day when Patti and her husband Bill drove into the parking lot of the Met. "I can't believe we're doing this," he told her. Her devotion to Baltimore's Cal Ripken Jr. had prompted her to suggest—strongly—that they spend the night at the park. "If I miss getting to see Cal, . . . " she said ominously—meaning getting close enough to nab an autograph. So Bill drove her to the stadium and they slept in their van.

I arrived at the Met at 9:30 on that Saturday morning, thinking the joint would be deserted since the gates didn't open until 10:45. But the Schoenbeins were first in a line that already numbered seventy-five or so. They had had tickets for three weeks, so why were they in line that early? Here's a clue: "I've got 70,000 baseball cards, including 250 Ripken cards," Patti told me. "I've been collecting since 1978. I've got two cutouts of him. I've got all his audios. Every commercial he's done, I've got on the computer."

In other words, Bill said, "It's a Ripken shrine."

As I chatted with them I realized the grand old game will survive every wound, even self-inflicted ones like the strike of 1994. It can't be slain, though it sometimes seems as irresponsible as a drunk driver.

I sat in the dugout and chatted with Ripken before the game. A single thought kept dancing through my mind: Patti Schoenbein would give anything to be doing this, but I just wanted to jot down enough notes for a column, watch a few innings, and go home. I was soured on big-time pro sports, and I was sorry that I was. I hoped Patti had gotten her autograph.

Fans had stood five deep along the right field wall, waving balls and bats and pictures at the man who had played more consecutive games than any other major leaguer. He signed as many as he could, but it was a mere fraction. I asked Ripken if he enjoyed signing autographs. "It's pretty fun," he said as he scrawled his signature across a poster. "I don't know that the actual writing my name is fun, but I like the interaction."

Was it also pleasant to return to the minors? The fellow who broke in with Bluefield, West Virginia, in 1978 smiled at the question. "It's good to *visit* the minor leagues," Ripken said. "There's a great quaintness to a minor league ballpark. It makes you remember. But all of us paid our dues to get to the big leagues, and I want to stay there." He enjoyed the camaraderie of the minors, Ripken said. Players spend a lot of time together off the field. They're playing in an unfamiliar city and know few people other than their teammates. Many young minor leaguers aren't married, so they rely on each other for companionship. They spend long hours together on buses during road trips. The best moments probably are in the minors, he said.

In 1995 Ripken broke a record that was once considered untouchable, the consecutive games streak that Lou Gehrig established in 1939. Ripken began his run in 1982, and on September 6, 1995, he played in his 2,131st consecutive game to eclipse Gehrig's mark. A lot of people were delighted. I wasn't. I grew up on the legend of Lou Gehrig, the Iron Horse, and I preferred that he retain the record. So many times as boy and man I had seen the flickering image of the dying Gehrig as he stood in Yankee Stadium on July 4, 1939, and told his fans, "Today I consider myself the luckiest man on the face of the earth." Why should I want his record to be broken? Besides, Ripken had participated in the strike of 1994, and there was something askew in cheering him for answering the bell at work when his and his colleagues' refusal to work had led to the World Series being canceled.

Ripken was thirty-eight years old on that day in 1999 (a year younger than Patti Schoenbein, old nosy here learned), and I asked him how much longer he could play. "I don't know," he said. "As long as I'm able, I guess." In fact, 2001 would be his final season.

When Ripken visited Birmingham, he had played in 2,704 major league games, the first in 1981. I wondered if he remembered it. "I sure do," he said. "I came in as a pinch runner and scored the winning run against the Kansas City Royals. I remember running out on the field at Memorial Stadium and thinking it was like a stage. The lights were on, and it was aglow, like a stage."

It was the beginning of a remarkable career. The tallest regular shortstop in major league history at six feet, four inches, he could field and he could hit. He won two Gold Gloves, and in 1990 he played ninety-five straight games without committing an error and made just three errors all season. In 1989 he broke Ernie Banks's record for shortstops with his eighth straight twenty-homer year, and then he stretched it to ten seasons. Ripken's consecutive game streak finally ended on September 20, 1998, against the Yankees when he asked Manager Ray Miller to keep him out of the lineup. He had played in 2,632 straight games, including 501 after he broke Gehrig's record.

I recalled the night he passed Gehrig, against the California Angels. I was clicking through the TV channels when I came upon a singular sight. Those who made up the sellout crowd of 46,272 at Oriole Park at Camden Yards were standing and applauding and screaming and generally going nuts because the game, and thus the record, had become official after the top of the fifth inning. The game was delayed twenty-two minutes and fifteen seconds as the crowd brought Ripken out for eight curtain calls. He took a victory lap around the park, shaking the hands of children, teenagers, security guards, and members of both teams. Now, I'm sure Cal Ripken Jr. is a nice enough fellow, but I reflected that those fans were paying a premium for tickets so that Ripken could make $6 million to play a game for nine months, and I could picture them dutifully going off to work to lay bricks and pave roads and repair automobiles day after day when they didn't feel like it, and I thought, hell, he should be applauding them.

One of the perks of being a sportswriter is that you could find yourself walking along a Birmingham street and chatting with a companion who just happens to be the greatest quarterback who ever lived. Johnny Unitas came to town for a speaking engagement a few years ago, and I accompanied him to the Alabama Sports Hall of Fame, a treasure trove of memorabilia that impressed even a fellow who had thrown touchdown passes in forty-seven consecutive NFL games. Unitas, who retired in 1973, played under rules that were drastically different from the ones that coddle the passing game of today. Assault and battery could be inflicted upon receivers downfield. Defensive linemen could head-slap a path into the backfield and then commit whatever mayhem they desired upon the quarterback without fear of a fine. Linemen had to block, not merely push with their hands.

So, as we strolled along on a sunny day, I asked Unitas how successful he would have been under today's rules. "I would have completed 75 percent of my passes," he answered. As it was, he completed 55 percent. Unitas wasn't bragging. He never boasted. He was a quiet fellow who let his talent, his confidence, and his unsurpassed courage speak for him. I asked a question and he simply gave me an honest answer. He believed he would complete three-fourth of his passes and he said so.

As we approached other pedestrians, it struck me as odd that no one seemed to recognize Unitas, one of the most famous athletes who ever lived. His trademark crew cut had given way to longer, parted hair, but his face hadn't changed much. It dawned on me that Unitas never looked like a ballplayer, and no one was spotting him as one now. It's funny what pops into your mind. I noticed his hunched shoulders and thought that my old elementary schoolteacher in Statham, Georgia, Miss Sue Perkins, would have chastened him for his poor posture. Correct posture was a big thing when I was a kid. I used to feel deliciously rebellious slumping in a chair while I did my homework in my bedroom.

I later read the words of Alex Hawkins, Unitas's teammate on the Baltimore Colts, who recalled the first time he saw Unitas. Johnny "was from Pennsylvania, but he looked so much like a Mississippi farmhand that I looked around for a mule. He had stooped shoulders, a chicken breast, thin bowed legs, and long, dangling arms with crooked, mangled fingers." Unitas, who played collegiately at Louisville, tried out with his hometown Pittsburgh Steelers in 1955. He never played a down in five exhibition games, and the Steelers cut him and gave him a bus ticket from camp back to Pittsburgh. The future member of the all-time all-NFL team cashed in the ticket and hitchhiked home.

Unitas and his young wife, Dorothy, moved in with her parents, and he got his old job back. He was a pile driver on a construction gang. He quarterbacked for the Bloomfield Rams, a local sandlot team, on a grassless field that was sprinkled with oil to keep the dust down. He was paid six bucks a game, and he took it home and gave it to Dorothy. Unitas didn't think the story was funny. He wanted an interviewer to know that the wolf wasn't at his door, that he made a decent salary on his construction job, but the six dollars was significant because he had made it playing football.

The Baltimore Colts, acting on the recommendation of Unitas's college coach, gave him a tryout in 1956. He stuck and got a contract for seven thousand dollars. It now hangs on the wall of the Pro Football Hall of

Fame in Canton, Ohio. In 1958, three seasons after he began playing for the Bloomfield Rams, Unitas led the Colts to the NFL championship. They beat the New York Giants 23–17 in Yankee Stadium in the first overtime game in league history. His tying drive was a drawing board example of the two-minute drill.

The Giants led 17–14 with 1:56 left in regulation play. The Colts had the ball on their own fourteen-yard line. With the Giants protecting against long passes, Unitas went to Raymond Berry on intermediate patterns. Three consecutive passes gained sixty-two yards and set up Steve Myhra's tying field goal with seven seconds remaining. Then Unitas marched the Colts eighty yards in sudden death overtime, mixing runs and passes. Alan Ameche scored the winner from the one-yard line with 8:15 elapsed.

It's been called the greatest game ever played, the game that lifted pro football to a new level of prominence. I remember watching it in black and white on TV and pulling for the Colts, because Unitas had already captured me. I was a general news reporter for the *Gadsden Times,* and I couldn't have guessed he and I would one day be strolling along a street in Birmingham. One who didn't believe it was the greatest game ever played was Johnny Unitas. "I never felt it was a particularly good game until the last two minutes and the overtime," he said. It was gilded by being the first OT contest in championship history and because it was played in New York, he noted. A much better game, Unitas said, was the one in which the Colts earned the division title. San Francisco led 27–7 at the half but Baltimore won 35–27.

Unitas was disenchanted with the modern pro football scene. Drugs and focus on the individual rather than the team turned him off. Talent shouldn't be a license for selfish behavior. He wouldn't want to coach, he said, because he couldn't put up with the "horse manure" modern coaches put up with, and he'd probably end up with a squad of just twenty-five players.

I was saddened, along with millions of others, when Unitas died of a heart attack at age sixty-nine in 2002. As much as his dramatic passing, I recalled his guts. In one game the Bears' Bill George grabbed his leg, rendering him immobile, and massive Doug Atkins pulverized him. His nose was smashed and slashed and his face was covered with blood. The crowd became deathly quiet, and trainers and doctors hustled onto the field. Atkins gazed down at Unitas and said, "Well, kid, that's about it for you today." Unitas looked at the ex-Tennessee star and said, "Not just yet it ain't."

With his nose nearly twice its normal size and his eyes swollen almost shut, Unitas returned to the huddle. On fourth down, with no timeouts left, Johnny called the same play on which he had been injured and threw a thirty-nine-yard touchdown pass to Lenny Moore to win the game 24–20. Sometimes after he was sacked hard, Unitas would call the same play and delay a split second longer before throwing the ball. The message was that he wasn't afraid, that the sacker might have won the round but Johnny was going to win the fight.

But when I call to mind my favorite image of Johnny Unitas he isn't wearing a Colts uniform and he isn't in victory lane. It is October 24, 1953, in Knoxville, and outclassed Louisville has just lost to Tennessee 59–6. In the dressing room after the game they are having to cut off Johnny's jersey and shoulder pads because he can't lift his arms. And the reason he can't lift his arms is because he has made so many tackles. He played defense, too.

Paul Hornung played for the greatest professional football coach, and he had wanted to play for the greatest college football coach.

Hornung was the handsome, blond, curly haired "golden boy" halfback of Vince Lombardi's awesome Green Bay Packers, and if he could have changed his mother's mind he would have suited up for Paul Bryant's Kentucky Wildcats instead of Notre Dame. Hornung is from Louisville, Kentucky. He wanted to play for the Bear, but his mom wanted him to go to Notre Dame. "Back in those days you went where your parents wanted you to go," Hornung told me during a visit to Birmingham for a speaking engagement in 2000.

For Bryant, Hornung was always the one who got away. Bryant even linked his leaving Kentucky to coach Texas A&M to Hornung. Bear was speaking at a dinner in Kentucky and he asked Hornung to stand. "He was the best recruit in Kentucky, and if I couldn't recruit him it was time for me to leave," Bryant said. Hornung replied: "I didn't have anything to do with that oil well you got in Texas." After the dinner Hornung told Bryant, "You've got to quit saying that every time you come back to Kentucky. You're going to get me killed."

Bryant said he would give scholarships to all five seniors on Hornung's high school team if Hornung would choose Kentucky. No dice. Anyway, a scholarship wasn't a guarantee of anything, Hornung reflected. "Bear would take his team to camp in the summer and break their backs. He'd take 120 and come back with about 40."

Hornung liked to remind Bryant: "Suppose I had gone to Kentucky. You left the next year. What would I have done?"

"I'd have taken you with me," Bryant replied.

Hornung was Lombardi's type player, and he would have been Bryant's. "I loved Coach Lombardi," Hornung told me. "The other players would say, 'Hornung, go in there and tell him he's working us too hard.' But I never won any of those arguments. He thought if you didn't have a bone sticking out of your leg you were all right."

Hornung was a quarterback at Notre Dame, but he moved to halfback at Green Bay. Never has the Notre Dame magic been more visible—and controversial—than in 1956 when Hornung won the Heisman Trophy playing for a team that went 2–8. No other man from a losing club has ever won it. Hornung knows what everyone else knows. "I would never have won the Heisman if not for the Notre Dame glamour," he said, "not in a year like we had. If, say, the University of Illinois had had the same record and I'd played exactly the same way for them, forget it." Tennessee fans were particularly miffed. The voting was the closest it had been up to that time. Hornung got 1,066 voting points and the Volunteers' Johnny Majors got 994. Majors had been the running, passing, punting tailback in the single wing offense of a 10–1 Tennessee squad.

Hornung's first year at Green Bay was 1957 and his final year was 1966. He missed the 1963 season because Commissioner Pete Rozelle suspended him for betting on NFL games. Still, in 1986 he was inducted into the Pro

Football Hall of Fame. Hornung could pass, run, catch, block, and kick, and he had a nose for the goal line. He led NFL scoring in three consecutive years. In 1960 he set the all-time record with 176 points on fifteen touchdowns, fifteen field goals, and forty-one extra points. On special leave from the army during the Berlin crisis in 1961, he scored nineteen points against the Giants in the NFL title game.

Twice the NFL's most valuable player, Hornung played for four of Lombardi's five NFL championship teams. And "team" was the operative word, for Lombardi stressed the team concept over individual glory. When the all-pro squad of the decade of the 1960s was named by the Pro Football Hall of Fame, the Packers accomplished something that no other team from any other decade in NFL history ever had and none has done since. They put at least one player from every position group on the squad: receiver, Boyd Dowler; offensive line, Forrest Gregg, Jerry Kramer, Jim Ringo; quarterback, Bart Starr; running back, Hornung, Jim Taylor; defensive line, Willie Davis; linebacker, Ray Nitschke, Dave Robinson; cornerback, Herb Adderley; safety, Willie Wood; special teams, punter Don Chandler.

Hornung told me a story that illustrates that great coaches don't, indeed, treat everyone the same. "You're making more than anybody on this team," Lombardi told him. "Maybe not in salary—Bart Starr and Jimmy Taylor are making more—but you're making it in commercials. I'm going to be on your ass, and that will let all the other players understand that nobody is sacred. Also, you need it and you can take it."

Hornung smiled at the memory. "He knew he had to treat Bart different from Paul Hornung and Jimmy Taylor," the former golden boy said. "He loved Bart. Bart was a wonderful extension."

Chapter 17

LET ME TELL YOU ABOUT a few of my friends, guys I never would have known if I hadn't lived the sportswriter's life. . . .

Do something nice for someone. You'll be glad you did.

One Saturday morning I phoned Harry Walker and told him not to plan lunch, that I was going to grill three T-bones and bring them to his home, and he and his wife, Dot, and I would make short work of them. It was an easy drive from my place in Trussville to the house in Leeds that he and Dot had occupied since the 1940s. We had a grand day. I can cook a mean steak, and these were perfect. Harry told me the same old baseball stories I'd heard many times, but that was part of his charm. Dot, a placid little woman who never seemed to be rattled by anything, caught up with her sewing.

Neither would live long after that day. Harry died on August 8, 1999, at age eighty, and Dot joined him on July 2, 2000. I was a pallbearer at her funeral and an honorary pallbearer at his, and on each occasion I remembered those T-bone steaks and was pleased I took the time and effort to grill them. Little things can mean a lot.

I visited the former major league batting champion (.363 with the Cardinals and Phillies in 1947) at his home frequently. Harry represented big league baseball as I had known and loved it when I was growing up, before it became the exercise in greed that it is today. When I was a boy I had a booklet on hitting by Harry "the Hat" Walker that, perhaps, had been a free premium with a box of cereal. I thought it was neat that in later years we had become fast friends. To imitate him, I even used to fidget with my baseball cap when I was batting.

Plus, Harry's spread was a fun place. I could bury myself in his collection of baseball memorabilia and clippings and listen to his firsthand stories about his friends Stan Musial, Joe DiMaggio, and Ted Williams. He had forty acres, and he made use of much of the land. He had a fishpond, and when they saw him coming to feed them, scores of fish would swarm to the bank and break the water at his feet, like hungry puppies begging for scraps. He had a batting cage, and major leaguers still visited Leeds for hitting instructions. He was a serious gardener, and he fought a running battle with rats that savored his cantaloupes. He hated those rats. He cursed them so spiritedly that I had to turn my head so he wouldn't see me laughing.

Harry was an anomaly, an old baseball player and manager who neither smoked nor drank. When he was four or five years old someone gave him a chew of tobacco. His mother caught him and made him eat it, and he never touched tobacco again, in any form. Harry never had a beer or a slug of liquor. The only alcohol he'd ever tasted was wine, and he found it "way too sour." Good gosh, the guy had never even had a cup of coffee in his life—though Dot had to have her coffee every morning.

Harry cussed like a fleet of sailors, though. But his profanity was as natural to him as breathing, and most of the time he was as unaware of it as he was of breathing. The former UAB coach wanted me to see the new press box the university had named for him, so I accompanied him to a UAB–Mississippi State game. We sat just behind the MSU radio announcer, who cupped his hands around the microphone, trying to censor Harry's language. "Why is that damned right fielder playing so deep against this batter?" Harry would ask me. "What in the hell is he thinking?"

I remember another visit I paid to Harry. This one was in Spain Rehabilitation Center in Birmingham, on his seventy-eighth birthday, October 22, 1996. He was recuperating from hip replacement surgery. That October marked an anniversary. Fifty years before, in the bottom of the eighth inning of the seventh game of the World Series, Harry had participated in one of the famous plays in baseball history, one that presented the Cardinals a 4–3 victory and the title over the Red Sox. Yet that play would be a source of consternation for Walker.

Enos Slaughter was on first base, and he scored on Harry's double to left center. For more than half a century baseball fans have seen "Country Slaughter's mad dash from first base to home" on movie and TV screens. And they've heard Walker's hit called a single. The Saint Louis newspaper correctly reported it as a double the next day, but a writer or two referred to it as a single. Slaughter perpetuated the more dashing version, and it stuck, Harry told me. "One guy wrote the story and made it more exciting," Walker explained. "Slaughter, everywhere he went, he said it was a single. One time Slaughter said it fell right behind shortstop. Then why was it relayed?" Slaughter, in fact, was stealing on the pitch, Walker said. "He was twenty-five or thirty feet before I hit the ball. He's stealing, but nobody talks about it. The other makes it more exciting."

The sport's ultimate authority, *The Baseball Encyclopedia,* records Walker's hit as a double, but some other sources still erroneously call it a single. The book *World Series: The Games and the Players,* for instance, reports: "Harry drove a single into center, in front of the fielder." Walker resented the fact that Slaughter got virtually all the credit for the play. I suspect that more than once he muttered to himself: "After all, somebody had to hit the darn ball for him to score the darn winning run." Although Harry's adjective would have been considerably saltier.

Walker played and managed in the bright lights of the major leagues, but Leeds was always home. Perhaps that love of the little town near Birmingham contributed to the confusion over his double. "Another thing that hurt, after the game was over I got in my car and headed for Leeds," he told me. "People were partying, but my baby daughter had just been born, and I thought I needed to be home. If I had stayed I would have gotten more publicity."

Harry expressed his love of Leeds to his friend John Russell in an offbeat scenario. Harry and John, who is co-owner of M and J Materials in Trussville, flew to Los Angeles where the Dodgers were honoring Harry's brother Dixie, another major league player. Fans were tailgating in the stadium parking lot before the game. Suddenly the two Alabamians saw a singular sight. "A woman was peeing in a slop jar," Russell recalled. Harry rolled the window down and shouted, "Lady, get your clothes on!" She began screaming and shaking her fist at them. Russell punched the accelerator, and they zoomed away from the angry, immodest Dodgers fan. "These people out here are crazy as hell," Walker told Russell. "I'm so glad I live in Leeds, Alabama."

I love for some reader or coach to tell me that sportswriters don't know anything about coaching. It gives me an opportunity to point out that I know a sportswriter who won two national baseball championships and who, at one time, was the winningest coach in any sport in Alabama collegiate history.

That would be Rudy Abbott, who retired as Jacksonville State University's baseball coach in 2001 with 1,003 victories. His Gamecocks won Division II national championships in 1990 and 1991. Not only is the JSU baseball park named for him, but so is the highway that runs beside it.

As I write this, my pal Rudy—who was a professional baseball player, a sportswriter, a sports information director, and a coach—is a first-term Calhoun County commissioner. I couldn't imagine why a guy who had just retired from the high-pressure life of coaching would want a headache job as a county commissioner. I phoned him the day after he won and said, "You're crazy as hell."

"You're about the twentieth person who has told me that," Rudy replied. "Nobody has said congratulations."

"Congratulations," I said, "but you're still nuts."

Rudy was a sportswriter for the *Anniston Star* when I first knew him.

George Smith, the sports editor, had hired him in the Smokehouse poolroom, a gone-but-not-forgotten emporium on Noble Street that I remember for its impeccably straight cue sticks and delicious open-faced steak sandwiches. Rudy's professional baseball career had not worked out, and that was why he found himself writing sports instead of playing. He had been a star pitcher at JSU, the author of two no-hitters, but playing for Lexington, North Carolina, in the minors he had thrown a ball that an opposing home run king had hit onto another planet.

"You've got to throw your best pitch to a batter like that," the manager said when he visited Rudy on the mound.

"That was my best pitch," Rudy replied.

"Then," the manger concluded, "you need to find another line of work."

It was the Pittsburgh Pirates who decided to take the chance on Rudy in the first place. A scout came to his daddy's grocery store in Anniston, and Rudy proudly told Pop: "Daddy, the Pirates want to sign me for five thousand dollars." His father, Harvey, motioned him over behind the meat counter, where he whispered: "Rudy, I know you want to play baseball, but I just don't have five thousand dollars to give those people."

Rudy saw himself becoming a newspaper managing editor some day. I was touched to read in a story about his retirement that he said his heroes are writers, folks who can string words on a screen or a sheet of paper like pearls on a necklace. When he was at the *Anniston Star* he even got to yell, "Stop the presses!" It was when John Kennedy was assassinated.

But he returned to Jacksonville State as sports information director in 1964. Dirty Wedgeworth, the baseball coach, became ill before the 1970 season, and Houston Cole, the JSU president, asked Rudy to coach the team until Wedgeworth returned.

"What are you going to pay me?" Rudy asked.

"Nothing," Dr. Cole answered. "You should fill in and help."

Wedgeworth never returned, and Abbott's temporary job became permanent. For years he coached baseball for free and continued to be the SID, but eventually he concentrated solely on baseball—and was paid for it. "I think I did a pretty good job for a fellow who never planned to coach," Abbott said. "For the first ten years or so that I was the baseball coach I didn't think of myself as a coach. I thought of myself as a sports information director who had a chance to get out of the office in the afternoon and coach a little baseball." Abbott coached JSU baseball for thirty-two seasons. Twice he was national coach of the year in Division II, in 1990 and 1991, when his clubs took national titles.

He and umpires struck sparks. "I've been thrown out of my share of games," Abbott said. "The strangest incident was at Clinton, Mississippi, against Mississippi College. It was game time and the umpires hadn't shown up. Their coach said, 'We've got a couple of guys in the stands who are good umpires. We'll have to use them or wait until the others show up.' Boy, did I fall for that. No coach should ever fall for that.

"One of their umpires was named Moses. I told him, 'I don't think they had the Moses in the Bible in mind when they named you, because you're a cheating devil.' He threw me out of the game. I got in the stands, and he threw me out of the stands. So I got in the team bus.

"When I wanted one of our base runners to steal, I put on the left blinker light of the bus.

"When I wanted the hit and run, I put on the right blinker.

"When I wanted to take the pitcher out, I blinked the lights.

"The umpire threw me out of the bus, too. I can't understand why he thought I was up to something."

They say football builds character. Well, I know for certain it builds characters, and it never built a more colorful one than Frank Howard, the longtime (1940–69) Clemson head coach.

Howard was a rotund, baldheaded, foul-mouthed, funny fellow. He had a knack for getting to the nitty-gritty of things, especially college football. "When we won they said I was folksy and colorful because I cussed and chewed tobacco," Howard told me. "When we lost they said I was a terrible role model for the players and everybody else because I cussed and chewed tobacco."

A group of visiting writers asked Howard if they could speak to a certain player. "Jones, get your ass over here," Howard bellowed across the practice field. When the writers mentioned his choice of words, Howard explained:

"If this was Harvard I'd say, 'Jones, please bring your derriere over here as quickly as possible.' If this was Princeton I'd say, 'Jones, kindly transport your posterior to this vicinity with all due haste.' But this ain't Harvard or Princeton so I'll just say, 'Jones, get your ass over here.' "

Howard appreciated shock value, and I'll never forget how he brought down the house at a Gator Bowl social affair before the 1978 game in Jacksonville. To set the stage: The season before, Paul Bryant's Alabama Crimson Tide had destroyed Woody Hayes's Ohio State Buckeyes 35–6 in a Sugar Bowl game that was hyped as a matchup of coaching immortals. Now Ohio State was about to play Danny Ford's Clemson Tigers in the Gator Bowl. Ford and Hayes were at the head table at a ritzy luncheon attended by Jacksonville dignitaries and prominent people from both universities. Howard, who was retired, was not on the program, but he stepped up to the podium and the first words out of his mouth were, "Hey, Woody, ole Bear beat the shit out of you, didn't he?" Everyone was shocked, but then the place erupted in laughter. Hayes managed a weak grin. Howard went on to tell a dirty joke or two that delighted most and offended a few in the audience.

Hayes generally made an ass of himself that day. He was sitting between a bigwig of the Jacksonville newspapers and a nationally prominent TV broadcaster (if memory serves, it was Keith Jackson) at the luncheon, but he spoke of "pipsqueak newspapermen" and laughed about shoving a TV cameraman. Full of himself, he said, "I'll have a brief press conference after the luncheon—and I guarantee you it will be brief." He laughed, but nobody else did.

Then, during the game, Hayes slugged a Clemson lineman named Charlie Bauman who had intercepted a pass and gone out of bounds near the Buckeyes' bench. Ohio State had been lenient with its loose cannon coach for a long time, but a national TV audience saw this disgraceful act, and the school retired him. A few months later I was chatting with Howard, and out of the blue he said, "I've been concerned about something, Bolton. Do you think what I said to Woody Hayes at that Gator Bowl luncheon somehow triggered what he did at the game?" I was touched, because an old friend was genuinely worried. "Frank, you didn't have anything to do with that," I assured him. "Woody Hayes has been out of control for a long time, and it was bound to catch up with him eventually. You didn't cause it."

I was having lunch with Frank and his wife, Anna, at their home in Clemson one day, and he told me how he got the best player he ever coached, fullback Fred Cone of Pine Apple, Alabama. I think of the story when fans get so excited or despondent about recruiting. "He never played high school football," Howard said. "My sister sent him to me. He wanted to go to Alabama or Auburn, but they wouldn't take him.

"My sister lived in Biloxi, Mississippi, next door to his sister. My sister called me and said she had a great player, but he had never played. I took him as a favor to her. I asked her later how she knew he was going to be so good, and she said she saw him dive off a diving board and he had a lot of muscle coordination. And people say there's no such thing as luck."

Howard always had a story to tell. The column I wrote when he died came easy—except for the part about deciding which stories to recount. He was Clemson's director of athletics, and he claimed that when Lake Hartwell was created a faction came to him asking that Clemson add rowing to its list of sports. "I heard one of them shells that you row cost seventy-five thousand dollars, and it don't bring in nothing. I told them I wasn't putting up no money for any sport where the players sit on their ass and win going backward."

He used to laugh at Paul Bryant's "itty bitty boys," claiming the Alabama players were heavier than the weights assigned to them in the program. Howard was in Tuscaloosa, and Bryant had the weight room scales adjusted and asked the Clemson coach to step up. Frank weighed about 270, and the scales registered him at about 220. "Damn, Bear, I owe you an apology," Howard said. "Them scales is right after all."

Bryant was one of Howard's favorite targets when Frank spoke at banquets. "Talking about Bear, he called me in 1941 and wanted a job as my assistant," Howard told me. "The smartest thing I ever did was not hiring him. If I'd hired him, within six months he'd have cut my throat, drunk my blood, had my job, and had us on probation for life."

Howard was called the Baron of Barlow Bend, homage to the minuscule community in South Alabama where he lived as a boy. He cultivated his hillbilly image, but the fact is he attended Alabama on an academic scholarship. He played under Wallace Wade, the school's first great coach. Wade later served as commissioner of the Southern Conference, a league that included Howard's Clemson teams. "One time he was up there talking to us coaches about blocking," Howard told me, "and he said he didn't want 'em throwing elbows up in their faces. He said, 'I just wonder who started this kind of coaching football.' I said, 'Coach, you know I played for you. Feel this knot in my arm. I know damn well my high school coach didn't coach that kind of stuff, and I know that knot is in my arm. I don't know how it got there, but I've got a pretty good idea.' "

When Howard came to Clemson as an assistant football coach he also was assigned the job of track coach—though he'd never seen a track meet. "My first day as a track coach, an ole boy asked me, 'Which form do you prefer with the javelin, American or Finnish?' Well, I hadn't never even heard of a javelin. I told him to go over to the library and check out a book called *Track and Field* by Harry Gill and do what he said do. Sho' nuff, he did, and he set a South Carolina record that held for thirty years.

"Most coaches overcoach."

Nobody can ever accuse B. J. Parker of having a big head.

"I'll never be a has-been," Parker said, "because I'm a never-was."

Parker didn't win many stock car races, but he leads lots of laps in the human race. I've known him for maybe forty years, lost untold games of golf to him, and traveled thousands of miles with him—and I honestly don't believe I've ever heard anyone say an unkind word about him. He's low key and affable, and race drivers like him because he was one of them and he understands their problems. They support his Southern All Star Racing and Southern Thunder Tour as he sanctions stock car and truck events throughout the South.

Parker, who lives in Graysville, Alabama, has never tried to get too big for his britches. His brand of racing fills the same size niche that the Birmingham Barons do. It's minor league, but it's fun. It's a poor man's NASCAR—and the last time I looked there were a lot more poor men than rich ones. As driver Ronnie Johnson once told Parker: "B. J., what you pay isn't hardly worth racing for, but it's just enough that we can't stay home."

Parker, who hit on his touring concept in 1982, does a good job of existing in the happy medium. "You can't have a purse so high that the promoter can't afford to pay it or so low that the drivers can't afford to put the equipment out there for it." He added, "And you have to pay the purse. There have been times when I had to borrow the money to do it, but you have to do what you say you'll do. A lot of little tracks have cut the purse when the crowd was small, but when people go to one of our races they know what they'll get." Parker's operation may be minor league, but it isn't bush league. He sanctions some one hundred races a year in Alabama, Tennessee, Georgia, Mississippi, South Carolina, North Carolina, Florida, and Kentucky. "I operate on volume," he said. "I have a lot of races and make a little out of each one."

Parker became a driver by accident—someone else's accident. He and his brother Avron fielded a short track car in 1958 with Avron as the driver and B. J. as the mechanic. But Avron cut off his toes in a lawnmower accident, and of necessity B. J. took over the steering wheel. "The old car was so bad I couldn't get anyone else to drive it," he said, "So I ended up driving it myself." He was a better driver than he lets on. He won a track championship at Cullman and a few races at Anniston and Sayre.

A scoring foul-up at old Midfield Speedway led to Parker's becoming a promoter. After the race, the drivers lined up to be paid, but promoter R. V. Parker (no relation) whispered to B. J. that he had no idea where anyone finished. What could he do? "I knew I had finished fourth," B. J. recalled, "and I went down the line and asked the others where they thought they finished. Then I told R. V. to call it out as the official finish and say the pay line would close in five minutes."

The next morning R. V. Parker asked B. J. Parker to have breakfast with him. "How would you like to be a partner in a race track?" R. V. inquired.

"I don't have any money," B. J. answered.

R. V. Parker, relieved to have averted a sticky problem the night before, said, "You don't need any money." So a promoting career was born at Midfield Speedway. That modest, accidental beginning would lead to Parker's being inducted into dirt track racing's national hall of fame in 2002.

His wife, Gail, has been with him every lap—though sometimes reluctantly. "At first I'd go somewhere with Southern All Star and lose money," B. J. said, "and she'd pout with her lips stuck out and tell me I ought to get a job like a normal person. The next week we'd make some money off a race and she'd hold on to the money pouch and say excitedly, 'Where are we going next? Where are we going next?' "

Rarely is he called anything but B. J., but Parker's name is Bervel James. "My parents named me Bervel because they thought I would grow up to be ugly," he said.

It's obvious that young folks of today don't have the regard for tradition and the events and personalities of the past that my generation does. But I was stunned when no Jacksonville State freshman athlete could identify Jodie Connell, the most notable football player in the school's history.

A few years ago JSU asked me to speak to its freshmen athletes, male and female, and I asked how many knew who Jodie Connell was. I didn't expect all or even most of them to know—but I was dumbfounded when not a single one had any idea. Connell was the gutsiest athlete I ever knew. He made the small college all-America team as a one-armed JSU guard in 1953. "Jodie had a handicap and didn't know it," his old coach, Don Salls, said. "He thought he had two arms and played like he had three." Jodie was named to JSU's all-time football team and was elected to the Alabama Sports Hall of Fame and the sports halls of fame of Etowah County and Jax State.

He lost his left arm just below the elbow when he was nine years old. He was swinging over an embankment with a chain around his arm when he fell twenty feet. The chain severely cut his arm. Gangrene set in, and amputation became necessary. It was shortly before penicillin became available, and a doctor said if the accident had happened a year later they could have saved his arm.

When his mother told him he would lose his arm, Jodie wept and said, "I always wanted to play football, but now I won't." But he did play. He pulled a rare quiniela by making all-state at Gadsden High in Alabama and at Lakeland High in Florida. Then he starred at Jacksonville State and even played minor league professional football for the St. Louis Knights. To top it all, Jodie weighed less than 180 pounds. When one coach marveled at his lack of heft and asked how much he weighed, Jodie replied: "I weigh 175 on the scales and 300 on a man's ass."

Jodie bristled when he read the word "handicapped" in stories about him. "A handicapped person is someone who can't tie his shoelaces with two hands." He told a reporter as he crafted a perfect Windsor knot in his necktie with one.

Jodie could be brought down, though. He suffered a separation of his right shoulder, and his right arm was in a sling. Jerry Bryan of the *Birmingham News* interviewed him for a story, and finally Jerry could stand it no longer. "Jodie, my curiosity is getting the best of me," he said. "What do you do when you have to go to the bathroom?"

Jodie answered, "That's when I find out who my true friends are."

Jodie loved to tell jokes and funny stories, and he didn't mind if the joke was on him. He ran for political office, and he stopped at a back roads country store. Some old geezers were gathered around the potbellied stove, swapping lies. Jodie introduced himself, said he'd appreciate their votes, and offered to buy everybody a soft drink.

"Let's grab taters to see who buys the drinks," one old fellow said.

"What's grabbing taters?" Jodie said.

"You see that barrel of spuds across the room? We'll all line up over here on this side of the store, and somebody will say 'go,' and the last one to grab a tater will pay for the drinks."

Jodie knew he could easily outrun the old guys, and he said okay. When one yelled "go" he raced to the barrel, snatched up a potato, and held it high.

No one else had moved. "You were the last one to grab a tater," the old guy said, "so I reckon you have to buy the drinks."

I liked the story so much that I adopted it for a scene in my novel *Water Oaks.*

The story Jodie told about the accident that cost him his arm swerved away from the facts. "We were real poor," he said, "and I was up in a persimmon tree eating 'simmons for breakfast when the limb broke and I fell."

Another favorite poor boy story: "We had a cloakroom at grammar school, and everybody brought their lunch in a syrup bucket and hung it on a nail in the cloakroom. I was too poor to have a syrup bucket, much less any food to put in it, so I'd go down the line and lift each bucket a little to see which one had the most food, and I'd steal it. One day I found this real heavy bucket, and I thought I'd have a great lunch. When I got it out on the playground and opened it, though, all that was in it was hickory nuts and a ball-peen hammer."

I was walking along a sidewalk in downtown Birmingham when I noticed my reflection in a plate glass store window. My belly was hanging over my belt. Disgusted, I sucked in my gut to see what I'd look like if I lost twenty pounds. That's all I did. "Hey, Charles Atlas!" a voice rang out. "I see you!" Of all people to have been driving by at that precise moment, it was Jodie. He never let me live it down. Jodie would get me in a group, flex his muscles, go through the posing routine of a body builder, and narrate: "Y'all should have seen him look at himself in that plate glass window. He'd do this and admire himself. Then he'd do this. Then . . . "

Jodie was a district director for the U.S. Department of Agriculture in real life. Jimmy Bryan of the *News* and I asked our agronomic buddy to go with us to Gainesville, Florida, where we would cover a football game. We drove down on Friday and checked into a motel. At 4:30 Saturday morning, a flickering TV screen and a voice woke Jimmy and me up. We wiped the sleep from our eyes to see that Jodie was watching a program about growing soybeans. "This is interesting," he told us. "Y'all need to get up and watch it with me." Naw, we didn't.

Jodie died from a massive stroke in 1983. He was just fifty-two years old. A few years ago his wife, Sara Lou, told me, "Jodie always said that trip he took to Florida with you and Jimmy was the most fun he ever had in his life." When I heard that, I reckoned that being woke up at 4:30 in the morning by soybeans was worth the aggravation.

The people of a city owe its sports teams their support, right?

Wrong.

"The word I hate most is 'support,'" Art Clarkson said. "I don't want people to 'support' me. I'm a private business, not a charity." He bristles when he reads that a franchise owner has threatened to pull his team out of a city if the people don't buy tickets. "If you don't succeed, it's not the city's fault. It's your fault."

I've always admired Clarkson because he never had the attitude that he was doing the public some beneficent favor by fielding sports teams and providing folks the privilege of attending his games. In an era when accepting responsibility for yourself is out of fashion, Clarkson is old-fashioned. "The first thing people think when they wake up is 'thank God I woke up.' Then they're glad they've got a job and got a family. The most important thing on their minds is not my sports team."

Clarkson's job is to sell a product—sports—just as another man's job might be to sell furniture or groceries, and he does it by knowing his business, by being clever and inventive, and by working hard. Clarkson is a diligent laborer. He owned baseball's Birmingham Barons, and he owned hockey's Birmingham Bulls, and now he owns indoor football's Tennessee Valley Raptors, which are based in Huntsville. He has forged a successful career in sports by "using common sense," a commodity that has joined responsibility on the list of endangered species.

When Clarkson got into hockey he didn't know how many players were on a side, but he brought the same savvy and common sense that had made the Barons successful. "In the minor leagues, with the advent of mass media, it's 80 percent marketing and 20 percent winning and losing," he said. "You're bombarded by so much competition, not just sports but everything in the media." In other words, a minor league team owner is competing with seventy-five TV channels that offer anything from sports to cop shows to cooking lessons.

Clarkson does it with promotions. Giveaway nights are big: go to the baseball park and get a free glove (with a company's name on it), to the hockey rink and get a free jersey, to the football arena and get a free football. Daredevils, comedy acts, and cut-rate tickets provided by businesses are standard. "I don't expect everybody who comes to a baseball game to be a baseball fan," Clarkson said. "We have to create an atmosphere of fun for mother and daddy and the kids."

Some people get into sports ownership for the wrong reasons, Clarkson said. Some are fans, which doesn't guarantee success. Some have become wealthy in other businesses, which doesn't guarantee success. "There are people who have been highly successful in their businesses, but nobody knows who they are, and they want to be recognized. They read and hear about people who own teams, and they want people to read and hear about them, so they buy teams. Let's say an orthopedic surgeon buys a sports team. Let's say he and I switch jobs for six months, that with no training I become an orthopedic surgeon and he becomes a baseball operator. We're going to have the same results."

Clarkson grew up in Los Angeles. He played football at Cal State–Northridge and signed a free agent contract with the Pittsburgh Steelers. He didn't make the NFL, but he played briefly in the Continental League. He was selling real estate and insurance when he read that the new World Football League would play in 1974. For weeks he badgered the Southern California Sun for a job selling season tickets until the club finally hired him, and a career in sports was born.

He cut his teeth on the WFL in Southern California and Memphis and on minor league baseball in Memphis and Wichita, and then he and some partners bought the Montgomery franchise of the Southern League and moved it to Birmingham, which had been without baseball for five seasons. Birmingham's team had pulled thirty thousand spectators in 1975, its last season before oblivion, but Clarkson's promoting energized the Magic City baseball scene, and the Barons drew two hundred thousand his first year, 1981.

Rickwood Field, which is now the oldest baseball park in America, was decrepit. Clarkson demonstrated to officials of the growing suburb of Hoover that it would be to the town's benefit to build a home for the

Barons, and in 1988 the club moved into Hoover Metropolitan Stadium. Rumors abounded that the park would not be ready by opening night, April 16. And they did cut it close, for workers were erecting the stadium gates and putting up stalls in the women's restrooms that afternoon. Clarkson knew he had to squelch the rumors, so he called a press conference for a ceremonial turning on of the lights. It was held on April Fool's Day—which though the press didn't realize it, was significant.

As a matter of fact, the park didn't even have electricity. Clarkson installed a fake switch in a dugout and secreted a construction worker in the outfield with a generator. When Clarkson flipped the switch for the benefit of the skeptical press, the guy fired up the generator and, lo, there was light. The press went home convinced everything was in order. On the video tape you can read Clarkson's lips as he whispered to himself, "Thank God the lights went on."

Clarkson sold the Barons in 1990. His stint as the owner of the Bulls followed.

He and nine other franchise owners organized the Extreme Football League that metamorphosed into arenafootball2, and his Tennessee Valley Vipers began play in 2000. The Vipers became the Raptors before the 2005 season and moved to the United Indoor Football Association, which Clarkson and eleven others formed.

Clarkson has had one heart attack, and I told him I am concerned about him because he seems constitutionally incapable of running in any gear except high. "Heart attacks are highly overrated," he replied.

Chapter 18

I'M FREQUENTLY ASKED IF, in my early years of covering the sport, I ever dreamed that Nextel Cup racing would become the hit that it is today. I knew it would. I knew the key was getting major speedways built, and I knew the big tracks eventually would come into being. I knew television would get wise when the sport's facilities matched its excitement. When I started covering Nextel Cup in 1962 it was a major league sport that was largely played in minor league ballparks. But, hey, that was just the circuit's fourteenth year of existence. Check the status of the National Football League in its fourteenth year.

There were only four superspeedways on the circuit in 1962—Daytona, Charlotte, Atlanta, and Darlington. Twenty-three of the fifty-three races were run on dirt tracks. Richard Petty won at the quarter-mile paved Huntsville Speedway, earning a first-place purse of $580. Many of the tracks that hosted races no longer exist, and others are solely venues for weekly shows. Races were run at such locales as Orange Speedway, Asheville–Weaverville Speedway, Rambi Raceway, Hickory Speedway, Greenville–

Pickens Speedway, Bowman–Gray Stadium, Piedmont Interstate Fairgrounds, Boyd Speedway, Valdosta 75 Speedway, Hub City Speedway, and the one with my favorite name, Dog Track Speedway in Moyock, North Carolina. Many drivers competed only in selected events. A field of sixteen ran at Huntsville; fifteen, at Piedmont Interstate; thirteen, at Valdosta 75.

One hundred-milers on half-mile tracks that paid a winner's purse of $1,000 were standard. Drivers and car owners negotiated with short track promoters for additional bucks called "show money." The amount depended on whether the driver was Richard Petty or Crawfish Crider. Fireball Roberts got $24,190 for winning the 1962 Daytona 500, and a kid named Cale Yarborough made $400 for finishing last. Dale Earnhardt Jr. earned $1,495,070 for winning the 2004 Daytona 500, and Mark Martin was paid $216,997 for finishing last.

The term "stock car" had long been a misnomer by 1962, but the automobiles were actual passenger cars that had been gutted and souped up. The races weren't as competitive as today's television-beholden events, and one reason was because the car makes did differ; they weren't stamped out with the cookie cutter that NASCAR uses to produce an IROC-like pastry. (The International Race of Champions, for those who don't know, is a made-for TV series that features identical cars.)

But more instrumental in the lack of competition was the fact there simply weren't as many strong teams and cars, and the difference in best and worst was incredibly glaring. In the fifty-three races of 1962, the tenth-place man finished an average of twenty-four laps behind the leader, and no tenth-placer was in the lead lap. In the thirty-six races of 2003, only three tenth-place drivers finished off the lead lap, and they were but one lap behind. So even the most hidebound, intractable geezer of a fan can't claim that, from a competition standpoint, the Nextel Cup racing of four decades ago was superior to that of today. But it was much more fun for a newspaper reporter to cover.

For years the Nextel Cup media corps was a fraction of what it is today. All the drivers knew all the writers, and the drivers were as accessible as your next-door neighbor. For instance, I might have strolled into Richard Petty's garage stall at Talladega and suggested we go to lunch at the Ark, a nearby restaurant that serves delectable catfish and that is a favorite of race drivers and fans. We'd board my car, and off we'd go, and then I'd interview him while we ate. Or Ned Jarrett and I might sit on a greasy garage workbench (a writer didn't wear his Sunday-go-to-meeting clothes to the track) while I jotted down notes. I might interview Fred Lorenzen while he waxed his race car. If I needed to talk to a driver during the first of the week or the off-season, I called him at home. I had his phone number. Heck, Bobby Allison's number was in the telephone book; anyone could call him.

Today a driver is more likely to be served up in a press conference in which everyone is fed the same info, or a writer will have to go through a PR flack for a one-on-one with a driver—who may be involved in shooting a TV commercial or making a corporate appearance. A writer can pull quotes off the Internet for a story and never actually speak to a driver. Davey Allison's home number was unlisted, and he wouldn't even give it to me.

The last driver I tried to phone for an interview was Kevin Harvick at Richard Childress Racing. I got a PR type on the phone.

"What do you want to talk to him about?" he asked.

I told him.

"How much of Kevin's time will you require?"

I told him.

"I'll ask him to call you. Goodbye."

Harvick never called. Guess he didn't have ten minutes to spare.

I've always said that Richard Petty was the greatest champion in any sport. For the press, he was available and quotable, and he'd sign autographs for fans until the world's supply of ballpoint ink ran dry. I remember when Jimmy Smothers, sports editor of the *Gadsden Times,* went to North Carolina to do a story on the Pettys and stayed in Richard and Lynda's home.

I was eating supper with Richard's son Kyle when he was a young driver, and I mentioned that, like his pop, he was a delightful interview. I'll never forget what he said: "Daddy told me that when I wrecked my day was over, but the reporters' day was just beginning. He said for me to stand there and answer questions until the last notebook was closed." And people wonder why I enjoyed covering racing.

Buddy Baker was one of my favorites. He drew word pictures because he knew writers loved them. Once he spun out in the opening moments while running up front at Talladega. He was left facing the oncoming field, though everyone dodged him. "I felt like I was running into the tunnel," he told me, "and the Alabama football team was running out of the tunnel."

Neil Bonnett also had a way with words. Perplexed by his race car that had a high roof and poor aerodynamic qualities, he groused: "I could wear a cowboy hat in this thing and it wouldn't touch the ceiling." Neil liked to tell about racing in New Zealand. They were gentlemen drivers, the short track promoter explained, and any time a car bumped or scraped another one there was a ten-dollar fine. Neil handed him a one hundred dollar bill and said, "Tell me when I've used this up."

Benny Parsons was a delight to cover. When he won the 1975 Daytona 500 in a huge upset, opposing crews applauded as he drove down the pit road toward victory lane. "It's one of the best things to happen to racing in a long time," crusty A. J. Foyt said. "I couldn't be happier," admitted Harry Hyde, the chief mechanic on Dave Marcis's car.

But anyone can have a bad day. Several of us were quizzing Parsons after a disappointing qualifying run at Talladega. A neophyte radioman from a small Alabama station asked him a legitimate question, and Benny uncharacteristically snapped, "That was a dumb question." The youngster was embarrassed. I said, "Benny, that wasn't a dumb question, and if I had asked it you wouldn't have said it was." Benny glared at me for a second, then his look softened and he said, "You're right. It wasn't a dumb question." He told the young fellow he was sorry and answered his question. Benny is a good man.

Ninety-eight percent of the drivers were cooperative when I was the racing beat writer for the *News,* but there were a few who were better left alone. For instance, life was too short to spend any of it wondering what sort of mood A. J. Foyt would be in on a given day.

I once phoned Rex White at his home, introduced myself, and said I'd like to talk to him for a few minutes. I didn't know him and he didn't know me, but the first and only words out of his mouth were: "I don't like the press."

"Okay. Bye."

Bill Elliott was no Kyle Petty. Elliott was testing at Talladega when he was first attaining prominence. We were standing in a lunch line in an infield building and I said, "Bill, could we talk for a few minutes?"

"What do you want to talk about?" he asked.

"Well, about racing."

"I'm tired of talking about racing," he grumbled, turning his back on me.

"I was tired of talking about racing ten years ago," I said, "but I've got to make a living."

So I interviewed Terry Labonte, the other driver who was testing that day, instead. The story wasn't as topical, but at least I didn't drive to Talladega for nothing, as Elliott would have had me do.

The next day the PR woman for Elliott's beer-sponsored team, Alexis Leras, who was an old friend of mine, apologized to me for his conduct. "Bill has been real busy," she said.

"I've been real busy, too," I told her. "Y'all are the ones trying to sell Coors, not me. The great thing about covering racing is that there are lots of other drivers out there I can talk to, and I assure you I'll never bother the guy again." And I didn't.

I always had more tact than to try to collar a driver for an interview when he was working on his car, but I never felt I had to apologize for offering him and his sponsor free publicity in a feature story. Even if I didn't mention the sponsor—and I usually didn't—the story helped put the driver and team, and indirectly the product, in the public eye.

Bonnett was always aware of doing a good day's work for his sponsor—even if its product wasn't his favorite. Neil, who was backed by Budweiser, would play in the golf tournament before a Talladega race, and he'd sip the contents of a red Bud can. What few knew was that he preferred Miller beer, and he'd have one of the tournament workers pour out the Bud and bring him a can refilled with Miller.

The winner of the first Cup race I ever covered, the 1962 Southern 500, wasn't determined until hours after the event ended. Junior Johnson was flagged the winner, but later the victory went to Larry Frank. It's difficult to imagine now, when the running order crawls across the top of your TV screen throughout a race, but scoring foul-ups weren't uncommon. In fact, in the third race after that Southern 500, a 300-lapper on a half-mile dirt track at Richmond, there was a mistake that seems beyond the realm of possibility. Most of the fans had left the track before Joe Weatherly was announced as the winner. In the original rundown, Weatherly wasn't in the top ten. He had been shortchanged nearly two dozen laps, and Jim Paschal was named the winner. Weatherly filed a protest and the mistake was rectified.

The sport was experiencing such beguiling, even charming, growing pains when I embarked onto the racing beat that I became curious about the earlier years, so I studied and interviewed and became a historian of NASCAR. Here's a scoring snafu for the books. Johnny Kieper was flagged the winner of a 250-lap Cup race at San Mateo, California, in 1955. Hours after the race, it was decided Kieper had run 251 laps. Good? No, bad, because Tim Flock had run 252 laps, and Flock was declared the winner.

In 1958 Lee Petty was named the winner of a Cup race at Concord, North Carolina, four days after the finish. Curtis Turner originally was awarded the victory, and Petty was given third place. Lee's wife, Liz, was his scorer. "That Mama Elizabeth has the fastest pencil in NASCAR," Turner complained after the outcome was changed.

Liz Petty was well known to all the drivers. One day Tiny Lund and Lee Petty got into a banging duel on the track, and it turned into a fight after the race. Richard Petty and his brother Maurice and their cousin Dale Inman joined in, and Jack Smith and Speedy Thompson tried to help Lund. Suddenly something cracked Lund on the top of the head, and he saw stars. Bang, bang, bang came the blows. It was Liz Petty, attacking him with her pocketbook. That broke up the fight. "I can't lick the whole goddamned Petty family," Lund admitted, as he struggled to his feet.

For years driving uniforms weren't required in Nextel Cup. On a sultry June 25, 1950, in Dayton, Ohio, Jimmy Florian took the lack of a dress code to extremes when he drove a Ford to that make's first victory ever on the circuit. Florian raced without a shirt. He climbed out of the car in victory lane clad in his pants and helmet and shoes. In the 1950s Coleman Lawrence used to race in plain old denim bib overalls. After Fonty Flock won the 1952 Southern 500, he stopped his car on the front stretch, bounded onto the hood, and led the crowd in the singing of "Dixie." He was wearing Bermuda shorts.

Speaking of dress codes, the *Anniston Star* had a woman racing writer named Marian Uhlman. She went to Talladega during race week, unaware of a NASCAR rule that prohibited women from wearing dresses in the garage area. What to do? Jim Hunter, the Talladega public relations director, solved the problem. Marian wore his pants the rest of the day and he wore her dress.

The surface was so rough on a half-mile dirt track in Wilson, North Carolina, in 1952 that it shook suspension parts off the cars, and in driving through the debris to win, Herb Thomas averaged just 35.398 miles an hour for the 100 miles.

The only Nextel Cup race ever won by a foreign car was the sanctioning body's first road race. It was run in 1954 on an airport course in Linden, New Jersey. NASCAR wanted the thing to have an international flavor so it opened the entry to foreign cars. Al Keller drove a Jaguar to the checkers. Joe Eubanks was second in a big Hudson.

NASCAR won't take away a victory now, no matter how illegal the car, but that wasn't always the case. Fireball Roberts finished first on Daytona's beach-road course in 1955, but he was stripped of the win nearly twenty-four hours later because he used illegal pushrods. Tim Flock was declared the winner.

I said Nextel Cup racing was a major league sport that was being played in minor league ballparks. I wasn't speaking entirely figuratively. In 1958 a race was run on a track in McCormick Field, a minor league baseball park in Asheville, North Carolina. Lee Petty's car got knocked into a dugout.

The old days of racing certainly were superior to today in one category—nicknames. Some who competed on the roundy-round were Madman

Mantz, Slick Smith, Skimp Hersey, Pee Wee Martin, Cotton Owens, Shorty York, Hub McBride, Bub King, Tex Keene, Pappy Hough, Runt Harris, Rocky DiNatale, Tojo Stephens, Crash Waller, Pug Blalock, Iggy Katona, Nook Walters, Snuffy Smith, Banjo Matthews, Possum Jones, Rat Garner, Soap Castles, Reb Wickersham, Legs Whitcomb, and a couple of Wimpys, Ervin and Sipple. The man with the name that was, unfortunately, the most accurate of the era was Slow Poke Travis, who finished nearly twenty-five miles behind the winner on the beach-road course in 1953.

The darndest story about the old days—the one that holds the past in the sharpest contrast to the present—is that of Jocko Flocko. In 1952 Tim Flock won the Nextel Cup championship, and in some races during that season and in 1953, a pet monkey named Jocko Flocko rode with him. Jocko wore his own little driver's uniform and goggles. Tim used to kid the other competitors that if he got tired during a long race Jocko would take over the driving duties.

Race cars used to have little doors over the right front tire. The driver could pull a chain and the door would open and he could check for tire wear. One day Tim pulled the chain and Jocko stuck his head down there and the tire scraped his head. He went nuts, squealing and thrashing about, and Tim had to pit and hand Jocko out the window to a mechanic. "It was the only time in history that a driver had to pit to put a monkey out of his car," Tim once told me without fear of contradiction.

There were no monkeys in Nextel Cup except grease monkeys when I started covering it in 1962, but it was still colorful enough and populated with characters of sufficient zaniness that I loved it. Human interest stories abounded, and I wrote them. The color green and peanuts were still the chief taboos. A green car had been involved in a terrible accident, and peanut shells were found in the pit area of a driver who had been killed. Joe Weatherly was in Birmingham for a Nextel Cup race in 1963, and when a green taxi appeared at his motel to transport him to the track Little Joe refused to ride and phoned another cab company. But money trumps everything else in racing, and the two superstitions became merely historical footnotes. Such sponsors as Gatorade, with its green cars, and Planters, with its Mr. Peanut, ruled.

Weatherly's pursuit of the championship in 1963 was an amazing story. Although he had won the title in 1962 and was the defending champ, he found himself without a full-time ride in 1963. Team owner Bud Moore provided him with a top car for the major races, but Moore didn't bother with the smaller events. Weatherly wanted to repeat as champion, though, so he bummed rides wherever he could, most of them incapable of winning. He won the title and set a record that no champ will ever break—by driving for nine different teams in 1963.

The strangest pairing in racing history occurred in 1964 when car owner Herman "the Turtle" Beam named Cale Yarborough as his driver. When Beam himself drove he stayed out of the way and always finished the race because he wouldn't tax the car by going fast. Thus his nickname. Yarborough, on the other hand, was the consummate charger. "If they castrated Cale," an admiring Dick Trickle once said indelicately, "they'd have to use a chainsaw."

Beam became increasingly peeved as Yarborough's charging tactics resulted in blown engines and other expensive damage. Finally, an incident at Nashville was the last straw, the one that split up Beam and Yarborough. "Tiny Lund's car went into the fence and caught fire," Yarborough told it. "Old Tiny jumped out of that thing and ran down the track. Well, I happened to be passing by, and Tiny himself ran smack into the side of my car and dented the door. Herman blamed me for it. He said if I hadn't been driving so fast I wouldn't have been at that spot at that particular time."

As the years passed, more and more superspeedways were built, and the sport acquired polish and stature. The pioneers who had run moonshine became former racers. Such stories as the one about Weatherly and Curtis Turner banging up rental cars as they raced each other on back roads and Little Joe finally driving his car into a motel swimming pool became folklore instead of current events.

I enjoyed Nextel Cup racing before, but the emergence of the Alabama Gang gave me a true rooting interest. Four men from Hueytown won 131 Cup races. Bobby Allison won 84; Davey Allison, 19; Neil Bonnett, 18; and Donnie Allison, 10. The first Alabama Gang victory was Bobby's, on

July 12, 1966. The last one was Davey's, on March 7, 1993. So for years we had dogs in the hunt.

I'll try to explain the difference in attending Cup races during the days of the Allisons and Bonnett and attending races afterward. It's like going to Little League games when your son is playing and then going to Little League games after he's through. It isn't the same.

Bobby's nailing the championship at Riverside in 1983 was one of the memorable stories of my career. He had finished second five times, and I knew how much he wanted the title. We flew to Los Angeles together and then motored on to Riverside in my rental car—but I insisted he drive it. "I've heard about the L.A. freeways for years," I told Bobby. "If we have a wreck on the way to the track, you're going to be behind the steering wheel. I'm not going to go down in history as the fellow who was driving when Bobby Allison got his leg broken in a highway accident and lost the championship."

Bobby had only to finish thirteenth at Riverside to take the title. He didn't try to win the race. He drove conservatively and finished ninth to beat out Darrell Waltrip in the standings. "I wanted to lead that race so bad I couldn't stand it," Bobby said. "And I could have led it easily. But the crew has never gone back on me, and that was our game plan."

I watched the race from Bobby's pit with crew chief Gary Nelson, and it was excruciating. Four unscheduled pit stops for problems made me realize I didn't have the nerves to be a crew chief. That night we went to Rocco's Italian Restaurant for a victory party, and Bobby raised champagne toasts to the crew that helped him win. On that happy evening I couldn't have dreamed what the years ahead held for the Alabama Gang.

What I would later call the Hueytown Horrors actually began in 1981 when Donnie Allison was seriously injured in a crash at Charlotte that effectively ended his career.

In 1988 Bobby Allison was injured in a life-threatening wreck at Pocono. He would never race again.

In 1992 Clifford Allison, Bobby and Judy's younger son, was killed in a practice wreck at Michigan.

In 1993 Davey Allison was fatally injured in a helicopter crash in the infield of Talladega Superspeedway.

In 1994 Neil Bonnett lost his life while practicing at Daytona. He had become a polished TV commentator, but he left retirement to return to the action of the track.

I had seen a fellow killed at a dirt track called Crystal Springs Speedway when I was a mere boy. I had seen Don MacTavish killed in a particularly gruesome incident at Daytona in 1969. I had seen Fireball Roberts fatally burned at Charlotte in 1964. But I didn't know them. I had been there when others I didn't know, such as Harold Kite and Larry Smith and Terry Schoonover, had lost their lives. But it was different when drivers I not only knew but counted as friends were killed.

Friday Hassler had been a dominator in Birmingham International Raceway's weekly shows, a thoroughly decent man I had interviewed on many Friday nights. He was killed in a crash in a qualifying race at Daytona in 1972. An opponent of many summer evenings on the Modified-Sportsman circuit won the second qualifying race. His name was Bobby Allison. "I knew the news and it broke my heart," Allison said. "But all I could do was hurt for Friday. I had to go and do my job."

Before the 1975 Talladega 500, Tiny Lund had played with my son Mitch at our motel. Lund was huge in anyone's eyes, but he must have been unearthly to a little boy. I can still hear them laughing as Lund regaled him with stories of racing and fishing. The race was rained out and rescheduled for the next Sunday. The only way I could take my vacation was to skip the 500 and let someone else cover it, and it became one of just two Talladega Nextel Cup events I missed while I was at the *News.* We were listening to the race on the car radio when we heard Lund had lost his life in a crash. I remember exactly where we were. We were on a back road near Suwanee, Georgia. Mitch broke down and cried. I cried. My wife, Sandra, cried.

One day I took my eighty-year-old mother to a testing session at Talladega Superspeedway. I introduced her to Grant Adcox, a friend of several years. He took it upon himself to explain the workings of the entire car to her, from the under-the-hood stuff to the rollbars to the tires. I told him how much I appreciated that act of kindness. After that, she always pulled for Grant when she watched a race on TV or listened on the radio, not realizing he had no chance of winning. I was in the press box when Adcox lost his life at Atlanta in 1989. During the excruciating fifteen minutes it took rescuers to extract him from his mangled car I vividly remembered the day he was so kind to my mother.

And when Dale Earnhardt was killed in the 2001 Daytona 500 I remembered his urging me to write a comprehensive history of NASCAR because "you were there, and if you don't do it, who will?"

For the last several years that I worked at the *Birmingham News* I dreaded going to races. I wondered who would be killed or maimed next. Just the other day I explained my feelings to Sonny Smith, the former Auburn basketball coach who has a racing program on radio: "If every year some player you knew well, someone you'd shared meals with, got killed in a basketball game, you'd get to the point that you didn't want to go to basketball games."

He said he understood.

Chapter 19

My forty-year career at the *Birmingham News* began in 1961 and ended in 2001, but it could have ended in 1963—along with my life.

I want to tell you a weird story. You may or may not believe this—it doesn't matter to me—but my wife, Sandra, has dreams and premonitions that come true. They're infrequent, but, I'll tell you, they command attention. One morning, distressed, she told me she had dreamed one of our favorite neighbors had a heart attack in a restaurant and died. A few days later he had a heart attack in a restaurant and died. She has dreamed of a number of automobile crashes that, indeed, did occur. And there was the time we were about to drive to Charlotte, where I would cover a race, when Sandra suddenly announced that she couldn't leave home because something terrible was going to happen. As I drove toward Charlotte alone, our son Mark, who was mountain climbing, fell sixty feet and was seriously injured.

At the end of the 1963 football season I was assigned to cover the Gator Bowl in Jacksonville, Florida, and then drive to Miami for the Orange

Bowl. Sandra was seized by foreboding when I left. She didn't want to be alone, so she stayed with my parents. She told them she had a premonition I would be killed during the trip.

I had a reservation at the Roosevelt Hotel in downtown Jacksonville. It was Gator Bowl media headquarters. But when I tried to check in, the person at the desk apologized because my room had inadvertently been given to someone else, and the Roosevelt was full. Not to worry, for they had gotten me a room at the nearby Robert Meyer Hotel. It was annoying, but I didn't think it was a big deal, and I checked into the Meyer.

North Carolina whipped Air Force 35–0 in the Gator Bowl game, but the week wouldn't be remembered for the game. The next morning, December 29, 1963, I was jarred from my sleep by a cacophony of sirens and bells. I looked out the window of my room on an upper floor and saw the Roosevelt was burning. The hotel in which I was supposed to be staying became a death trap. Twenty-three people lost their lives in what remains the worst disaster in Jacksonville's history. Faulty wiring was suspected as the cause of the fire that started in the ceiling of a ballroom.

At 7:40 A.M. the lobby was filling with smoke, and a doorman telephoned the fire department. The blaze was extinguished, but not before it had created a stealthy assassin—poison black smoke that ascended through elevator, plumbing, and electrical shafts, choked hallways, and crept under the doors of many of the three hundred rooms that were occupied by five hundred guests.

Some guests wet towels and sealed off the space beneath their doors, but others who didn't think so fast opened their windows and created drafts that sucked the smoke into their rooms. A woman jumped to her death from the twelfth floor. An elderly couple leaned out their window and held hands—and they were still holding hands in death when firemen reached them. Some made it to the roof and were rescued by helicopters. Some tied sheets together to make ropes and escaped. A man led a young Arkansas woman to safety. She was Donna Axum, Miss America of 1963.

I phoned Sandra at my parents' home and told her I was safe in the Robert Meyer Hotel, that I couldn't get a room at the Roosevelt. The terror that had overwhelmed her vanished immediately. I drove on to Miami, and she didn't worry about me for the rest of the trip.

I often think about that strange sojourn to Florida. I wonder about the fate of the person who got the room that was meant for me at the Roosevelt. Did he or she (or they) die? Did they escape? I'll never know. I do know that I went on to thirty-eight more years of newspapering, of writing columns and features and game stories. I wrote seventeen books, including eleven volumes of nonfiction and six novels. I wrote numerous magazine articles.

I have a theory that my writing has been read more than that of any other Alabamian. I wrote four columns a week for thirty-one years for the *News.* If each was read by fifty thousand people (a conservative estimate), that's 10 million readings a year. And that doesn't include the millions of readings of my feature stories, game stories, and other articles at the *News* and other papers and my freelance material.

I've written some things I'm proud of. One stands out above all the rest, because of the good that it accomplished, so it certainly brings me the most satisfaction. Big Oak Ranch, John Croyle's refuge for abused, unwanted children, was young and on shaky financial footing. John and I saddled a couple of horses and rode through a stream into a pasture. It was winter, but the weather was decent, and we tied our horses to a bush and flopped onto our backs in the dead grass and gazed at the clouds.

John was troubled. The ranch was at a crisis point as it struggled in its mission to help the helpless. It needed money and it needed it in a hurry. I returned to the office and wrote a column about little boys who had been subjected to devastating cruelty and about the ex-Alabama football player who was trying to help them. Christmas was fast approaching, and perhaps the column nudged readers into a giving spirit, for weeks later Croyle spoke words that delighted my soul: "That column produced $75,000 in donations. Without that money, Big Oak ranch would have gone under." If, indeed, I saved Big Oak Ranch, how could that column not be the favorite piece of writing these fingers ever produced?

I have no doubt that God intended that I be sprawled on my back in a pasture, listening to John Croyle, that day. I believe that God intended for me to lose that coin flip in a country high school and win my wife of all these years; that he meant for me to find a job as a flunky at the *Anniston Star* instead of one at Sears or Goodyear or Alabama Power; that he wanted me to notice an ad in the classifieds for a real writing job at the *LaGrange Daily News* when I wasn't looking for one; that it was his will that, as the elevator doors were closing, John Bloomer mention as an afterthought a vacant sportswriting job at the *Birmingham News.* Some would scoff and say that these things were merely random happenings, but I don't believe that.

And I believe that God intended that I be at my desk at the *Gadsden Times* and that I say and do the right things when a troubled high school girl appeared one day in the 1950s. A few years ago a woman telephoned me from Calhoun County. She said, "When you worked at the *Gadsden Times* you changed my life. I didn't know where you went after you left Gadsden, but the other day I saw a copy of the *Birmingham News* and noticed your byline, and now I want to thank you." She was born with a cleft lip, she told me, and that condition had an overwhelming effect on her life. When she was a little girl she'd hide when company knocked on the door. She kept her head down, never looking anyone in the eye. In the 1950s a teacher assigned her to interview me at the *Gadsden Times,* where I was a columnist and reporter. She froze. She told the teacher she couldn't do it. The teacher insisted, and the girl came to the newsroom of the *Times,* in a panic.

"I sat beside your desk and talked to you," she remembered, "but I kept my head down and my hand over my mouth. I wouldn't even look up. Suddenly you slapped my hand away from my mouth and said, 'You're a pretty girl, and I don't want to see you covering your face again.' I can't explain it, but that changed my life. I walked out of that office with confidence and with my head held high. I was a different person from then on."

She married, had a nice family, and became a successful tax accountant with several pediatricians as clients. She asked if I remembered the day she visited me at the *Gadsden Times.* I was sorry to have to admit that I didn't, but I'm glad our lives touched in that unlikely place.

A visitor to the sports department of the *Birmingham News* changed my life for the better. One day in 1972 a fellow introduced himself as Dave Akens, head of Strode Publishers in Huntsville, and said, "I've been reading your newspaper writing and I like it. I want you to write a book for me."

Akens wanted a book on the history of sports in Alabama. I thought the subject was too broad to have much appeal, so I suggested one that was more focused—a history of University of Alabama football. None had ever been written; Paul Bryant and his teams were riding high; and it seemed a natural. Akens reluctantly agreed to let me write the Alabama football book. *The Crimson Tide* was published in time for Christmas sales in 1972, and it did, indeed, sell a lot of copies.

Akens, suffice it to say, was not much of a football fan. He questioned my choice of title. "It could be confusing because Crimson Tide means the golf team and the tennis team and all the other Alabama teams," he said. I smiled and assured Dave that when an Alabama fan heard the words Crimson Tide he didn't think of the tennis team.

Akens didn't know a lot about football, but he could count book sales. Because of the success of *The Crimson Tide,* he launched Strode's College Sports Series. With my help, Akens enlisted sportswriters and others from across the nation to write histories of universities' football programs. Notre Dame, Penn State, Oklahoma, Southern Cal, Stanford, Tennessee, Texas, Washington, Texas A&M, Syracuse, Ohio State, Michigan, and Georgia are a few of the schools that got the Strode treatment. I think Dave was delighted that I talked him into publishing *The Crimson Tide.*

It was natural that I follow the Crimson Tide with a history of Auburn football. *War Eagle* was published in1973. I wrote other nonfiction books dealing with stock car racing, Alabama basketball, Alabama football, and Georgia football.

I believed I could write fiction, and I undertook the crafting of a novel that would be titled *Water Oaks.* Published in 1980, it was set in the 1950s in the fictional village of Hempstead, Georgia, which is based on Statham, one of the towns in which I lived as a boy. I was excited when a Hollywood production company bought a year's option on *Water Oaks.* An option locks up a book for a period of time, during which the production company seeks investors to provide the financing to make a movie.

Alas, Hollywood had sex, *Jaws,* and *Star Wars* on its mind at that time. "I couldn't get the backing to make a film," the head of the production company told me after a year, "because there were no tits, sharks, or robots in your book." When another of my novels, *The Lost Sunshine,* was optioned, I knew better than to get my hopes up for a movie deal. Nothing came of that option, either. *The Lost Sunshine,* too, lacked the TSR formula for success.

The best of my six novels, I think, is *Nancy Swimmer: A Story of the Cherokee Nation.* For eight months before I wrote a word, I researched the scandalous, horrifying mistreatment of the Cherokees by the governments of the United States and Georgia. American history isn't all heroes and star-spangled banners. The Trail of Tears is America's equivalent of Japan's Bataan Death March. It has been estimated that four thousand of the sixteen thousand Cherokees died during their incarceration in concentration camps and on the Trail of Tears, the death march to Oklahoma.

I'm a writer. That's what I do. I knew I would continue to write books, and that made what was already an easy decision—to retire from the *Birmingham News* in 2001 at age sixty-five—even easier. I'd have one job instead of two. (In fact, I've published a novel, *Turn Left on Green,* and this book since I retired.) But I would have retired anyway, even if it had meant being gradually lobotomized by watching afternoon television every day. My interest in big-time sports was withering. I didn't care which spoiled millionaire was hitting a home run off which spoiled millionaire between work stoppages. I didn't care which hideously tattooed NBA dopehead was caught with drugs. I didn't care which NFL thug had beaten up his wife.

Good ole boys from Hueytown and Timmonsville and Randleman have been replaced by photogenic boys from California and Indiana and Connecticut on the stock car speedways. Performing in the draft isn't enough; a fellow must be able to perform in a commercial. "You've got to be pretty," team owner Felix Sabates put it. A sponsor wants a driver who can "juke and jive. He has to go into the boardroom and talk to the people. There are a lot of drivers out there today, their career is pretty much history, because they cannot go to that next level, even though they may be pretty good drivers. But they don't have that marketability."

The battle cry of Smokey Yunick, the legendary mechanic—"All right, sonsabitches, let's have a race!"—seems as dated as "Remember the Alamo!" My gosh, stock car racing, the last bastion of pure dee, unvarnished competition, has become as slick a production as the stick-and-ball sports. I can't watch it on television because there are so many commercials that I lose the flow of the race in my mind.

Wake me and tell me I merely dreamed it, that college football coaches aren't really being paid a million dollars a year (and in some cases much more). That's downright obscene. Think how many buckets we could buy with a million dollars—to put under the leaking roofs of our elementary and high school classrooms across the state. Some Auburn and Alabama fans became miffed with me because I referred to the universities as football factories. Well, when a history teacher makes a million bucks, I'll call them history factories.

The other night I watched a 1925 silent movie, *The Freshman.* I was amused by a line in the film that could apply to Alabama and Auburn and dozens of other schools. The fictional Tate University was described as "a large football stadium with a college attached."

Auburn and Alabama were continually snagged in controversy. I was tired of writing about their foibles, and I was looking forward to retirement. The games had become almost incidental. NCAA probations, sex scandals, players in trouble with the law, intrigue, dissension, revolving doors for coaches, the demise of loyalty—where have you gone, Joe DiMaggio? And Travis Tidwell and Harry Gilmer? I could sympathize with an Auburn beat man who told me, "I've got to where I jump every time my phone rings, because I wonder what they're into now."

And I could sympathize with a young reporter from one of the state's small newspapers. At his request he had just been transferred from main news to sports, and he was sitting beside me in the Alabama press room as we both wrote about a press conference that dealt with football coach Mike

DuBose's misadventures. "If it's going to be like this," the kid said in a pained voice, "I might as well have just stayed on the police beat."

My wife, Sandra, and I drove up to Sewanee, Tennessee, in August 1999 so I could gather material for a feature story on the one hundredth anniversary of the greatest football team in southern history. The 1899 Sewanee squad went 12–0, shutting out eleven opponents. The Mountain Tigers embarked on a twenty-five-hundred-mile train trip and beat five foes—Texas, Texas A&M, Tulane, LSU, and Ole Miss—in a span of six days.

We were in one of the scenic, peaceful, civilized spots on the planet. That night we sat on the patio behind our room in the rock motel on the campus of the University of the South and breathed clean, invigorating air and remarked on the brilliance of the stars. Up there on the Cumberland Plateau, away from the artificial light of towns and cities and shopping centers and interstates, we realized we hadn't seen the stars so clearly in decades.

We had a pleasant drive down the mountain and through the countryside the next day, but when we arrived home I noticed the light on the answering machine was blinking. The message from the office told me to hustle to Tuscaloosa for a press conference regarding the fate of Mike DuBose, who was in hot water because of his relationship with one of the school's female employees. So much for the glorious stars and sweet mountain air of Sewanee. I turned to my wife and said, "When I reach sixty-five in two years, if I say I might not retire from newspapering, just speak two words to me: 'Mike' and 'DuBose.'" I didn't literally mean I'd retire because of DuBose, of course, but at that moment he was a painful reminder that the focus of my job had switched from the games themselves to the off-the-field crap. The era of the Toy Department seemed prehistoric.

I'm not saying that, in retirement, I have no interest in Auburn and Alabama football. After forty years of gridlock, I don't care to battle the traffic to and from the games, but I watch them on television while a T-bone sizzles on the grill. I just don't have the interest required to write columns about them. I don't know or care who the second-string right tackle is or whether the latest coaching rumor is true or false.

I have not become antisports, as some have suggested. I like sports. I delight in watching my grandson Cory Bolton play football for Springville High School. I enjoy attending football games at Jacksonville State. The state high school basketball Final Four is great entertainment. I even "compete" if you don't insist on too strict a definition of the word. I jog three miles six days a week and run in five-kilometer road races. One day I brought home a handsome, engraved medal. "The good news is that I won in my age division," I told Sandra. "The bad news is that I was the only one in my age division."

It's the conflicted, money-mad, marquee sports scene that has turned me off. For several years I was acutely aware that my interest in the major stuff didn't match the interest of the fans, the people for whom I was writing. That made me uncomfortable. I had to force myself to read the sports pages. Now that I'm retired I don't have to read them and rarely do.

Dealing with fans, incidentally, is an adventure unto itself. If "fan" isn't short for "fanatic," it should be. I should write a few paragraphs about fans.

One day I was digging slots into a hillside at my home and installing three-foot sections of railroad crossties to serve as steps up to the front porch. It was raining, and I was wet and muddy and tarred with creosote. Sandra came to the door and said, "You have a phone call."

"I can't come to the phone," I said. "Get a number."

She went inside, returned, and told me, "He says it's urgent. It can't wait."

So we put down newspapers across the floor, and she stretched the phone cord as far as it would stretch, and I stood dripping on the carpet and said hello, and the voice on the other end said: "I hate to bother you, but I've just got to know something. Who are you for, Alabama or Auburn?" I couldn't believe my ears. I wiped the rain from my eyes and roared, "I'm completely neutral. I hope they both lose every damn game they play."

The caller hesitated for a moment and then said, "Oh. Well, goodbye."

I didn't hope they'd lose every game they played, of course, but at least that nailed whichever one he was for. I hoped they'd both win every game they played, because it made my job easier. It's easier to write about winners than losers. Yet, many fans cannot accept that it is possible for a person to hope both Alabama and Auburn win—but not skip a beat in his life if either or both lose. What's difficult for some fans to accept is that a sports columnist can simply be doing his job, calling them as he sees them. I think they picture themselves at the columnist's desk, praising their favorite and deriding the opposition—so that surely must be what the columnist is doing.

Now, perhaps you are an Alabama or an Auburn supporter, and you are protesting that my descriptions don't fit you. I can only say what a country music singer said years ago when some welfare organization complained about the song "Welfare Cadillac." He asked if they were on welfare and driving Cadillacs. When they said no, he replied, "Well, then, I'm obviously not referring to you, am I?"

Fans have written me letters in which they cursed me. Pitied me because I was so ignorant. Wondered how much Alabama or Auburn was paying me under the table. Suggested I move to Auburn or Tuscaloosa where I would feel at home. Informed me they were canceling their subscriptions. I rarely answered a critical letter. I had written whatever I had written in my column; the fan had said his piece; and I figured anything beyond that was merely arguing. Besides, the *News* insisted on employees being polite to readers, no matter how dense they were, so I wasn't allowed to say how I really felt—that I couldn't have cared less if they canceled their subscriptions.

A sports columnist must adopt the mind-set of a basketball referee. He can't have rabbit ears. If he has a thin skin, he won't last forty-six years in the newspaper business. Besides, he should remind himself that no matter what he writes, not everyone will agree with him. I could write that the earth is round, and if fifty thousand people read it, one thousand would argue that it is flat. And that's just in Auburn.

Several years ago I wrote a column that ran on April 1. I did everything to alert the readers it was an April Fool's column but phone them individually. I broke the news that Alabama was recruiting Siamese twins to play in the offensive line. They were joined at the hip, and they were a particularly valuable commodity because the NCAA had ruled they counted as only one person. Besides, they were the catcher on their high school baseball team. One was right-handed and one was left-handed, and they had never allowed a passed ball. A couple of weeks later a Crimson Tide fan phoned me and, in all seriousness, asked, "How is Alabama coming along in recruiting those Siamese twins. Do you think we'll get them?" I asked myself, if one reader bothered to call, how many others are wondering the same thing but not calling? It was scary to think those people could breed and vote.

Fans almost always go along with the party line and against the columnist when there's a conflict, but there was one refreshing instance when they didn't. When Terry Bowden was coaching Auburn football, the school scheduled Florida State, coached by his father, Bobby, for games in 1999 and 2000. When Terry departed and Tommy Tuberville came on board, Auburn canceled the games with FSU and replaced the Seminoles with Appalachian State and Northern Illinois. I wrote that it was a shameful retreat that flew in the face of what college football was supposed to stand for and that Shug Jordan must have been turning over in his grave. The words of the school fight song, "War Eagle, fearless and true," were ringing hollow. If the coach didn't think they could beat Florida State, how could his players believe him when he told them they could beat Florida? My lead on one of the columns I wrote on the subject was "War Chicken!"

I expected to receive the usual protests from Auburn fans. I had not only criticized AU football but also blasphemed against the sacred battle cry. But the protests didn't materialize. Instead, fan after fan told me he or she was embarrassed by Auburn's running away from Florida State and thanked me for writing about it. One stranger even stopped me in a parking lot to say it. I think I got one negative response.

I tried to be fair where Auburn and Alabama were concerned. The larger question is does the *Birmingham News* play it down the middle? I think it usually does, though fans of either school no doubt could cite instances that seem to indicate otherwise. What's more likely than a conspiracy is just plain old poor judgment, incompetence, deadline pressure, or the left hand not knowing what the right hand was doing. But, of course, folks prefer conspiracy theories.

But I'll never forget one incident that must have infuriated every Auburn fan who heard about it—and I suspect plenty of them did hear about it. One Monday morning in the 1960s Benny Marshall came to work shaking his head and telling me, "You won't believe what happened at the game Saturday." It seemed that Alabama had whipped Auburn at Legion Field and after the game Benny was chatting with a tall, baldheaded fellow. Vincent Townsend, a prominent executive of the *Birmingham News,* who was an avid Alabama fan, approached them with a huge smile on his face. He slapped Benny on the back and said, "Well, Mr. Marshall, we beat those bastards again!" Unbeknownst to Townsend, the fellow who was standing beside Benny was Jeff Beard, Auburn's director of athletics.

On a lighter note, I still smile, years later, when I recall a phone call from one fan. I had written a supposedly clever column about professional wrestling. A woman phoned and invited me to watch some "real" wrestling. A high school tournament was upcoming and she thought I would enjoy it. When I thanked her for the invitation but politely declined, she asked, "Do you know anything about high school wrestling?"

"I know one thing about it," I said. "I know you've got a son on the team or you wouldn't be going, either." Bless her heart, she laughed and said, "I've got three sons on the team."

When I told Tom Arenberg, the sports editor of the *Birmingham News,* that I would be retiring, I had the satisfaction of knowing the Bolton name would continue on at the *News* for years. My son Mike not only is the best writer, reporter, and columnist in the sports department, he's the best on the entire paper. He's the best I've ever read anywhere at finding and crafting "hey, Mabel" stories, human interest zingers that have subscribers still talking a week later. ("Hey, Mabel, you've got to read this piece about . . . ")

At the retirement party the *News* gave for me, someone asked, "Aren't you a little sad to be leaving the newspaper business after all these years?"

I said, "The only thing I'm a little sad about is that after all these years I'm not a little sad."

I thanked the *Birmingham News* for giving me an opportunity in 1961 when I needed one, thanked my friends for being my friends, and when I ate my last bite of finger food at the party I was retired.

And I lived happily ever after.

Index

Page numbers in italics refer to photographs

Abbott, Rudy, 194, 226–228
Adams, Bill, 125
Adams, Doug, 211
Adcox, Grant, 249–250
Akens, Dave, 255
Alabama Journal, 40
Alabama Gang, 58, 85, 247–248
Alabama Renegades, 21
Alcindor, Lew, 4
Alexander, Bill, 121
Alexandria (AL) High School, 29, 30–31
Ali, Muhammad, 75, 211–214
All American Bowl, 100
Allen, Phog, 151
Allison, Bobby, 57–60, 61–62, 64, 69, 75–81, 85–86, 111, *131,* 241, 247–248
Allison, Clifford, 248
Allison, Davey, 58, 79, 86, 111, 176, 241, 247–249
Allison, Donnie, 57–60, 64, 73, 80–81, 85–86, 247–249
Allison, Ed, 60
Allison, Judy, 111, 248
Alumni Gym (Auburn), 19–20
Ameche, Alan, 219
Anderson, Mike, 148
Andrews, Bob, 119
Anniston Star, 32–33, 118, 123, 203, 226–227, 245, 254
arenafootball2, 238
Arenberg, Tom, 262
Atkins, Doug, 220
Atlanta Hawks, 110–111
Axum, Donna, 252

Bailey, Sam, 193
Bailey, Tom, 1
Baker, Buddy, 64, 242

Bank, Bert, *135*
Banks, Ernie, 216
Barfield, Doug, 142, 164–165, 167
Barker, Jay, 88, 186, 189–190
Barkley, Charles, 142–144
Bartow, Gene, 47, 103–104, *133,* 145–148
Bartow, Murry, 148
basketball; the college game in Alabama, 136–139; games between the University of Alabama and University of Alabama-Birmingham, 138–139
Bass, Marvin, 95
Bassett, John, 90
Bauman, Charlie, 229
Beam, Herman "the Turtle," 247
Bear, Roger, 85
Beard, Jeff, 262
Beard-Eaves-Memorial Coliseum (Auburn), 124
Beasley, Marlene, 199
Beasley, Terry, 53, 162, 191, 194, 197–199; book "God's Receiver," 198–199
Beck, Ed, 155
Beech, Jim, 174
Bennett, Claude, 103, 148
Berbick, Trevor, 214
Berry, J. W., 119
Berry, Raymond, 219
Big Oak Ranch, 205–206, 253–254
Birmingham Age-Herald, 46
Birmingham Americans, 89–91, 93–95
Birmingham Bandits, 89
Birmingham Barons, 52, 207–211, 231, 236–238
Birmingham Barracudas, 89, 99–100
Birmingham Bolts, 89
Birmingham Bulls, 89–90, 236, 238
Birmingham Fire, 89, 99
Birmingham International Raceway, 56, 58, 62, 63–65, 69, 70, 73, 85–86, 249
Birmingham News, 1–5, 7, 12, 14, 27, 38, 42–47, 49, 50, 52–54, 56–57, 73, 81, 85–86, 95, 106, 112, 116, 118, 138, 140, 145, 148, 153, 162, 175–176, 179, 182, 187, 196, 242, 249–251, 253–256, 260–263
Birmingham Post-Herald, 61
Birmingham Stallions, 89, 91–92, 96–98, 102, 180
Birmingham Steeldogs, 89, 196
Birmingham Thunderbolts, 88
Birmingham Turf Club, 101
Birmingham Vulcans, 89, 95
Bisher, Furman, 153
Bite, Mike 5
Bloomer, John, 42–43, 93, 254
Bockrath, Bob, 186
Bodine, Geoff, 8
Bolton, Clyde, *128–135;* attends Jacksonville State, 29–31; writes a good deal, 253; books: "The Crimson Tide," 5, 17, 255; "Turn Left on Green," 41, 66, 256; "The Basketball Tide," 136; "They Wore Crimson," 205; "War Eagle," 255; "Water Oaks," 255; "Lost Sunshine," 235, 256; "Nancy Swimmer," 256
Bolton, Cory, 9, 259
Bolton, Mark, 34, 38, 251
Bolton, Mike, 34, 38, 162, 262
Bolton, Mitch, 34, 136, 249
Bolton, Netta, 1, 109
Bolton, Sandra, 31–32, 34, 37, 38, 59, 87, 101, 106, 111, *135,* 136, 249, 251–252, 258–259
Bonds, Tommy, 117
Bonnett, Neil, 55, 58, 64, 85–86, 242–243, 247–249
Booker, Tommy, 3
Boozer, Reuben, 31
Bostick, John, 126
Bounds, Brad, 154–155
Bowden, Bobby, 104, 261
Bowden, Terry, 164, 170–171, 261
Bowerman, Don, 117
Bradberry, Buck, 205
Brickhouse, Richard, 85
Brock, Dieter, 162
Brown, Cindy, 210–211
Brown, Dale, 157–159
Brown, Rickey, 117, 126
Brown, Watson, 104
Browning, Al, 14, 184
Bryan, Jerry, 46–47, 234

Bryan, Jimmy, 2, 38, 47, 53, 54, 95–96, 99, *131,* 162, 194, 196, 235
Bryant, Mary Harmon, 173, 175
Bryant, Paul "Bear," 3, 7–8, 12, 13–18, 23–28, 47–50, 75, 82, 123–124, 137, 146, 157, 161–162, 164–170, 173–183, 185–186, 193, 203, 220–221, 229–230, 255; autobiography "Bear," 4, 15, 28, 48
Bryant, Paul, Jr., 176
Butkus, Dick, 198
Butts, Wally, 14, 20, 48, 49, 109, 165–166
Byers, Walter, book "Unsportsmanlike Conduct," 157
Byrd, Jeff, 197

Caldwell, Ray, 52
Callahan, Ralph, 32
Canadian Football League (CFL), 89, 97, 99
Cappelletti, John, 178
Carr, Gregg, 191, 201–203
Carter, Billy, 87
Carter, Jimmy, 87
Carter, Nick, 108–109
Carter, Rosalyn, 87
Cathey, John, 33
Chandler, Gov. A. B., 155
Chandler, Jennifer, *129*
Charles, Tommy, 67
Cherokees, 256
Chevrolet Frontenac, 65
Clark, Cotton, 194
Clarkson, Art, 236–238
Clay, Cassius Marcellus, Jr. *See* Ali, Muhammad
Coker, Bill, 35
Cole, Houston, 227
Coleman, Tonto, 160
Coleman Coliseum (Alabama), 120, 124, 140
Coleman, Jeff, 174
Continental Basketball Association, 89
Collier, Blanton, 50
Cone, Fred, 230
Connell, Jodie, 233–236
Connell, Sara Lou, 235–236
Cook, Beano, 197
Copeland, John, 172
Corso, Lee, 107
Cosell, Howard, 212
Cox, John, 152
Crawford, Eddie, 115
Cremins, Bobby, 146
Crider, Crawfish, 240
Crisp, Hank, 116
Crowe, Jack, 9, 10, 22, 104–105
Crowell, Burl, 158
Croyle, John, 105, 205–206, 253–254
Curry, Bill, 169, 177, 180–183
Curry, Eric, 172, 191

Darlington Southern 500, 70–72; speedway, 239
Davidson, Sheryl, 21
Davis, Bob, 22–23, 123, 141, 159
Davis, Kermit, 146
Davis, Owen, 122
Davis, Paul, 165
Davis, Stephen, 171
Davis, Tim, 3
Daytona 500, 74, 80, 82, 111, 240, 242, 245, 250; International Speedway, 82–83, 239
Dean, Dizzy, 52
Dee, Johnny, 116
Derozier, Art, 141–142
Dietzel, Paul, 50
DiNardo, Gary, 88
Dixie Bowl, 90
Dixie Speedway, 59, 61
Dodd, Bobby, 27, 50, 180
Donahue, Mike, 9–11, 17
Donnell, Rich, 199
Dooley, Barbara, 168
Dooley, Vince, 50, 109–110, *132,* 167–168
Dotsch, Rollie, 92, 96, 102
Douglas, Leon, 117, 126
Drew, John, 110–111
Drew, Red, 164
DuBose, Mike, 8, 177, 185–187, 257–258
Dunbar, Betsy, 163
Duncan, Jerry, 24
Dunn, T. R., 117, 126
Durham, Hugh, 139–140
Duron, Rev. Denny, 94

Dye, Pat, 34, 105, 144–145, 164–170, 181, 202

Eagles, Tommy Joe, 144–145
Earnhardt, Dale, 27, 75, 250
Earnhardt, Dale, Jr., 240
Eaves, Joel, 51, 109, 120, 122–123
Elliott, Bill, 243
Ellis, Cliff, 145
Ellis, Paul, 126
Eubanks, Joe, 245
Evans, Janet, 211
Extreme Football League. *See* XFL

Fairgrounds Speedway. *See* Birmingham International Raceway
Falwell, Jerry, 100
Farmer, Charles "Red," 57–63
Faulkner, William, 86
Feldhaus, Allen, 122
Fibbe, Jimmy, 122
First Baptist Church, Montgomery, 40, 41–42
Florida Blazers (WFL team), 93–94
Flock, Fonty, 80, 245
Flock, Tim, 80, 244, 245–246
Flocko, Jocko, a monkey, 246
Florian, Jimmy, 244–245
Flournoy, Brownie, 163
Fonda, Jane, 153
Ford, Danny, 229
Ford, Frank, 144
Foreman, George, 211, 213–214
Foster Auditorium (Alabama), 50–51, 116, 118–119, 125
Foster, Jim, 84
Fox, Al, 38
Foyt, A. J., 65, 242
Fracchia, Mike, 3
France, William "Big Bill," 66, 69, 72, 82–85
France, William, Jr., 83
Franchione, Dennis, 177, 186–187
Francona, Terry, 209
Frank, Larry, 72, 244
Frazier, Joe, 211–214
Frederick, Rex, 121
Frederickson, Tucker, 191, 204–205
Freedom Riders, 40–41
Fuller, Mike, 191, 204
Fullwood, Brent, 105, 170, 191

Gadsden Times, 36–38, 39, 128, 219, 241, 254
Gant, Harry, 61
Garrett, Goober, 126
Gehrig, Lou, 216–217
George, Bill, 219
George, Eddie, 171
Gilbert, Porter, 121
Giles, Chris, 147
Gill, Harry, 231
Gillman, Sid, 26
Gipp, George, 26
Gloor, Tom, 56–57, 69, 70, 72
Goff, Ray, 111–112
Golden, Bobby, 193
Goodyear tires, plant in Gadsden, 31
Goostree, Jim, 23–24
Gordon, Jeff, 76
Gorgeous George, 212
Gossom, Thom, 191–193
Gotta, Jack, 90, 92–96
Gottfried, Mark, 140
Graves, Ray, 50
Griffith, Johnny, 47, 49–50, 109
Grillo, Ron, 178
Grizzard, Lewis, 2, 66
Guepe, Art, 50

Hagan, Cliff, 120
Hall of Frame Bowl. *See* All American Bowl
Hallman, Curley, 8
Hardekopf, Bill, 210
Hardin, Paul, 148
Harmon, Bob, 70, 72
Harraway, Charley, 94–96
Harris, Henry, 125
Harrison, Phil, 34, 35
Hart, Henry, 121
Harvick, Kevin, 241
Hassler, Friday, 64, 249
Hawkins, Alex, 218
Hayes, Bobby, 96

Hayes, Woody, 229–230
Hayley, Lee, 125, 142
"He Hate Me," XFL player, 88
Helderman, Frank, 39
Helderman, Frank, Jr., 37
Helmlinger, John, 122
Hemingway, Ernest, 56
Hemphill, Paul, 14, quoted, 52–53
Henley, Terry, 194–195
Hill, Dick, 146, 148
Hilyer, Jim, 8, 91, 102–104
Hobbs, David, 123, 138, 140
Hodges, Cosby, 57
Holmes, Larry, 214
Homer, Jim, 116
Hood, Hooker, 65–66
Hoover Metropolitan Stadium, 207–209, 211, 214, 238
Hornung, Paul, 220–222
Housel, David, 114
Houston, Alan, 150
Howard, Frank, 228–231
Huber, Lee, 156
Hudson, Wendell, 125–126
Humphrey, Bobby, 195–196
Hunt, Bobby, 205
Hunter, Jim, 245
Hunter, Scott, 199–200
Huntsville Speedway, 76, 239–240
Hurlbut, Jake, 3
Hutsell, Wilbur, 164
Hyde, Harry, 242

Inman, Dale, 244
IROC (International Race of Champions), 240

Jack, Gerald, 184
Jackson, "Bo" (Vincent Edward), 104–105, 170, 191, 200–202, 204
Jackson, Keith, 229
Jackson, Wilbur, 193
James, Fob, 107
James, Pat, 25
Jarrett, Ned, 241
Johns, Layton, 121–122
Johnson, Dwayne, 172
Johnson, Eddie, 111, 123
Johnson, Gary, 101
Johnson, Junior, 65, 71–72, 76, 78–79, 244
Johnson, Ronnie, 232
Jones, Alton, 62, 64
Jones, Carl, 69
Jones, Snoozy, 8
Jones, Wallace, 156
Jordan, Lee Roy, 48, 190
Jordan, Michael, 75, 207–211
Jordan-Hare Stadium, 121, 165
Jordan, Ralph "Shug," 12, 13, 16–19, 22, 47, 50, 91, 102, *129,* 161–165, 173, 177, 188–189, 191–192, 204–205, 261

Kabase, Ace, 45–46
Keller, Al, 245
Kelley, Willie, 70, 72
Kennedy, Andy, 147
Kieper, Johnny, 244
King, Martin Luther, Jr., 40
King, Mule, 117
King, Reggie, 126
Kite, Harold, 249
Klem, Bill, 28
Knight, Bobby, 6, 116, 117, 147, 158–159
Kolen, Mike, 197
Ku Klux Klan, 17, 37

Labonte, Terry, 243
LaGrange Daily News, 33–35, 128, 254
Lambert, Paul, 141
Lancaster, Harry, 156
Landers, Ann, 24
Lane, Bob, 91
Larsen, Don, 34
Laslie, Carney, 26
Latimer, Scoop, 49
Lawrence, Coleman, 245
Lebo, Jeff, 145
Ledford, Cawood, 152
Leeburn, Don, 167
Legion Field, 2–3, 5, 14–15, 23–24, 93, 101
Lemmons, Abe, 4, 121
Leras, Alexis, 243
Lewandowski, John, 145
Lewis, Tommy, *131*

Lindsey, George "Goober," *134*
Liston, Sonny, 211
Littlejohn, Joe, 84
Logue, John, 112
Lombardi, Vince, 25, 180, 220–222
Lopez, Nancy, 100
Lorendo, Gene, 18–19, 162, 165
Lorenzen, Fred, 241
Lowry, Walton, 46
LPGA, 90, 100
Lund, Tiny, 244, 247, 249
Lynn, Bill, 120–121, 123

MacTavish, Don, 249
Maestri, Don, 160
Majors, Johnny, 50, 221
Maloof, Gavin, 99
Manning, Archie, 164
Marcis, Dave, 242
Maravich, Pete, 149–151
Maravich, Press, 150
Marinaro, Ed, 197
Marks, Bobby, 28
Marshall, Benny, 3–4, 14, 27–28, 42, 45–46, 47–49, 50, 51–54, 56, 70, 85, 262; books "20 Grand," 52; "Winning Isn't Everything," 14
Martin, Ashley, 10–11
Martin, Eddie, 114
Martin, Jim, 46–47
Martin, Mark, 240
Martin, Wayne, 47, 53
Massey, Chris, 100–101
Matlock, John, 95–96
Matthews, Banjo, 73, 246
McCallum, Scotty, 148
McCarthy, Babe, 51, 152–154
McCarty, Buford, *131*
McCord, Keith, 117
McCorvey, Joe, 47
McElveen, Greg, 117
McEwen, Tom, 53
McGowan, Frank, 46
McGowen, Dick, 205
McGriff, Bill, 121
McKay, Arch, 40
McKenzie, Jim, 175
McKenzie, Mike, 6
McLemore, Rev. Bill, 161–162
McMahon, Stephanie, 88–89
McMahon, Vince, 88
McNair, Kirk, 107–108
Mears, Ray, 119, 123, 152, 159–160
Memorial Coliseum (Kentucky), 153
Mengelt, John, 120–121, 123
Miller, Ray, 216
Mincher, Don, 210
Mincy, Jerome, 147
Mira, George, 94, 96
Mitchell, Mike, 123
Mitchell, Steve, 147
Montgomery Advertiser, 38–39, 41–43
Moore, Bud, 79–80, 247
Moore, Jeff, 144
Moore, Lenny, 220
Morris, Chris, 144
Morris, Johnnie, 59
Moseley, Frank, 26
Murray, Anthony, 117, 126
Muskewitz, Al, *132*
Musso, Johnny, 68, 96, 190
Myhra, Steve, 219

Naglem, Browning, 185
Naismith, James, 151
Naman, Don, 64
Namath, Joe, 3, 4, 5, 174, 190
NASCAR, 58, 60, 66, 70, 73–75, 77–79, 82–83, 85, 231, 239–240, 244–245, 250
Nash, Cotton, 119, 153–154
National Football League (NFL), 89, 92, 94–95, 99, 100
National Invitation Tournament (NIT), 126, 138
National Women's Football League, 21
N'diaye, Mamadou, 145
Neighbors, Billy, 3, 48, 190
Nelson, Gary, 8, 248
New Jersey Generals (USFL), 97–98
Newman, Zipp, 45–46
Newton, C. M., 6, 116–117, 121, 123–126, 136–139, 150–151, 158–160; book "Newton's Laws," 126
Newton, Evelyn, 126–127, 137

Newton, Joe, 123
Nextel Cup, 29, 55, 58, 61, 63–64, 69, 70, 73–81, 85–86, 239–240, 244–245, 247, 249
Nix, Lloyd, 18
Nix, Patrick, 171
Nixon, Richard, 86–87
Nordholz, Mike, 120
Norton, Ken, 211–214
Norwood, Scott, 97
Nugent, Tom, 106–107

O'Brien, Al, 7
O'Connor, Carroll, 192–193
Oldfield, Barney, 65
Oliver, Bill, 164, 171
O'Neal, Shaquille, 158
Owens, James, 163, 193
Oxford Plains Speedway, 77

Palmer, David, 202
Pardee, Jack, 94, 100
Parker, Avron, 232
Parker, "B. J." (Bervel James), 58–59, *132*, 231–233
Parker, Gail, 233
Parker, R. V., 59, 232
Parkinson, Jack, 156
Parsons, Benny, 242
Partridge, Kent, 171
Paschal, Jim, 73, 244
Patterson, Floyd, 211
Patterson, Gov. John, 40
Patterson, L. P., 38, 39, 43
Pell, Charley, 193–194
Pell, Ward, 194
Perkins, Ray, 169, 177–180, 182–183, 190
Person, Chuck, 144
Person, Wesley, 144
Pete Maravich Assembly Center, 150
Pettit, Bob, 120
Petty, Kyle, 241, 243
Petty, Lee, 87, 244, 245
Petty, Mary Elizabeth "Liz," 244
Petty, Maurice, 80, 244
Petty, Richard, 55, 65, 73, 75–76, 78, 80, 85–86, 239–241, 244
Phillips, Arthur, 33
Phillips, Eddie, 126, 140
Pietkiewicz, Stan, 123
Pilney, Andy, 50
Polk, Bob, 146
Porter, Chris, 145
Powell, Dee, 23
Price, Mike, 187
Professional Drivers Association, 85
Professional Bowlers Association, 90
Putnam, Bill, 93–96

Rawson, Larry, 205
Reed, Matthew, 94, 96
Regal, William, 88
Reynolds, Burt, 106–107
Reynolds, W. Ann, 148
Rice, Bobby, 107–108
Richard Childress Racing, 241
Rickwood Field, 52, 64, 237
Riley, Hayden, 51, 118–120, 124
Ripken, Cal, Jr., 214–217
RISE program, 184
Roberts, Fireball, 65, 74–75, 79, 240, 245, 249
Robinson, Oliver, 147
"the Rock." *See* Johnson, Dwayne
Rockne, Knute, 26
Roosevelt Hotel fire, 252–253
Rose, Grayson "Pappy," 66–69
Rotton, J. P., 65
Rozelle, Pete, 221
Rupp, Adolph, 51, 115, 119–120, 124, 146, 149, 151–152, 154–157
Rupp Arena, 153
Russell, John, 226
Rutherford, Johnny, *133*
Rutledge, Jack, 3
Ryan, Charles, 37
Ryan, Nolan, 105

Sabates, Felix, 256–257
Salls, Don, 233
Sampson, Ralph, 147
Sanders, Apple, 150
Sanders, Rex, 82

Sanderson, Wimp, 118, 123, 126, 137–141, 157–158
Schoenbein, Bill and Patti, 214–216
Schoonover, Terry, 249
Scott, Xen, 17
Seale, Bill, 160
Self, Tom, 5
Sewanee, 258
Sewell Hall (Auburn), 163
Shannon, Robert, 147
Sharpe, Jimmy, 167
Shaw, Arthur, 38
Shively, Bernie, 119
Shula, Mike, 187
Sidle, Jimmy, 191, 204–205
Simmons, Johnny, 195
Sims, Neal, 91, 176
Sington, Fred, 113–114, *130*
Sinkwich, Frank, 198
Skinner, Bill, 160
Slaughter, Enos, 225
Sloan, Steve, 178, 190
Smith, Barry, 203–204
Smith, George, 118, 123, 194, 203, 227
Smith, Jack, 244
Smith, Larry, 249
Smith, Sonny, 118, 139, 141–145, 250
Smith, Taylor, 33
Smothers, Jimmy, 241
Southern All Star Racing, 58, 231, 233
Southern League, 211
Space Jam, movie, 211
Spinks, Leon, 214
Splane, Vince, 155–156
Sports Arena (Auburn), 50, 116, 121–122
Sprewell, Latrell, 140
Stabler, Kenny "Snake," 23, *135,* 188–190, 200
Stallings Center, 184
Stallings, Gene, 27, 107–108, 169, 177, 182–186, 190, 202; book "Another Season," 184
Stallings, John Mark, 183–184
Stallings, Ruth Ann, 183–184
Starr, Bart, 116, 222
Steptoe, Nero, 65–66
Streit, Judge Saul S., 157
Sullivan, Pat, 53, *134,* 162–163, 191–192, 194–198
Swinford, Wayne, 110

Talladega 500, 85, 249
Talladega Motorsports Hall of Fame, 74
Talladega Short Track, 61
Talladega Superspeedway, 8, 63–64, 69, 73, 77, 81–84, 86, 114, 242–243, 249
Taylor, Jimmy, 222
Tennessee Valley Raptors, 236, 238
Thomas, Frank, 26, 181
Thomas, Herb, 245
Thomas, Jabe, 73
Thomas, Joab, 177–178, 180
Thompson, Speedy, 244
Thornton, Charley, 116
Tinker, Billy, 121
Tinker, Wallace, 121
Todd, Richard, 4
Tohill, Billy, 96
Toretta, Gino, 172
Torso murders, 36
Townsend, Mickey, 54
Townsend, Vincent, 54, 85–86, 262
Trammell, Pat, 3, 48, 175
Travis, Slow Poke, 246
Trickle, Dick, 247
Trimble, Murray, 3
Trippi, Charley, 49, 198
Tuberville, Tommy, 164, 171–172, 261
Tucker, Bobby, 121
Turner, Curtis, 78–79, 81, 244, 247
Turner, Rory, 170
Tyson, Judge John, 174–175
Tyson, Mae Martin, 175
Tyson, Marc, 175
Tyson, Mary Harmon, 175

Uhlman, Marian, 245
Underwood, John, 48
Unitas, Johnny, 217–220
United Indoor Football Association, 238
United States Football League (USFL), 89, 91–92, 96–97, 99, 100

Van Hoose, Alf, 46–47, 50, 86, 112–113
Vaught, John, 50
Vitale, Dick, 146

Wade, Wallace, 17, 174, 181
Walker, Dixie, 226
Walker, Dot, 223–224
Walker, Harry "the Hat," 208, 223–226
Walker, Herschel, 97–99, 201
Walker, Wade, 50
Wallace, George, 125
Wallace, Gerald, 140
Waltrip, Darrell, 64–65, 76, 248
Waltrip, Michael, 74
Wannebo, Matt, 9
Warner, Marvin, 96
Weatherly, "Little Joe," 79, 244, 246–247
Weathers, Ronald, 46
Wedgeworth, Raymond "Dirty," 227
Werblin, Sonny, 174
White, Gerald, 144
White, Rex, 242–243
White, Ronnie, *133*
White, Tarzan, 108–109
Whitworth, Jennings B. "Ears," 177
Williams, Art, 99–100
Williams, Carlos, 147
Williams, Steve, 96
Williamson, Richard, 167
Willingham, Larry, 96, 163, 191
Winston Cup. *See* Nextel Cup
Wooden, John, 4, 75, 145–146
Woodruff Hall (Georgia), 19
World Football League (WFL), 89–90, 92–97, 100, 237; World Bowl, 93–94
World Hockey Association, 89
World League of American Football, 89, 97, 99, 100
World Wrestling Federation, 88
Wright, Steve, 25–26
Wyatt, Bowden, 50

XFL, 88–89, 97, 238

Yarborough, Cale, 65, 240, 247
Yates, Brock, 61
Yearout, Gusty, 188–189
Young, Jerry, 146
Yunick, Smokey, 257